Best Wishes Vern!

Trust this will take you, pleasantly through a few hours of our cold winter!

best regards
Dennis Fisher
Jan '91

NONE OF THE ROADS WERE PAVED

Robert H. Hahn

Fitzhenry & Whiteside

None of the Roads Were Paved

© Fitzhenry & Whiteside Limited 1985

All rights reserved. No part of this publication may be reproduced in any form, or by any means, without permission in writing from the publisher.

Fitzhenry & Whiteside
195 Allstate Parkway
Markham, Ontario L3R 4T8

Printed and bound in Canada by John Deyell Company

Canadian Cataloguing in Publication Data

Hahn, Robert H. (Robert Henry), 1920-
  None of the roads were paved

ISBN 0-88902-980-6

1. Harmony Kids (Musical group). 2. Hahn, Robert H. (Robert Henry), 1920-   3. Musicians - Canada - Biography. I. Title.

ML421.H37H33 1985   784.5'0092'2   C85-099160-9

Acknowledgments

TO THE MEMBERS OF MY FAMILY who assisted in the recall of many events chronicled in this book, my thanks.

This story is for those people who may, as they turn these pages, remember the time when this country was very young. How fortunate some of us were to have lived through this historic time. The book is also for young people, my own children included, so they might better understand their heritage and know that strong and enduring roots were planted and nourished for them — and that it wasn't always easy.

I dedicate the book to Mom and Dad — true pioneers in this great land. Mom read the final draft just before she died. She was pleased. Dad, whom I describe in the book as "the greatest entrepreneur I have ever known," would have been pleased too, I think.

To Donald Croker, my gratitude. Without your help and encouragement the manuscript would have been a whole lot less.

Lastly, I thank my wife, Neva, for her love and understanding, and for arranging the "quiet time" needed to complete a project as ambitious as this.

* * *

All the events, places, dates, and people written about in this book are real. A few names are fictitious to avoid unnecessary embarrassment.

Chapter 1

THE LAND WAS PARCHED AND DRY, the surface cracked and scarred. The world was grey. Nothing moved except the odd lonely tumbleweed as it danced its way across the barren landscape. Hot, smothering, clinging dust blew over farms where there was no sign of life. If anyone lived there, no one was visible. Windows were covered to keep the unremitting dust from seeping in. If there were cows or horses, they must have been inside the barn. Tractors had been covered with shrouds of abandonment, only the rusty tips of the exhaust stacks showed. Fences were covered in drifting talcose dust and here and there, in the lee of a building, a few fence posts could be seen, staggered like skeletal fingers in surrender to a vast and empty sky.

It was a picture of total desolation. This rich and productive land gave up completely in the drought and Depression years that broke the heart of the west. Nowhere was it worse than in Saskatchewan.

Along with the drought and the wind came hordes of grasshoppers so thick they dimmed the western sun. Rampaging across the cropland like a crawling, moving blanket they obliterated everything in their wake. There was crop-rust and saw-flies, unemployment and frustration; foreclosure and dispossession, and an unrelenting, burning sun. The crops withered as the once-fertile soil dried up; and so did the dreams of my Dad and countless others. The prairies had died.

The Depression era of the Thirties is looked upon by many westerners as the ultimate betrayal of nature and man. It left an indelible imprint on the people. This is the image of the prairies, the farms and the towns that I grew up with, and is burned in my memory like a brand. This is how it was. This is how I remember it. Who could forget *eight years* with no rain!

The history of the United States, as depicted in its folklore and motion pictures, conjures visions of covered wagons forging ever westward from the east. This is not how Canada was settled. The opening of Canada's west was not a ceaseless movement by easterners in covered wagons. Railways played a major role.

Many immigrants who homesteaded the prairies had little or no knowledge of eastern Canada. Landing from ships which docked along the Atlantic coast, they boarded trains which took them directly to the pioneer areas of the western plains. They brought with them their own language and their own culture which was foreign to the life style and traditions of Upper and Lower Canada. Their contact with the east was one of merely passing through.

They had a strong sense of brotherhood through a common background. They were mostly poor Europeans. Thus there developed a strong bond of community. It was the only way they could survive.

Theirs was a frontier spirit and they were hardy and tough. Many had little or no education and found it difficult to express their frustration in words. They had little contact with the world outside. It was alien to them and they felt self-conscious, insecure and threatened. They could cope with the many hardships thrust upon them by the whims of nature but they were distressed at having to live in what many felt was pseudo-colonial status foisted upon them by 'that thing back east' — the political and financial establishments of power.

In the main it was this kind of people who forged the foundations of the west and in so doing transposed themselves from foreigners into westerners. The type of farming they engaged in was different from that in the east, and westerners had little to say about the prices they were paid for their crops. Again, those decisions were made for them back east. Decisions that did not realistically take into account the very special problems of the west. Westerners did not have control of their own destiny. The east decreed where track was to be laid, where the townsites would be built, the rates the railways would charge. All these things were imposed upon the westerner.

My Dad was born in Tavistock, Ontario, in 1890. His father and grandfather before him had also been born in the province. Five generations of Dad's family are buried in two cemeteries in Heidelberg, Ontario, with headstones dating well back into the 1700s. Two of Dad's brothers fought with the Canadian armed forces in World War I. Dad not only *was* Canadian, he *felt* Canadian. But more than that, he became a *westerner*.

He went west in 1908, as he used to say, "following the steel." When the railways were being built, and where the terrain was right, a town would spring up. He helped to build stores and houses, hip-roofed barns, and even the grain elevators which still dot the prairie landscape. Just when a town got comfortable, but before it could embrace him, Dad would uproot and leave — following the steel and searching.

In 1910 he arrived in Eatonia — a widening in a dirt road across the empty flatlands that stretched as far as the eye could see. There were a few bedraggled, sun-bleached, paintless houses but there was also plenty of precious water. It was sweet water, and like an oasis in the desert it brought the steel of the railway and the immigrants: the new Canadians, the new 'westerners.'

Eatonia, where I was later born, became an important railway town in the early days of the west. It soon had a roundhouse where trains were serviced, and a coaling station. Dad got caught up in the excitement and bustle of this burgeoning frontier town. His restlessness subsided. He had found what he was looking for — he was home. He made the long trek to the Dominion Lands Office in Saskatoon and on October 20th, 1910, in exchange for the princely sum of ten dollars, he became the proud owner of 160 acres of virgin land. He had filed on his first homestead.

Peter and Maria Folz, with their seven children, arrived in Saskatchewan from Austria in 1906. One of these children, who was only six years old at the time, was to become my mother. Two more children were born after the family arrived in Canada. In 1914 Maria Folz died and hers was the first recorded burial in the local cemetery.

In the spring of 1916, as soon as the roads were passable, my Dad was touring the district with a load of Singer sewing machines. "Every home should have one," he used to say, for he was the area representative. The Folz family not only bought a sewing machine, but Peter Folz found he had also acquired a very aggressive suitor for his sixteen-year-old daughter, Mary.

As with most early European immigrants, Peter was not only the father, he was the supreme authority. His word was not to be questioned. Having been exposed to little else but misery and deprivation during their lifetime, the family was terribly unsophisticated, uneducated, and subservient to the head of the family. While their newfound freedom in a land such as Canada would allow the children to go to school, Peter, in the only tradition he knew, saw little need to send them. To him education was not a requisite; the ability to work was. The girls were taught to plant and tend the garden and to cook and sew. The boys learned how to tend livestock and keep farm machinery in good repair. During seeding and harvest periods everyone, boys and girls, big and small, worked in the fields.

When Dad appeared on the scene, Mom was swept off her feet by his swashbuckling style. Peter and his older sons resisted this intrusion into their life, and when Dad asked for Mom's hand in marriage he was told to leave the farm and never come back. Mom wouldn't dare to stand up to her father but a clandestine courtship ensued. Notes were passed through a trusted neighbour.

On July 22nd, barely three months after they met, Mom and Dad were married. My parents' wedding picture shows a handsome couple. Dad had a Barrymore-type profile and, according to Mom, the buccaneering style of an Errol Flynn. He was just a mite short of six feet tall with a lean waist and broad shoulders. Mom was very pretty, an elegant but sturdy five feet of love, determination, and adherence to the biblical axiom that it was more blessed to give than receive. Mom's two younger sisters came to live with them. She had mothered the girls since Maria died. The first thing Dad arranged was for them to start school.

When my sister Marie was born she was the first of the new Hahn family. We were all to become a part of a risky, exciting, and always unpredictable musical journey where none of the roads were paved.

Chapter 2

The 'flu epidemic of 1918 swept the prairies like a biblical plague. Hundreds died, and because Dad was a cabinetmaker by trade, he built coffins to bury the dead. As Mom tells it, "Hardly anyone was not touched by a death somewhere in the family. Ours was no exception. From the time Marie came down with it, until your father started building her tiny coffin, was no more than two days. This was the only time in all the forty years we were together I saw your father cry. I'm afraid I wasn't much help to him 'cause your brother, Lloyd, was only four weeks old at the time." There was a long pause in the telling before Mom spoke again. "Of all the good and bad times we went through together, I guess I remember this part as the worst."

When the 'flu epidemic had passed, the need for coffins and funerals was still there so Dad took a two-week course in Saskatoon and learned how to embalm bodies. Then he revamped the back of a Model T into a hearse and for the rest of the time we lived in Eatonia he was the town undertaker.

Dad had a shop on the main intersection of town. He was the delegated Fire Chief and part of his shop had space allocated for the storage of a fire wagon. Originally designed to be pulled by horses, it had a wagon tongue sticking out front. The few times it was ever used it was always pulled by hand by the town's volunteer firemen.

Dad seemed to be into everything. He collected empty beer bottles from the town kids. He paid a penny each and resold them for a nickel. I arrived on the scene a year after Lloyd and as soon as I was able to walk we would spend most of our weekends scouting the roads around town looking for empty beer bottles. Once a month a truck would stop by and pick up the empties from the rear of the shop.

Dad was the Pontiac car dealer in Eatonia. He had a service station out front with gasoline pumps which had to be worked by hand. In the back was a garage where he repaired all makes of cars. In those days, the most popular cars were Model T Fords and 490 Chevs. If you could afford it you could also buy an Essex or a number of more expensive cars. One farmer even owned a Marmon. Dad had the franchise for Hart Parr tractors and Oliver farm machinery as well as being the area representative for Singer. He was the only shoemaker in town and had three heavy-duty machines for sewing leather. He repaired binder canvases. He was a tinsmith and had machines for cutting and shaping tin-plate and zinc sheets. He had soldering and welding equipment and a turning lathe, powered by a gasoline engine. He made eavetroughs and tin waterproof linings for watering troughs. He made stove pipes to fit any need and could even make elbows when a stove pipe had to turn a corner. It seemed there was nothing he couldn't make or fix.

The roaring Twenties was the era of Prohibition. In a booming frontier town like Eatonia there was room for a good bootlegger. Dad recognized the opportunity and went into the liquor business. He had a contact in Yorkton, the main distribution centre for booze in the province, and periodically a truck with two burly drivers would arrive, generally in the middle of the night, and stack a dozen cases of whiskey in the back room where Dad stored his coffins and prepared the dead bodies. The whiskey was usually dispensed with great dispatch within the next couple of days.

The west teemed with bootleggers. There just weren't enough Mounties around to police the whiskey trade, which went on in every town in the three prairie provinces. The suppliers were well organized, well financed and well connected politically. Only twice were we visited by the Mounties during Dad's tenure in the liquor trade. The first time he had been tipped off two days before and when the police arrived to search the premises not one bottle could be found.

The second time was more exciting. As luck would have it, Dad had a corpse in the back room with instructions to give it the full treatment as it was being shipped back east for burial. This meant it would require a great deal more preparation than usual.

When the word arrived that the Mounties were coming they were already in town. Dad held a hurried conversation with Mom and then went into the back room and locked the door. The Mounties arrived in all their splendour and Mom let them in. She told them they were welcome to look around but they'd have to wait a short while before they could search the back room as her husband was working there and under no circumstances could he be disturbed.

"He's an undertaker, you know, and when he's working on a body, no one is allowed to bother him until he unlocks the door — you know, with the children and all."

The Mounties wandered through the rest of the house, looking through cupboards and under the beds. Not finding anything, they went outside and looked through the sheds and storage bins. Finally they came back into the house and sat down in the living room to wait. They kept casting nervous glances at the locked door, and about half an hour later the key turned in the lock and Dad emerged in a long smock. The Mounties introduced themselves and asked Dad if he would mind if they looked in the back room.

"Look all ya want," Dad said. "But I hope ya got strong stomachs. I'm not quite finished with the poor chap and it's kinda messy back there."

We saw Dad give a knowing wink to Mom as the Mounties entered the room. They came out a couple of minutes later, their faces ashen. They thanked everybody for their cooperation and left.

Dad hadn't done any work on the body at all except to make sure it was fully exposed, with powdered plaster-of-Paris sprinkled everywhere. There were syringes sticking in both arms. What he had done was stash fourteen cases of whiskey inside a half-dozen stacked coffins.

Bootlegging became increasingly risky. Dad began regular runs into Montana and North Dakota at remote border crossings. At this, Mom finally talked him into giving up the liquor business. The void was quickly filled by another man who owned a brand new Marmon, which could outrun anything the Mounties were driving, and certainly moved along at a better clip than Dad's converted hearse.

Dad thrived on the bustling pioneer atmosphere of these early days. He was, by any measurement, the greatest entrepreneur I have ever known. With all the activities he was involved in, things went smoothly for the Hahns. Eatonia, with a population of around 300, was the kind of town all kids should grow up in. I remember my childhood as being very happy. Only two things marred this otherwise pleasant period in my life.

The first was that I wet the bed. Overnight camping trips with the Scouts or staying over at a friend's place were out of the question. I was terribly conscious of this problem, which set me apart from the other kids. As personal as the problem was, it certainly was no secret. Every kid in town knew about it and brought it to my attention and the attention of everyone else in earshot.

"Bobby Hahn — Bobby Hahn — thinks he's so smart 'cause he plays the piano — bed pisser! — bed pisser!"

Kids can be cruel and I suffered all through my childhood from an affliction I didn't understand and couldn't do anything about.

The other problem was having to take piano lessons every Saturday afternoon from a very scholarly and rather pompous English farmer named George Gledhill. Dad had built some of his buildings in exchange for two years of piano lessons for Lloyd and me. Our first impression of Gledhill was that he just didn't like kids. In retrospect, he was very serious about his teaching and could not tolerate any lack of interest or application on our part, as he himself was totally dedicated to his charge. He had no sense of humour and his manner was quite intimidating. It only took a couple of Saturdays for us to realize that piano lessons were not going to be much fun.

Gledhill carried an ornate cane which was used to maintain a rigid tempo by whacking the floor. It was also used to rap our knuckles whenever we made a mistake. He was all business and neither Lloyd or I would dare *not* to have practiced all the scales and exercises he heaped on us week after week.

Every day, after school, we'd hurry home and practice an hour each, getting ready for Gledhill's Saturday visit. Lloyd had to work harder than me. He spent all his practice time just working on Gledhill's lesson for that week. As I got into the routine, I found myself making up pieces as I practiced. I'd start off with the best of intentions playing scales, first with one hand, then the other, then both hands together. After working on my lesson for maybe fifteen minutes, my attention would wander and I'd find myself playing little songs or making up melodies. Mom never knew the difference — as long as she could hear the piano, she assumed I was practicing. In the two years we took lessons from Gledhill he never gave us one piece to learn but by the end of that time I could play every song I'd ever heard and dozens more that I'd just made up.

Our house was full of music. Dad was a pretty good musician. He played several instruments but principally drums, and he led the only orchestra in town. The front of his bass drum had a painted silhouette of a naked lady in a spider web and around the outer circle of this remarkable lady were the words "Hahn's Jazz Azz." (I never understood it either). Mom often took Lloyd and me to the dances when Dad was playing, but we always had to leave early as dances went on into the wee hours of the morning. Before going home Lloyd and I would make a fast trip around the grounds and rarely did we not find at least a dozen empty beer bottles.

The first Thursday in every month a man with a horse and buggy came to town with a film projector and boxes of film reels. He would put on a silent movie in the town hall and the place would be packed. Admission for kids was five cents, which I didn't always have. There were a number of ways you could get in for nothing. On the day of the movie two kids would be picked to go up and down all the streets hollering: "Show tonight — Town Hall — *Birth Of A Nation* (or whatever happened to be playing that month) — Starting time, 8:15." One kid would be given a bell to ring and he would walk a couple of hundred feet in front of the 'hollerer.' The two kids picked each month would get in free. I was only picked once as the bell ringer.

One time I was desperate. I had no money and the two kids had already been picked. The man was setting up his screen and projector when I sidled up to him nervously and asked if I could have a word with him.

"Look, kid — if you're gonna tell me you ain't got no money and ya want a free pass to the show, forget it! If I let every kid in who didn't have the money, I wouldn't make enough in this town ta pay for my horse's oats."

"It's true I don't have the money," I replied, "but I was wondering if you'd let me watch for nothing if I played the piano while the people are coming in and when you change the reels."

I was only eight years old but I had finished my two years with Gledhill and I really knew a bunch of songs.

"Let me hear ya play something," he said, motioning me over to the piano.

I sat down at the piano and played *The One Rose* — a Bing Crosby recording which had just come out and was very popular.

"How many songs d'ya know, kid?" he asked.

"Enough so's I won't hafta play the same song twice all night."

"Okay, kid, ya got the job."

When I first started, I would only play as the people came in and when the reels were being changed. The second month, when the show was over, I played *God Save The King* and everyone joined in the singing. The man looked very pleased. As the months went by and as I got more comfortable I began making up music to fit the action of the picture. It didn't take long to discover that all I needed were four basic kinds of music. I needed a piece for the villain or the bad guys, one for storms and earthquakes, one for the chase sequences and something pretty for the love scenes. I worked hard to build a private library of pieces to fit these needs. I got into trouble with the chariot race in *Ben Hur* and after that, if I didn't feel secure, I just wouldn't play if the action required something outside my library.

In a town as small as Eatonia, everybody knew everybody else. Nobody ever complained about my music and sometimes they would even applaud if I happened to get lucky fitting the music to the picture. Besides, the music helped drown out the noise of the film projector.

Though I didn't know it at the time, the extreme discipline demanded by Mr. Gledhill plus all of the creative freedom I was allowed playing for these silent movies was to be invaluable to me in later life.

I played the pump-organ during Sunday school at the United Church and on Saturday mornings I played for the Lutherans. Their service was held in German but I soon reached a stage where I knew most of the hymns. If the minister picked one I didn't know, the congregation would simply sing it without me.

The church in Eatonia was very important to me in these early formative years. It did not sit on its lot in stark testimony to some architect's creative dream. It was a simple clapboard structure, plain and utilitarian. Everything in our town revolved around it. It's where life began with christenings, where life moved forward with weddings, where it was renewed with Holy Communion and where it ended with funerals. It's where the Scout group and Girl Guides met. It's where the annual "Father and Son" banquets were held. It's where we gave extra in the collection plate to the missionary fund for poor kids in other parts of the world. It's where the townsfolk and the farmers for miles around met in fellowship. If someone missed coming to church, a neighbour would check to be sure he was all right.

In later life, I had occasion to attend services in bigger churches in big cities in different parts of the world but never did I experience a more truly wonderful feeling than walking out of the United Church in Eatonia after a service and shaking hands and being thanked by the minister, just like the grown-ups.

Everything embraced in the words "peace on earth — goodwill toward men" happened in Eatonia at Christmas. We never had to worry about Christmas being 'white' — it always was. All the farmers added sleigh bells, especially for going to church and between their tinkling music, the crisp, clean snow and the beautiful carols, Christmas in our obscure little prairie town was always a very special time. We'd get a package of presents from our grandparents in the east and the gifts we exchanged between ourselves and our friends were mostly handmade. So were the decorations in our house.

Another exciting time was Hallowe'en. The whole town would let its hair down. All gasoline, oil and kerosene came into Eatonia in 45 gallon drums. At any given time a couple of hundred empties could be found lying around waiting to be picked up. All the kids in town became proficient at riding these empty barrels up and down Main Street, making a hell of a noise rattling over the gravel or bumping up and over the wooden sidewalks. On Hallowe'en, the first item on the agenda was to roll all the empty barrels we could find into the middle of Main Street and block all the traffic. The grownups knew it was going to happen and made alternate arrangements to park their cars or tether their horses. For days before, everyone had been working on their costumes. The girls would dress as boys and the boys as girls.

One Hallowe'en I had one of Aunt Carrie's dresses on with the hem pinned up loosely. I had lipstick and rouge plastered all over my face and along with about twenty other town kids was busy pulling a four-horse seed-drill up Main Street. Suddenly, the hem on my dress came loose and as I tripped over it and fell, the seed-drill kept right on coming. I barely had time to cover my head before the drill discs ran over the length of my body. They cut like knives through everything from Aunt Carrie's dress to Aunt Katie's brassiere and patent-leather high-heeled pumps. The kids dragged me into the drugstore where they stuck patches on me wherever I was bleeding, which was every six inches, the distance between the discs. In no time I was back on the street, my dress cut in strips and tatters, little the worse for the experience.

We always did our 'trick or treat' at the front doors of the houses before we started dumping over the outhouses at the back. It wouldn't work the other way around. The challenge was to make sure that every outhouse in town had been tipped over before the night was through. One elderly lady, who lived alone, would fasten hers to the ground with guy wires connected to four iron stakes that were pounded into the ground, three feet deep. Every year was the same. We'd just snap the guy wires with wire cutters and over it'd go, just like all the others.

On two occasions we didn't win. One man sat in his outhouse all night with the door open and a shotgun in plain view. The other time, unbeknownst to us, another man had had his outhouse moved ahead four feet. The hole had been covered over lightly with flimsy slats and a layer of grass to make it look like the surrounding terrain. As we approached the rear of the outhouse in the dark the first four boys fell in, and by the time we extricated them our enthusiasm had waned.

Another Hallowe'en was rather special. One of the kids had a team of horses and a stone boat. A stone boat is built very low to the ground so that heavy objects like big stones can be rolled onto it. We headed for the town dump where we loaded the half-decayed remnants of what had once been a horse. The carcass was crawling with worms and maggots. Once loaded, we hauled this foul-smelling hulk back into town and deposited it in the vestibule of the school. Mission accomplished! School was cancelled for two days until the town fathers could clean up the mess.

Meanwhile, some of the bigger boys were waiting for a particular farmer to arrive. We'll just call him Olaf. He drove a big freight wagon and his horses were pitifully scrawny and thin. Their manes and tails had never been brushed and it was obvious Olaf didn't take good care of his animals. The matter had been discussed at church meetings and though some of the church elders had spoken to him about it, Olaf politely told them to mind their own business.

Olaf finally arrived, tied up his team, and went sauntering down Main Street, headed for Asnin's store. As soon as he was out of sight, the boys unhooked his team and dragged his wagon around the back of the school. By this time, the rest of us had arrived and there must have been at least thirty of us busy dismantling the big freight wagon. All the wheels were taken off and the body taken apart. Piece by piece, the components were hoisted with a block and tackle onto the roof of the school. Here, the wagon was reassembled and the block and tackle taken away. The wagon stayed up there until the following spring. Nobody could figure how we got it up there in one piece and certainly, no one could quite figure out how to get it down. Olaf moved out of our district a short time later and nobody missed him.

Every small town in Saskatchewan had a Chinese café. In town after town, they were called either the "New York Café" or the "Canada Café." Two Chinese gentlemen operated it, Jim Kow and Chin Sam. Although much has been written about the sad exploitation of the Chinese during the building of Canada's railroads, little has been written about their contribution to the heritage of this country. They were a part, albeit a small part, of every community in the west. Although they were accepted as part of the community, their culture did not allow the same degree of integration as immigrant Caucasians. While a Swedish man might marry a German girl or a Scottish man might marry a Ukrainian girl, most Chinese remained bachelors, as there were few Chinese women allowed into the country during that period. Still, theirs was a meaningful contribution to the beginnings of our country — they too were the early pioneers. Transients could rent rooms over the Canada Café, and when the trains spent the night in Eatonia, the crews would use these rooms.

Trains were an important part of my growing up. It upset me when a train arrived during school hours and I couldn't be there to meet it. I am not talking about the super-efficient diesel-powered trains of today; I am talking about *real* trains — *steam* trains — huge, powerful, intimidating, frightening monsters that could pull a mile-long string of boxcars loaded with grain. Eatonia had a "Y" configuration of tracks which ran about half a mile out of town on two gradually separating tracks. If we happened to get a friendly crew, they'd let us ride a boxcar up and down the "Y" as the cars were being separated and assembled in the right order. Those were wonderful times.

A stockyard had been built just off the railroad right-of-way. We'd sit on the fence for hours as the cattle were shunted from one corral to another and finally up a loading ramp into one of the cattle cars.

The steam engine would sit and wait with steam hissing from a hundred places, seeming to know we were all watching. Then there would be a tremendous surge of power and the drive wheels would spin on the tracks, showering sparks in all directions. Steam would gush out of release valves and this beautiful iron monster would slowly begin to move. You could see a sweating fireman shovelling coal into the glowing furnace as the engine went by, the engineer waving and blowing a long, ear-shattering blast on the whistle. A train whistle, up close, is fearful, but when it's far away, it has a haunting, mournful sound. You could hear a train an hour before it arrived as it blew its whistle at every crossing. I can still hear that melancholy cry. I'd lie in bed at night listening and wondering where the train had come from and where it was going.

One day a bunch of us watched a train come in and the crew bed it down for the night. When they had finished, a man with a kit bag came over to me and asked for directions to the café. He was black — the first black man I'd ever seen. I was slightly in awe of him but kind of proud as I led him up the street towards the café with all the other kids trailing behind.

"So this is Eatonia," he said, as we sauntered along. "Heard a lot about this place — what's your name, son?"

"Bobby," I replied, my eyes focussed straight ahead.

"Well, Bobby, me 'n you's gonna be good friends. I'll be comin' here regular for a while and it'll be nice havin' a friend in Eatonia."

We had arrived in front of the café and I was looking down and kicking some gravel.

He put his kit bag down and put his hands on my shoulders. "You never seen a black man before, son?"

"As a matter of fact, no I haven't," I replied. "Are you that way — like all over?" I asked and I could have bitten my tongue as soon as I said it.

He was smiling. "Son, you go home and tell your folks you met your first black man today. Tell them his name is Johnson and that he's gonna be your best friend — okay?"

"Okay, I'm gonna tell 'em soon's I get home, Mr. Johnson," I babbled as he turned and went into the café.

I did tell Mom about Mr. Johnson and that he was going to be my friend, but I couldn't seem to get around to explaining that he was black. I met his train three or four times a month. Finally, I asked Mom if I could bring my friend home for supper on his next trip and she agreed. When I arrived a few days later with Mr. Johnson, I was surprised to learn that neither Mom, nor her two sisters who were living with us had ever seen a black man either. He was very friendly and put everyone at ease with stories about moving to Canada from the States and how much he loved living in Canada. He became a regular for supper when his crew was in town and we got Christmas cards from him long after he stopped coming to Eatonia.

Every prairie town had a 'Jew's store.' Ours had the imposing name *The Eaton Supply Company Limited* and was owned by Mike Asnin. No one ever referred to it by its real name, it was simply known as the Jew's store. In Eatonia, no one had any aversion to calling it that, nor was anyone even remotely aware there might be something wrong in using that terminology. There wasn't. Asnin dealt in groceries and drygoods and his store really smelled good. When no trains were due, I loved hanging around his store and, generally, Asnin didn't seem to mind. With my total immersion in the Bible stories I learned in Sunday school and having had to memorize every last word in the Ten Commandments, the idea of ever stealing anything never occurred to me. Periodically, Asnin would give me a fig or a prune out of one of the bins, but I wouldn't have dreamed of taking one without his permission.

Mike Asnin had a deep faith in the people of the area and he never stopped supplying credit to anyone, based on the good crops that would surely come — next year. In the back of the store was an area outfitted with long benches and some comfortable old chairs. On Saturdays, when the farmers came to town, this space was a gathering place for the wives and smaller children. I loved hanging around watching these ladies. Most were immigrants from European countries and it seem perfectly normal for them to breast-feed their offspring in the back of Asnin's store as they held animated conversations with their friends and neighbours. To me, reared in a rigid Victorian environment, looking at these ladies feeding their babies was sheer fascination. Some of their tits were enormous. Old man Asnin was forever interrupting my reveries by grabbing me by the ass of my pants and marching me out the front door. When Asnin was angry he lapsed into German and his voice went up about an octave. I knew enough German to know what he was saying and even if I hadn't, the pitch of his voice would have told me to get out of there as fast as I could.

We had two boarders. One was the town druggist and the other ran one of the grain elevators. They didn't sleep at our house, just had their meals there, for Mom was a great cook. The druggist had a crush on my Aunt Katie who was only sixteen (or at least we thought he did). After school Aunt Katie worked in the hardware store to earn a little money for 'women's things,' and save for Christmas and birthday presents. One afternoon, I came home from school and found nobody home. In my nosey way, I started snooping around the house and under some things in Aunt Katie's dresser drawer, I found 85 cents. For some unexplainable reason, I stuck the money in my pocket. It never really occurred to me that I was stealing. Before I could do anything, somebody came in and then I couldn't put it back. I ran down to the Jew's store and after some browsing I bought seventeen toffee bars at a nickel each. It was only then that the realization of what I'd done hit me. I ate one hurriedly on my way home and hid the others under a pile of lumber in the back yard. I didn't feel good about what I'd done and worried about it the rest of the afternoon.

The conversation that night during supper felt strained. Normally the two boarders would kid around with my aunts and Mom but there was a tension in the air that night. As soon as supper was over, they both left. Then Dad tapped his knife on the table, which meant 'silence,' and I knew something was coming.

"I think Katie has something she wants to talk about but before she does, maybe there's something we should do first."

I looked down at my empty plate, afraid to look up. I sensed everyone around the table was looking at me.

Dad spoke again. "Just a little exercise to test your memories. You first, Lloyd — let's see if you remember all the words in the second Commandment."

Lloyd looked over at Dad, a surprised expression on his face. Memorizing parts of the scriptures was a part of going to Sunday school. We knew many of the Psalms, word for word, some of the better known Bible stories like "The Good Samaritan" and certainly all of the Ten Commandments. Lloyd's voice sounded almost automated as he began: "Thou shalt not make thee any graven image, *or* any likeness *of any thing* that *is* in heaven above, or that *is* in the waters beneath the earth: Thou shalt not bow down thyself unto them, nor serve them: For I the Lord thy God *am* a jealous God, visiting the iniquity of the fathers upon the children unto the third and fourth *generation* of them that hate me."

I sneaked a look around the table. Mom was smiling; my two aunts looked rather bored and Dad's face was expressionless as Lloyd went on.

"And shewing mercy unto thousands of them that love me and heed my Commandments."

"Very good, son," Dad said. "Now we'll see if Bob remembers his . . . let's see now . . . why don't you take a couple of the short ones . . . what about the fifth."

"Honour thy father and thy mother," I said quickly.

"Very good. Now, what about the eighth."

It was then I realized I was a dead duck. My head was almost touching the table as my voice intoned the words, "Thou shalt not steal."

"Now, Katie, what was it you wanted to say?" Dad asked quietly.

Aunt Katie's voice was very deliberate as she spoke. "Somebody took 85 cents out of my dresser today. It was there when I went to school this morning and it's gone now."

Dad crashed the table with his fist and all the dishes jumped. "Now, somebody took that money and I want to know *who* and I want to know *now.*"

I sat up straight as a board and I must have had guilt written all over me as I whispered. "I took the money."

"Well then, give it back to your aunt and get up to your room — I'll be up in a few minutes."

"I can't," I said. "I spent it."

"You spent it! What on?"

"On toffee bars. I ate one and I hid the others out back."

"I see," Dad said, his voice ominous. "S'ppose ya just go out back and get 'em."

I went outside and came back a few minutes later and dumped the 16 toffee bars on the table.

"Seein's how ya like toffee bars so much you'd steal yur aunt's money to buy 'em, tell ya what we'll do." Dad's voice was almost friendly as he continued. "Ya realize ya can't steal and not be punished, don't ya?"

"Yes sir," I said.

"Well — how'd ya like to eat all those toffee bars before ya leave the table?"

I couldn't believe my ears. I loved toffee bars. What kind of punishment was this?

"And we're all gonna sit right here and watch 'til ev'ry last one is gone," Dad said. He shoved the pile of bars over in front of me and said, "Okay, get started."

The first couple of bars were fantastic. The third one began sticking in my teeth and I asked Mom for a toothpick.

"No toothpicks," Dad said gruffly. "Just keep eating."

Before I could swallow the toffee, it had to be chewed until it was soft. Each bar seemed harder than the one before and long before I got to number eight, my teeth seemed loose in their sockets and my jaws began to ache. Around 10 o'clock, Dad excused everybody so's they could go to bed but he just sat there watching as I took the wrapper off number nine. It was 2:30 in the morning when I finally swallowed the last bite. I could barely open and close my mouth. I have never eaten toffee since.

In the fall I would spend hours on the edge of town looking out over the prairies. What a good time of the year this was, with the grain ripe and ready for harvest. The pump house roof was one of the best places for watching. It was pretty high and nobody could see me. The roof was slanted a little, with slats about a foot apart almost like a ladder so's you couldn't slip.

I'd lie on my back, my eyes squinting a kind of focus which allowed me to see only what I wanted to look at. I could shut out the bustle of the roundhouse and look right past it just by squinting a certain way. All around, the world was gold and waving gently, except when I'd look straight up. Nothing is higher or bluer than a prairie sky in autumn. White, fluffy clouds float aimlessly. As long as I kept my eyes half-focused, nothing could have been more peaceful and nowhere could the world have been more in tune with itself.

All I had to do to shake myself out of this tranquility was to open my eyes wide. Then the world came alive with frantic activity. The period between the ripening of the grain and the harvest was short. Dozens of extra men would arrive from the east, mostly riding in empty boxcars, to help with the harvest.

Binders with slithering blades would cut the grain, which fell backwards onto a moving binder canvas. It was pushed into a neat bundle on the one end of the binder canvas, and when a sheaf had accumulated it was automatically tied with twine and ejected onto the ground. Men followed the binder, arranging the sheaves into stooks. There was a knack to 'stooking' and many an eastern rookie spent frustrating hours getting the hang of it. Once the stooks had had their time in the sun the threshing outfit moved onto the farm. The stooks were loaded onto hay racks and one sheaf at a time fed into the thresher. These were marvelous machines, belt-driven in those early years by a steam engine which boosted the power in its boilers by burning some of the straw it was ejecting. Wheat poured out of a big spout on the thresher into a wagon box and the stripped straw was blown into a huge stack.

The steam engine was a magnificent machine, too. Except for a slight hiss of escaping steam, it was practically noiseless but very powerful.

As soon as the threshing was finished the outfit moved on to the next farm, leaving behind full granaries and huge straw stacks. When the straw had been allowed to settle for a few days the town kids built tunnels in them. I spent many a happy hour playing in them. It was a part of every prairie kid's growing up.

Those were good days for Dad, too. The farmers' harvesting equipment had to be made ready and Dad usually hired a couple of extra men to help him with the repairing of binder canvases, sharpening the cutting blades, and fixing worn or broken parts. The good years were also a good time for farm machinery sales. Dad was a wheeler-dealer and he'd accept worn machines, knowing he could put them in good repair, as down-payments on new machines. He'd take lien notes against the day the farmer would sell his grain. By 1928 he had dozens of secondhand farm implements and tractors sitting on a vacant lot and lien notes against farmers amounting to more than $80,000. On paper we were well off, but we never seemed to have any money. Mom was always charging her groceries at the Jew's store.

In autumn, everything was fat. The prairie chickens were fat; the badgers and ground hogs were fat; the ducks and geese arriving in orderly 'V's and landing on the newly-harvested fields were fat; even the gophers were fat.

Catching gophers was a lot of fun and a source of pin money for the town kids. In spring, these little prairie rodents would dig up the seed as fast as the farmers got it into the ground. During May and June, if the gopher community was getting out of hand, the government would pay a bounty of from three to five cents for a gopher tail.

When there was water in the sloughs or along the railroad grade we'd go out with a couple of pails and an old washtub and drown them out. Gophers dig a hole and then a whole network of extra bedrooms connected by tunnels. We could pour a couple of washtubs full of water into the hole before he'd come out, looking like a half-drowned rat. We'd quickly put him out of his misery and deposit his tail in our pockets. When there was no water the process was slower. We'd take a long piece of binder-twine and form a slip noose on one end. We'd wait until we saw a gopher go down a hole then quietly put the noose around the entrance. We'd string our twine back until we were perhaps fifty feet away and wait. A gopher is very cautious. He would stick his head up for a split second and immediately disappear. Gradually he would get braver and braver and eventually stick his head all the way out and look around. One quick yank on the twine and that was it. Another gopher — another tail.

The relationship between my two aunts, my parents and the rest of us kids was unique. The aunts weren't that much older than Lloyd and me and had to observe the same family discipline. One of the extra freedoms they enjoyed, which was denied Lloyd and me, was access to Mom's True Story Magazines. That didn't mean we didn't read them whenever we had the chance. The locale of the stories was generally some remote part of the world like New York or Hollywood, even Paris. The men depicted earned as much as $60 a week, which was pure fantasy. People went to parties on yachts big enough to have their own orchestra on board. Though it was all quite ridiculous the stories were intensely interesting to me. The love aspects also became a part of my fantasies as a young, growing boy. It was another world but I would never see it nor did I believe in all of it. Most of it was so far-fetched, especially when I looked around at the simple life of our little town.

Between those stories and the time I spent on the pump house roof or lying on my back on a straw stack, I spent a great deal of time daydreaming. I was happy and contented, but I knew that somewhere out there was a bigger world where people did more than eat and sleep and go to school and church. If it was printed in a magazine some of it must be true. More and more I fantasised. When Bing Crosby made a recording he had a whole bunch of musicians playing in his orchestra — why couldn't I be one of those musicians? Or maybe I could play hockey for the Toronto Maple Leafs — or be a singer like I saw at the travelling Chautauqa show. Even better, maybe I could be an engineer on the trains and go anywhere I wanted and eat in restaurants all the time.

When I was six my sister Kathleen was born and when I was eight Aunt Katie married a farmer from the next town.

During summer holidays, Lloyd and I would take turns spending a month each with Aunt Katie and Uncle Garner. I learned how to ride horses and Uncle Garner even let me drive his tractor. Because Katie knew about my bed-wetting this was one of the few places I could go and not be embarrassed. Uncle Garner was one of four brothers and each had a quarter-section of land. Their Dad also owned a half-section. Between them, they farmed 960 acres and they pooled their resources during seeding and harvest times. About half of their land was seeded in wheat and the other half was summer fallow, which means that half the land was allowed to rest every second year. The summer fallow was used to graze cattle, horses and other livestock.

During one of these summer holidays — I guess I must have been nine years old — I can remember standing on the front porch with my aunt and uncle watching a big black cloud forming on the horizon. Minutes later, the cloud was overhead and the heavens opened and spewed disaster — thunder and lightning and hailstones as big as eggs raining down and rattling on the tin granaries. Garner stood with tears in his eyes as he watched a year's labour go down the drain in less than five minutes.

When the stock market crashed in the fall of 1929, the effect was felt immediately on the prairies. That same year the drought hit and cash crops disappeared. When farmers couldn't grow cash crops the whole economy suffered. The towns existed because of the farmers, and when the crops failed everyone felt it. Crops had been good through most of the Twenties. Most farmers were well off and owed very little money. They bought more land and began to mechanize their farms. During the Twenties, 25,000 tractors, tens of thousands of cars and trucks, and more than 5,000 expensive combines were sold in Saskatchewan. Dad's business boomed selling farm implements and cars and on paper, he made a lot of money. With crop failures and the price of wheat falling to 50 cents from $1.25 a bushel — and no wheat to sell, it was impossible to retire their debts. The spectre of financial ruin descended on everyone, and few had the resources to survive.

The drought was not an overnight disaster. You didn't wake up one morning and find the land had given way to drifting dust. It just stopped raining. Seed didn't take hold in the hard-caked soil, grain didn't grow and there was nothing to harvest. The Saskatchewan triangle, with Saskatoon as its apex and the U.S. border as its base, produced almost $100 million worth of wheat in 1927. By 1936, this had shrunk to $3 million. Almost eight years went by with literally no rain.

Because the process was gradual, and because there was always next year, the federal government remained apathetic, viewing the drought as something which would correct itself as soon as the rains came. There had been droughts before but they had always been followed by good years. The east did not recognize the extent of the western problem until much of the damage to the west and its people was irreversible.

Blowing topsoil drifted across fields and roads making many of them impassable. Dust covered fences and reached the roofs of farm buildings. It was relentless. It blew in through cracks around windows and under doors. By 1935 the disaster area covered 18 million acres, or a quarter of all farms in Canada. The federal government finally recognized the worst calamity in Canadian history was in the making on the western plains.

In 250 municipalities there was almost total destitution and the distribution of 'relief' had become Saskatchewan's biggest industry. The people who administered the relief programs were themselves on it. School teachers went unpaid and most municipalities defaulted on their debentures.

The price of everything the farmers produced went down and stayed down. Those who remained on their land wore out their machinery and had no resources to keep it in repair.

Dad began building "Bennett Buggies" and "Anderson Carts." R. B. Bennett was the prime minister of Canada, and during the late Twenties, J. T. M. Anderson became the first-ever Conservative premier of the province. The Bennett Buggies were converted from the larger, more expensive cars such as Essex, Terraplane, Pontiac, and McLaughlin-Buick. Dad would remove the motor and drive train and reassemble the steering mechanism on to a hitch with a wagon tongue so the vehicle could be pulled by a team of horses. The steering wheel was removed and the finished conveyance was really the body of a car pulled by a team of horses. Anderson Carts were similar but, Anderson being a lesser politician than Bennett, his carts were converted from lesser automobiles such as Fords or Chevs. The ride was certainly better on tires with tubes than on the normal, bumpy, iron-rimmed wagon wheels, even though it meant having to carry a repair kit for fixing flat tires.

What was happening in Saskatchewan was also happening in the bordering provinces of Alberta and Manitoba. Our American neighbours were going through the same drought. In Oklahoma, Arkansas, and Nebraska, people were leaving in droves. The 'Okies' and the 'Arkies' loaded their belongings on to beat-up old trucks and headed for the promised land, California.

For a long period, optimism prevailed among the hardy settlers in southern Saskatchewan. Somehow, next year would be better. Dad took stock of the $80,000 in lien notes owed him by the farmers. After counting the heartbreak he put the notes back in a tin box under the bed. People borrowed all they could from the banks against next year's crop. They ran up bills in Asnin's store and lived on the future — one good crop with prices high was all they needed to turn themselves around.

Most held on as long as they could, then started to move. A sign would go up in Asnin's store announcing an auction sale, and a family would be gone. Many moved west to British Columbia, but many more took advantage of a government plan and moved north where the survey had been extended and new homesteads were available.

Even if the rains came it would be years before the land would be productive again. Dad had a decision to make. He joined a group of farmers who were going north to look around. When he returned a few weeks later he had filed on a homestead in the far north. The site was only nine miles from the end of the survey in northern Saskatchewan and not too far from the Alberta boundary. When he got back, he showed us on a map where we would be living. The map was a calendar from the Saskatchewan Wheat Pool. The calendar was the same every year and the map showed the province in detail. As the survey moved farther and farther north, the map, unfortunately, had not been revised to show these newly-surveyed areas. On the top of the calendar, over the map, was a wide, narrow picture showing a harvest scene and a field of wheat stooks. Off to the right was a grain elevator with the words Saskatchewan Wheat Pool and on the left, behind one of the wheat stooks was where out new homestead would be. Right off the map!.

Dad began disposing of most of his farm equipment. He traded farm machinery until he had a dozen head of cattle and six horses. After the trading was finished we, too, put up a sign in Asnin's store announcing our auction sale.

Two railway freight cars were loaded with farm machinery of every description. All of Dad's tools, accumulated over a decade, three industrial-type sewing machines, some dismantled chassis from Model T Fords, farm wagons with extra wheels and rims, a blacksmith's forge and anvil, tin and zinc sheets, two seed drills, sets of harrows, a hay mower, a brand-new binder still in crates, plows of various sizes, tinsmithing machines for cutting and crimping plus a complete set of lasts and a heavy metal base used for repairing shoes, a gasoline-driven lathe, and all the assorted paraphernalia collected over twenty years went into the railway cars. On the last day before we were to leave another cattle car was loaded with the livestock. The cars went on their way to St. Walburg, the end of the railway in the north.

Aunt Carrie was now married and living in St. Walburg. She and her husband made arrangements for the cars to be unloaded when they arrived. They also arranged for a fenced-in pasture for the livestock. None of the cows were milking.

The night before we were to leave, there was a farewell party for us in the church hall. There were speeches, a lot of well-wishing and a few tears. We said our goodbyes and promised to write and tell everyone how we were getting along. I could hardly wait for the next morning and the excitement of this new adventure. I was ten years old.

Chapter 3

THE MORNING DAWNED under foreboding skies but it wasn't only the sky that looked that way. The atmosphere around the house was troubled as furniture and personal belongings were moved this way and that. It was as though someone had died and this was the final dispersal of his possessions. We said goodbye to things we had grown up with and would never see again. The neighbours had gathered around to help us pack the few essentials we would need to begin life all over again.

Our old piano was somewhere under the pile, securely lashed to the corner posts. No way would it be left behind. Unkind words had been said about it when we were struggling with Gledhill's lessons, but it was an old friend now and no one in the family would have dreamed of parting with it. Somewhere, too, was a wooden box containing two guitars, a banjo, a fiddle and Dad's set of drums. Even though we were going off the map it wouldn't be the end of the road as far as music was concerned. The instruments would have a meaningful place in our lives in the months and years to come. They would become our livelihood later, when we changed from homesteaders into wandering minstrels.

The truck was a hybrid, assembled by Dad. The motor and drivetrain were from a Reo Speed Wagon truck. It had a Ruxell Ford rear end and how these mismatches were put together was a tribute to his ingenuity. On one of the running boards a larger-than-normal tool kit had been installed, just in case.

All the materials for repairing flat tires and a rugged over-size tire pump were stowed. Flat tires were a way of life. Apart from the short stretch of highway between Regina and Moose Jaw which had an asphalt surface, all other main highways in Saskatchewan were gravel. The secondary roads were merely graded and everyone had the gear to extricate themselves from the mud if it rained.

Most of the roads were known as 'washboard' because the surface was like the corrugated washing board on which clothes were washed and scrubbed. On the gravel roads, ridges would form a few inches apart, and the more the traffic used the road the deeper these ridges would get. A few hours on one of these highways and your teeth felt loose.

Mom and Dad sat in the front cab with the baby, Joyce, the future singing star, who was only a few months old. Lloyd was eleven, Kathleen was four and I was ten. We were sitting high on the load on top of our mattresses. As we pulled out to the last goodbyes of the assembled townsfolk, you could feel the truck was pulling a heavy load and once we hit the washboard at Kindersley, 44 miles away, the going would be painfully slow.

From Eatonia to North Battleford was 240 miles and most of it was washboard gravel all the way. From North Battleford to St. Walburg was another 110 miles and the road had no surface at all. It was to be a bone-shaking, rough and bumpy 350 miles. That was as far as the truck would take us. From then on it would have to be wagon and horses, north for another 80 miles to the homestead.

Saskatchewan is very symmetrical, almost a perfect rectangle except that the southern boundary, which borders on the states of Montana and North Dakota, is slightly longer than the northern border with the North-west Territories. When the province was surveyed, correction lines were made to allow for the differential. There was a correction line, as I remember, every six miles as we moved north. Each correction line was only a matter of a few rods but it made it possible for complete sections of land to be surveyed.

At Kindersley the skies darkened and the winds began to blow, at first in fitful gusts, then stronger, picking up the dust, which ran like whirling dervishes across the parched earth. In no time the hot wind sucked the surface of the prairie into a rolling, billowing, dust cloud that effaced the daylight and suffocated the sun into a ghost of dull red glow that could barely be seen. Dad had to turn on the lights. Most of the driving was in first or second gear. As the wind increased, visibility went down to ten or twelve feet in front of the truck. At every correction line Lloyd and I had to walk on either side of the truck, hollering instructions to Dad to make certain he was driving down the middle of the road. We tied bandanas over our faces to keep the dust out but our faces were soon black. The dust seeped through everything on the truck. Our mattresses were covered with a thick, powdery coating and almost unrecognizable. Somewhere under them, covered with a blanket, was Kathleen. Mom had baby Joyce completely covered up. Luckily we had no flat tires, and when night came we figured we had gone about 50 miles.

We pulled off the road. In minutes we had Dad's tarpaulin hooked up over the truck and Mom was soon cooking a meal on a small camp stove. We all took turns minding the baby while Dad checked under the truck. A couple of mattresses were brought down and the dust banged out. We were all very tired and sleep came easily in the moan and whistle of a now-diminishing wind.

The next morning dawned bright and sunny with no wind at all and we made much better time. Riding high on the load it is difficult to describe how flat and uninteresting the prairies of Saskatchewan can be. As far as one could see, in any direction, everything was the same. On trips west in subsequent years I was astonished to see how lush and green the prairies can be, especially in the spring and early summer when the grain crops are three or four inches high, but on our trip north it was a silent and vacant world. The only noise was the rattling, jarring vibration of the truck that seemed to get louder as the prairie silence deepened.

The second day we did much better, even with two flat tires. Counting the correction lines we estimated we had covered about 130 miles giving us 220 to go to St. Walburg.

The third day the landscape began to change. Here and there were patches of green and the odd stunted tree. The terrain became a little more rolling and, with the heavy load, the truck spent most of its time in low gear as it groaned and complained its way up the slight inclines.

That night, by the light from a coal-oil lantern, Dad wrote a long letter home to his folks in Ontario and another to his sister in Detroit. Some of these letters were made available to me in later years and served to remind me of many of the details, long since forgotten. They made me wonder why there was so little communication between us children and our parents, especially Dad. He bared his soul in letters he wrote to his sister. He didn't have that kind of communication with us, even with Mom. In our family, there was never any display of love or affection. We had great admiration for Dad, and Mom was a warm and caring person, but there was little show of feelings. We grew up having learned to mask or hide them. The normal relationship enjoyed by most children with their parents, the closeness of family, the hugging, the touching, was totally absent in our house. Naturally I was not to know this, as what we were going through was all we had ever known and therefore was right and natural. We were developing complexes and hang-ups that would have been an analyst's Utopia.

It wasn't our job as kids to worry about what we were going to eat, or even *if* we were going to eat, let alone where we were going. Dad did all the worrying and Mom just went along, never questioning. We just sat on top the mattresses and looked out at this whole new and wonderful adventure.

Looking back, the last way to describe it would be as hardship. It was all very exciting; we were going somewhere!. And nothing was happening to us that wasn't happening to many other families. We had uprooted and left, not sure what was waiting for us except that somewhere, up north, things were supposed to be better.

I have often wondered what went through Dad's mind. There he was, with a wife and four kids, an old truck with most of his earthly belongings on it and driving into the unknown. How alone he must have felt when he went to sleep each night. How much better it would have been for all of us if he had allowed us to share his plight.

Two days later we passed through North Battleford, the first *big* city we children had ever seen. It had a population of over 5000. Only Regina, Saskatoon and Moose Jaw were bigger. Even today, the population of Saskatchewan is less than half that of either Toronto or Montreal.

Dad was anxious to keep going, so our first experience of a big city was fleeting. That night we camped well past North Battleford. The next day, the world on either side of the road began to change. We were no longer on the prairies. Tall stands of trees dotted the countryside and the terrain was hilly and rolling.

We were no longer in the dust bowl. The fields were green and we saw cattle and horses, fat and sleek, grazing contentedly. Some of the buildings were painted. For the first time we were seeing the world in colour when we had become so accustomed to it in nondescript shades of grey. Before we went to bed Dad dug an axe out of the tool box, chopped two logs into two-foot lengths and flattened one side of each.

"Gotta feelin' it's gonna rain," he said as he strapped the logs on to the running boards. "We may need these if it does."

The next morning, sure enough, it was raining. It woke us all as it beat a gentle tattoo on the tarpaulin.

"God, that sounds good," Dad said as he pulled on a jacket and stepped out through the flap. We dressed quickly and followed him, Kathleen right behind us. The rain was warm and felt good as it ran down our smiling faces. Kathleen ran back into the lean-to where Mom was dressing the baby.

"Somebody's throwin' water on us," she complained.

Mom smiled. Kathleen, at four years of age, had just seen rain for the first time in her life.

The rain kept up most of the day and we didn't make very good time. We were no longer on gravel and the roads were muddy and full of ruts. Some of the hills could only be negotiated a few feet at a time. Dad unstrapped the two logs he had prepared and looked at Lloyd and me as he surveyed a gentle incline up ahead.

"I want one of you on each of the runnin' boards," he said. "As soon as we start slowin' down, jump off an' stick the logs, flat side down, under the back wheels so's we don't roll back. Okay, here we go!."

He gunned the motor to a high-pitched whine and released the clutch. The truck moved ahead a few feet and Lloyd and I blocked the rear wheels. Over and over, the process was repeated. We were splattered with mud from the spinning wheels, but it worked and we finally reached the brow of the hill. Then the logs would be loaded and we'd ride the running boards, the truck careening down the hill until it stalled again going up the other side.

Dad coaxed and cajoled; he pleaded and cussed. "Come on, ya sonofabitch — go — go!" and he'd push the accelerator to the floor. Mile after arduous mile we laboured until the sun went down and we had to stop for the night. We were still about 30 miles from St. Walburg when we went to bed, tired and bedraggled.

The next afternoon we pulled into St. Walburg and were greeted warmly by Aunt Carrie and her husband, Andy. Andy was a Caterpillar tractor expert working on railway grades which would extend the lines farther north. This was a never-ending election ploy. Whenever an election came up, one of the campaign promises invariably was to extend the line north, but as soon as the election was over the railway grades would disappear into the muskeg as the work was discontinued. Uncle Andy followed the construction business wherever it took him and the year we moved north he was busy keeping heavy earth-moving equipment in repair for a large construction crew based in St. Walburg.

He had arranged to rent a house for us and had supervised the unloading of the freight cars when they arrived. We all got busy unloading the truck and getting some semblance of order into what would be our new home for the next few months. It was August, 1930, and the Depression was choking the hearts out of the people. St. Walburg was still 80 miles from the new homestead but nothing could be accomplished that year. Buildings would have to be erected before we could move onto this piece of virgin land and it was too late in the year to start that sort of construction. It would have been winter before anything had a roof on, so Lloyd and I were registered at the local school, just across the street from the rented house, and Kathleen began her first year at school.

The following spring, when school was over, we began moving up to the homestead. We had only two horses left and eight head of cattle. During the winter we had lived mostly by disposing of some of the livestock we had brought with us and what Dad felt was excess farm machinery. He also sold the old truck for a pittance. We were left with enough farm machinery to meet our needs, together with Dad's tools and workshop machines.

The 40 mile road north to Loon Lake, while only a bush trail, wasn't too bad. But the 40 miles from Loon Lake to the homestead was another story. Much of it passed through muskeg. While a road of sorts skirted the worst of the muskeg areas, there was no way to get around one called "The Big Muskeg." Going north, it *had* to be crossed. It was about an eighth of a mile across and a lake of thick, stinking, oozing mud, anywhere from one to five feet deep, the surface thinly covered with clumps of grass and moss. Jump up and down on a clump of grass and the muskeg would ripple all around you for a hundred feet. Getting stuck, or breaking the surface of this muck was not unlike getting stuck in quicksand. You kept going down until you hit firmer footing, and in many instances the muck would almost cover a horse.

The first loads were small and light — the tools we would need for building, most of Dad's workshop tools, some of the lighter farm machinery, etc. There had only been light spring rains and the muskegs, even the big one, didn't present any major problems.

On our first trip north we couldn't help but wonder what all the fuss was about. Lloyd and I were left on the homestead to keep an eye on the first load. We had a small tent and ground sheets, a .22 rifle with a couple of boxes of shells, some salt, a 100 pound bag of flour mixed, half-and-half, with ground wheat which had been run through an oat chopper so the flour would last longer. We also had a couple of rolls of wire for snares, some fishing line with spoon hooks and matches packed in tin boxes to keep them dry.

It would take Dad about two weeks to return to St. Walburg, do what had to be done there, and return with another load. In the meantime Lloyd and I were left to fend for ourselves. This became an interesting period for us because for the first time we were really together, just the two of us.

With the lack of any outward show of affection in our family, there had always been an emotional void between us and a degree of rivalry which started back in Eatonia. Mom had arranged for us to begin our first school year at the same time. This wasn't done by holding Lloyd back a year, rather I was allowed to start a year early when I was only four. We both jumped grade two and I know this bothered Lloyd at the time as he was eighteen months older than me and I guess he figured he should have been eighteen months smarter. Then there was a certain resentment because I had attracted attention with my piano playing. Lloyd refused to play for anyone but the teacher, while I never missed an opportunity to play whenever I was asked. This was counterbalanced somewhat by my bed-wetting and Lloyd rarely missed a chance to bring this up. In Eatonia we had had our own little circles of friends and didn't need each other. Things were different now.

The first day after Dad left, we wandered over to the adjoining homesteads to look around and find out who our neighbours were. Only two 'quarters' had been filed on. The next quarter north was owned by Lizzie and Ted Boening, a brother and sister. Though they were very hospitable we could see just by looking around that they didn't have very much. We were scouting to see if we might get an invitation for supper or maybe even mooch a couple of quarts of preserves or whatever. Nothing doing.

The man across the right-of-way from us was a bachelor and his place was a shambles. We wouldn't have eaten there if we *had* been invited. His cabin was filthy.

"You kids got any rope over ta yer place?" he asked.

" 'Fraid we don't," Lloyd answered. "Why?"

"Well I got this horse, Nellie — sonofabitch she got away on me 'bout a month back. Haven't bin able to catch 'er since. Keep seein' 'er hangin' 'round but can't get close 'nough ta snag 'er. If I had some rope, maybe I could get a lasso over 'er fuckin' head."

God, he talked dirty. He never did catch that horse. Not all the time we lived in the north. It must have been the only wild horse up there. We'd often see her running with the other horses or just grazing but she wouldn't let you near enough to catch her.

It was getting on in the afternoon by the time we got back to our place.

"I'll make some biscuits outta the flour," Lloyd said. "Why don't you set a couple of snares and see if we can catch a rabbit. I see all kinds of 'em 'specially down by the creek. Set the snares down there and while you're waiting there's a big patch of blueberries just over Boening's fence."

I grabbed a pail and some snares and walked down to the creek. You could see little paths in the underbrush so I figured small animals had their own little network of highways and I was right. The snares looked very professional — you could hardly see them and they were securely tied to willow clumps. I went back up the hill and into Boening's blueberry patch. The blueberries were ripe and lush. For each one I put in the pail, I ate one 'cause we hadn't eaten all that day. I could smell the smoke from Lloyd's fire and I figured if I got lucky with one of the rabbit snares we'd have a fine meal, what with Lloyd's biscuits or muffins or whatever they were going to be when he was finished. The pail was finally full of berries and I wandered back to the creek bed to check the snares. The first one had been disturbed but there was nothing in it. As I turned along the creek to check the second one, I could see all hell breaking loose up ahead. I ran towards the ruckus and stopped abruptly. There was something in the snare but it sure as hell wasn't a rabbit.

I ran back part way up the hill and hollered at Lloyd. "Get down here, quick, I got somp'n in one of the snares but you're gonna hafta help me with it."

Lloyd came running and whatever it was was in its last throes, the snare pulled tightly around its neck. We waited a few minutes to be sure and edged closer.

"What is it?" I asked.

"Not sure, but it looks like a red fox."

Sure enough, that's what it was and it was sad because you could see it was a mother and must have babies somewhere. Its eyes were bugging out and there was no doubt it was dead.

"Whadda we gonna do with it? We can't just leave it here stinking up the place. We gotta bury it, or somethin'."

"Unhook the snare," Lloyd said, "and we'll drag it over and dump it in the fire."

So that's what we did. In the following years, when we really tried to snare fox for their skins, we were never successful. This was the only time we ever got one and it was out of season and worthless.

By the time we were finished getting rid of the fox, Lloyd's biscuits looked more like shoe leather interspersed with bran. Supper that night consisted mostly of blueberries and tea we made out of dandelions. When we went to bed that night we felt we'd had a pretty good day, all in all, except we both felt bad about the fox.

The next morning we got a fire going and Lloyd went out to set a couple of snares. I was just sitting around waiting and gazing into the fire, day-dreaming and there, not more than 50 feet away sat a rabbit. Slowly I sneaked into the tent and got the .22. It made a loud click as I shoved a shell into the breach and I was hoping the rabbit hadn't heard it. Wrong! When I crept out and looked around, it was gone. Stealthily, I worked my way through the trees and a couple of hundred feet later there it was, sitting up on its haunches smiling at me. I couldn't have been more than 30 feet from it. I carefully raised the rifle until I had it in my sights and pow! Down it went.

Lloyd came running when he heard the shot and together we skinned and cleaned it. We took it down to the creek and washed it then rigged up a spit and strung it over the fire. Rabbit for breakfast wasn't our usual fare but we were getting hungry. Just as we were cleaning up the last of the bones, a guy in a buggy came tearing into the clearing.

"Name's Gus," he said as he jumped down and tied his horses to a tree. "Your old man stopped by my place on his way out — told me if I was goin' by ta stop in and see if you little farts is okay."

I looked over at Lloyd. It seemed like everybody we'd seen since we arrived used dirty words.

"Brought ya a couple sacks o' potatoes," he continued as he rummaged around the back of his buggy. He hauled the two bags over and leaned them up against a tree. "One bag's fer eatin' and the other's fer plantin' — you got a shovel?"

"Yeh, we got a couple of shovels."

"Here's what ya do then," Gus said as he dug one of the potatoes out of the sack. "Each of these eyes is a seed, so's all ya do, ya cut the potato into quarters, like so." He proceeded to cut the potato in four pieces and when he finished he grabbed one of the shovels.

"Now, ya dig down 'bout a foot, then turn the sod over and beat the shit outta it with the back o' the shovel, like so. Then put some of the dirt back into the hole and stick a piece o' the potato in, like so. Then cover it up nice an' easy and pat it all down, like so. Think ya can handle that?"

"Seems pretty simple," Lloyd answered.

"If ya get 'em in in the next week or so and we don't have an early frost, leastwise yer folks'll have potatoes come winter. Now, get yer asses in gear 'cause we're goin' fishin'."

"Whadda ya mean, fishing?" I said, "we're supposed to be watching all this stuff."

"Horseshit! — there's nobody in a hunert miles o' here gonna bother this stuff. Now, let's go," he continued as he untied the horses.

Lloyd found the fishing line and spoonhooks. We jumped on the buggy seat beside Gus and he tore off, winding his way through the trees on to the road leading north. The road zigged and zagged gently within the confines of a 60 foot wide strip that had been surveyed and cleared of trees. It was four miles to the village of Goodsoil, which was merely a widening in the road to accommodate a general store and few other assorted buildings. Gus didn't even slow down — he went breezing right through.

"Where exactly we goin'?" Lloyd asked.

" 'Bout five miles up — right where the Waterhen runs outta the lake. Best damn fishin' around — jackfish, maybe fifteen, twenty pounds and stupid. Bite anythin' you throw in and fight like hell."

Gus drove his team like he was going to a fire. He kept slapping the reins along their backs and hollering at them. Sitting on the outside of the narrow buggy seat, I had to hang on all the time or I'd fall off, especially when the road swerved to the left.

The road from Goodsoil to the river was an Indian trail that twisted and turned its way through the trees. In what seemed no time at all we cleared the woods and gazed out upon a beautiful lake.

"There she is — Big Island Lake — see out there," Gus said, "You could fish that fucker the resta yer life an' never in the same place twice. Whitefish bigger'n you." He paused as he jockeyed the buggy around some tree stumps. "Wrong time o' year for whitefish — besides ya need all kindsa worms and crap — smart bastards."

He drove along the shore line to a small cove. We jumped down and helped unhook and unharness the horses. He put halters on them, tied long tethering ropes to the halters and secured them to a tree.

"Now, they gotta 'nough rope ta get to the water if they wanna drink or they can eat grass if they wanna or just lie on their big fat ass. Whadya say yer name was?" he asked me.

"Bobby. But growups gen'rally call me Bob."

"Okay, Bob, scout 'round and bring us a pile o' dry brush. We'll getta fire goin'. Here, take this hatchet, help ya ta dig it out. What's yer brother's name?"

"Lloyd."

"Hey, Lloyd, cum over here and get this axe. I want ya ta cut a whole swath o' those green willows and pile 'em up right here," he said, pointing. He bent down and picked up a handful of dried grass and tossed it in the air and watched as it floated down gently in a northeasterly direction.

"Sonsabitchin' mosquitoes gonna chew our ass off tonight. Gotta build a good smudge fire. When ya get finished that brushin, I wantcha to move the horses. See that big tree?"

I nodded.

"Well tie 'em ta that one — and hustle yer ass, we ain't got all day."

Gus set about building a fire and he sure knew what he was doing. After the dry brush I had gathered took hold, he heaped the fire with some dry deadfall, then even bigger logs he had us drag down. He waited till the fire was a big glowing mass of embers then he dumped some of Lloyd's green willows over the embers. A long, heavy cloud of smoke drifted up and blew gently in the direction of the horses.

"Now, that'll keep the flies off 'em," he said.

The sun was going down over the lake. Lloyd and I sat under the smoke cloud and looked out over this breathtaking but peaceful scene. I'd gone camping a couple of times when we lived in Eatonia but I'd never stayed overnight before.

Gus took his .22 and disappeared up the side of the hill into the dense brush. A couple of minutes later we heard a shot, then another one. Gus came out of the bush carrying two birds.

"Prairie chickens," he announced. "Big and fat this time o' year. Ya know how ta clean 'em?"

"We've never done it, but if you show us, we'll learn real quick,"

We all sat down on a log sticking out into the water and Gus handed one of the birds to us. When we had plucked all the feathers off he took his hunting knife, slit the bird open, dug inside and pulled all the innards out and threw them out into the river.

"You're not supposed ta do that," I said.

"Horseshit. Fish'll clean that up 'fore it turns the first bend."

He sure seemed to know everything. He threw his hunting knife over to Lloyd and I could see my brother gritting his teeth as he slit the bird open. Gus watched, a kind of faint smile on his face. He took both birds and swished them around in the river until he was satisfied they were clean. He found a long green willow to use for a spit and strung the birds out over the glowing coals.

"There's a pail with a handle on it — over there beside the buggy wheel," he said, looking at me. "Go down and fill it up 'bout three-quarters — an' make sure there's no bugs or rabbit shit floatin' 'round in it. We'll make us some tea."

We had us some meal that night. Gus had biscuits in a sack and a quart jar of some kind of preserves that tasted like pumpkin.

Gus checked the horses' tethers to make sure they weren't tangled then banked the fire with a few more big logs and lots more green willow bows. Smoke wafted gently over the camp site.

"Better get yer butts ta bed early 'cause we're goin' fishin' soon's the sun comes up," he said.

Sleep came easy — it had been a long and exciting day.

It seemed that we'd just gone to sleep when we heard Gus throwing more logs on the fire and making tea.

"Half the day is gone — get yer asses movin' — time ta go fishin'."

I hadn't wet myself and that made me feel good.

"Cept fer the tea, we got nothin' ta eat till we catch it, now let's go."

Lloyd grabbed our fishing lines and spoonhooks and we all moved down to the water.

"Ya know how ta tie the hooks on yer line so's they ain't gonna come off?" Gus asked.

"Just tie a good knot, isn't that enough?"

"Bullshit. Here, lemme show ya." Gus proceeded to tie a very fancy knot on to the hook. Then he laid the line out about a hundred feet and cut it. He tied the second hook on the remaining line, then tied the end of each line to logs about 50 feet apart.

"Now, lemme show ya how to get this fishin' business started. First ya wet the line, like so. Then you arrange the line in a neat pile in front of ya so's it ain't gonna tangle. Ya take the hook, like so, and just like you was gonna lasso a cow, ya swings it in a circle 'round yer head and let the circle get bigger'n bigger'n, then pow! — ya let 'er go, like so."

Gus released the hook and it went sailing out over the water. The pile of line was almost gone when we heard the light splash as the hook hit the water. He must have thrown it about 90 feet. Slowly he started reeling it in, making sure it fell into another neat pile in front of him. The spoonhook shimmered through the water.

"That's all there is to it," Gus said. "Take ya a couple o' throws till ya get the hang of it but ya should be able to get most o' the line out every time, long's ya don't hook each other when yer swingin' 'er. If you take that log over there and Lloyd takes this one, ya should be outta each other's way. If ya catch anythin' that doesn't have teeth like a shark, it ain't a jackfish 'n' you can throw it back.

He walked back towards the fire and we saw him dig a gallon jug out from under the buggy seat. He took a big swig and sat down, leaning up against a log, his jug beside him.

Anybody says they've gone fishing, doesn't know what fishing is till they've fished the Waterhen River right where it runs out of Big Island Lake. Every second throw we caught a fish, and when we didn't catch one, we could see it in the clear, clean water trying its damndest to grab the hook before we yanked it out of the water. We threw the fish back as soon as we caught them except for one beauty we were going to eat.

I went back to ask Gus how to clean the fish. He was sleeping so I tapped him gently to wake him up. Boy, was he mad. He threw me his hunting knife, told me to scale the fish and when I had all the scales off, slit it down the middle and clean out the insides.

We finally got the fish nice and clean and made sure by swishing it around in the water. When we got back to the fire Gus was up, staggering around, and you could see he'd really been into his jug.

"Put some lard in that big fryin' pan and soon's it's melted, curl the fish up and fit 'er in. Ya gotta keep turnin' 'er over. Peel some potatoes and boil 'em in one of those pots an' don't fergit the tea. I'm goin' in fer a swim 'n' see if I can get rid of this fuckin' headache."

Geez, did that fish taste good . . .

"Next time," Gus said, "we'll bake it in mud and all the bones'll just lift out."

We were just finishing eating when a big batch of birds landed on the lake. There must have been a million of them.

"Wild ducks," Gus said. "Gotta get us one. If we's quiet, they'll come driftin' this way with the current. We jus' go down and hide behind those logs and wait."

He grabbed the .22 and we got behind a pile of logs at the water's edge and waited. Sure enough, they came drifting right at us. squawking and hollering. Some got caught in the current and Gus drew a bead on one and fired. They took off like a bunch of hornets but one was left flopping around.

Gus jumped up. "Got 'im," he hollered. "Now one of you swim out there and get 'im."

I looked at Lloyd and he looked at me. Finally, Lloyd spoke up. "But neither of us can swim."

"Can't swim? How'n hell d'ya think we was gonna get that fuckin' duck without somebody fetchin' it?"

He was really mad and the duck was comin closer and closer. Gus looked at us disgustedly and ran up to the horses. He untied one and with only its halter on jumped on its back, clothes and all, and headed for the river. The horse didn't seem to mind at all. It plowed right into the water and started swimming. Gus grabbed the duck as it floated by and in no time he was back on dry land. He sure knew how to do a lot of things, Gus did. He turned back into his friendly self again before he went to sleep that night, especially after Lloyd and I said we would clean the duck if it was the same as the prairie-chicken. Gus said it was.

When I woke up the next morning, I'd wet myself and I was really embarrassed. Gus saw immediately what had happened.

"Pissed yerself, eh kid?" he said, but his voice wasn't mocking or sarcastic. "Probably my fault fer hollerin' at ya yesterday. Ya do that often?"

"Yeh," I answered, looking down, "almost every night."

"Well don't worry 'bout it. I had a friend, way back — pissed hisself till he was fifteen, sixteen, but we figured a way an' got it stopped and he never did it again. I'll explain it to ya one of these days, now stop cryin' and let's get outta here. I gotta get home an' feed the pigs."

I'd hidden my problem ever since I could remember, or at least I'd tried to and now here I was, talking about it with a grown person and he wasn't laughing at me and he knew all about it. Gus just seemed to know about everything.

When we got back to the homestead everything was as we'd left it except that somebody had left a panful of homemade sausage, all covered over, and a quart of green tomato pickles.

Before Gus left we both thanked him for taking us fishing.

"No big deal," he said, "I was goin' anyway — glad ya could come along. You make sure now to get those potatoes planted in the next couple o'days."

So Lloyd and I went to work and got the whole bag planted. The rows were kind of haphazard but the potatoes didn't know the difference.

When I remember back, the summer of '31 was one of the best of my life. Gus took us fishing one more time, and all kinds of people would stop in and leave us things to eat. Every couple of weeks Dad would arrive with another load, and he could see we were doing just fine. He was really pleased about our planting the potatoes.

One one trip, well into the summer, Dad took Lloyd back with him and I was left alone. Lloyd was gone more than two weeks but he showed up one afternoon chasing a cow. He had chased it all the way from St. Walburg and he couldn't go very many miles each day as the cow was milking. Now at least we'd have fresh milk every day.

Sometime in August Dad arrived with a load and brought another man with him.

"Boys, I want ya to meet Charlie. Charlie's gonna be with us for the next while — helping with the last of the moving and getting us started with the building."

Lloyd and I shook hands with Charlie who had one of those powerful grips that make you wince. We noticed he walked with a bit of a list, kind of to one side. We found out later he'd had infantile paralysis when he was a child and his left arm was almost withered away. He did have some strength in the fingers, enough that when bridling a horse he could lift his bad arm up with his good one and his fingers could hold a buckle while his good arm was tightening the straps. Whatever might have been missing in his left arm was more than made up for in his right. He was really strong and I don't ever remember anyone besting him in an arm-wrestling match.

Charlie was a sort of hired man but we were careful never to use that expression when he was around. It was 1931 and the Depression was at its worst. The government had relief programs but we wouldn't be eligible until the whole family had move on to the homestead. However, as an interim measure to help us to get started, the relief officer agreed to pay Charlie $5 a month for working for us and Dad was paid $5 a month for keeping him.

One of the first things Charlie did was wander around the building site, marking it with stakes. He showed Dad the best locations for the house and barn, even the outhouse. He carried a divining rod of green willow and marked the spot where Lloyd and I were to start digging a well.

"Should hit water not more'n eight, ten feet, if'n know what I mean."

Charlie stuck that line, "if'n know what I mean" on the end of almost every sentence. When he'd be talking with Lloyd or me we'd anticipate it and say it with him. He'd just laugh because he had a good sense of humour.

In September Dad and Charlie made one more trip. They brought back a big tent that Dad had sewn big enough to hold two double beds and a stove. They even brought the stove, a restaurant type with an oven large enough to hold two dozen loaves of bread. It also had a 20 gallon reservoir on one side, so we usually had hot water for washing. The tent had a vent sewn into it for a stove pipe.

Through September we were all busy cutting down trees and clearing the area for the buildings. Then we began cutting logs and snaking them to the site. All the buildings would be built of logs and each log had to be prepared by removing excess branches and all the bark. The ends were sawed to length and dovetailed to fit tightly with the log forming the next wall. The process went slowly because Dad, with his carpenter's training, wouldn't settle for anything less than the best. September flew by and when October came, with the smell of autumn in the air, the buildings were far from completed. Most of the walls were up but there were no floors in the house. We wouldn't need a floor in the barn. The most difficult job was still ahead — raising the ridge poles on both buildings. Once these were up the roof could go on.

A more urgent priority was to move the balance of our belongings up from St. Walburg. This would include the last of the heavy farm machinery, the heavier of Dad's shop tools like the big sewing machines, the lathe, all of the tinsmithing machines and blacksmithing gear, and all our household furniture. It would be a very big and heavy load. Along with it, Lloyd and I would be chasing seven head of cattle; two more cows which were milking, and five two-year-old steers. The Boenings had a heavy team of Clydesdales and Dad arranged to borrow them plus another team from Gus. We had a big freight wagon with a hayrack-type box, large enough to hold everything as we headed back to St. Walburg.

It was nice to see Mom and the girls again and have a good home-cooked meal. They had moved in with my aunt and uncle until we could come and get them. We started loading the hay rack with the last of our things. A special pen had been built for two pigs we would be bringing back. The load was piled high with the lighter things like furniture with the heavier machinery on the floor. When you looked at it, you couldn't help but wonder how anything could move it, even a six-horse team.

"That's a big fucker, Harvey," Charlie said to Dad, "if'n know what I mean. No problem getting up hills, might be a problem holdin' 'er goin' down, if'n know what I mean."

Boening's team had a heavy set of harness, especially the leather traces which hooked from their collars to the actual pulling gear on the wagon. The harness also had heavy leather 'Dakota' team breeching which fit around their rear ends to hold the load going down hills.

The horses were strung out in three two-horse teams, one in front of the other. We had Gus's team out front as they were the fastest, with ours in the middle and Boening's hooked on to the wagon. Only the back team had any control when it came to steering as the wagon tongue was hooked on to their collars. This, too, was the only team of the three that could hold the load going downhill. The other two teams were only used for pulling.

There was a last-minute change of plans as Charlie's father showed up to hitch a ride as far as the Beaver River. He was well into his sixties, so Charlie rigged up a comfortable seat for him on one of our big chairs in the corner of the load. The old man had only a small knapsack with a few belongings, and a gallon jug of what he called "moose milk" which he jealously guarded. He didn't communicate too well or maybe he felt it wasn't necessary. When he did have anything to say, it was usually a complaint about something or other. He got himself comfortably settled, took a swig out of his jug and was asleep before we even got started.

It took most of the morning loading the pigs into their pen, assembling the seven head of cattle and harnessing the horses. Charlie was everywhere, checking the latch on the pig-pen, explaining to Lloyd that it would be best if he were to lead the one cow and stay as close to the load as possible while I brought up the rear and kept the other cattle bunched as best I could. Lloyd and I were to change places every few miles, as it wasn't going to be easy chasing and keeping the cattle together. "Goddamn steers gonna be in the bush all day, if'n know what I mean. Get yerself a long green willow whip and keep whackin' 'em on the ass, that'll straighten 'em out," he said. "We ain't gonna be makin' all that good time and we'll be makin' lotsa stops to give us a chance to regroup ev'ry once in awhile, if'n know what I mean. Coupla hills between here an' Loon Lake gonna give us some trouble, if'n know what I mean. Six horses gonna pull it okay but that back team ain't gonna hold 'er back goin' down, if'n know what I mean. Best ya take this buggy whip'n ride one of the middle horses — snap the asses off the front team and we'll havta race it down, if'n know what I mean." Dad kept nodding understanding because he could see exactly what Charlie meant.

Charlie then gathered up all the reins which were two for each team. He climbed the front wagon wheel and pulled himself up on top of the load. One set of reins was extra long and he threw one of them backwards over the load. He carefully assembled all the reins between the fingers of his withered hand, then, grabbing the long one strung out with his good hand, he whipped it out over the heads of the lead team. When he had fed it almost all the way out he waited just long enough then flicked it slightly. The rein snapped over the lead team's heads with the sound of a bullet. They jumped to attention. All six horses leaned into their harness and we started slowly moving. Dad walked alongside, prodding any horse that wasn't doing its job. Lloyd grabbed his cow and I brought up the rear of the caravan, hollering and snapping my willow whip in all directions.

Charlie seemed to be about 50 feet high and magnificent, snapping that long rein right where he wanted it. Those horses knew who was boss.

"Yehhh-hooo," he yelled as we pulled out of St. Walburg. A couple of miles out, he pulled the outfit up on the brow of a hill. "No goddamn way we gonna hold this load down that hill, if'n know what I mean," he said to Dad. "Best ya get on one of yer own horses and when I tell ya, rake 'im in the guts like ya had spurs on and snap the asses off the front team with yer whip. I'll hold 'er best I can but you better keep those two teams out fronta mine or we're gonna have horses splattered 'round from asshole to breakfast, if'n know what I mean."

Dad got on Tony, the smallest of our team and Charlie stood up on the load and flicked his rein. The hill wasn't all that steep but the heavy load started rolling and gaining momentum. We could see Charlie straining to hold the back team but it was a losing battle. The wagon rolled, faster and faster and all of a sudden we saw Charlie flick his rein out over the front team.

"Go ya bastards — slap 'em on the ass, Harvey, give 'em hell, harder, harder — go, go yehhh-hooo!"

They went. When they reached the bottom all six horses were at full gallop with a couple of tons of disaster right on their tails. This process was repeated a number of times before we reached Loon Lake and each time I wondered if we would make it. We did, and by the time we arrived it was getting dark. The sun sets early in October in the north. Lloyd and I were dead tired what with chasing ornery steers all day. I felt I'd run 100 miles even though we'd only come less than 40. We pulled into a tall stand of pines and made camp.

Dad got a big fire going and strung a pot of stew over it that Mom had prepared. Charlie's old man found himself a spot near the fire, took a long swig out of his jug and went back to sleep.

Charlie and Lloyd and I unharnessed the horses and gave them a generous helping of oats. Then we had to catch all the loose cattle and stake them out on ropes so they wouldn't wander off. Charlie showed us how to tie knots that wouldn't slip, and when the cattle were tended to we moved back to the horses.

"One thing you fellas gotta learn is to take care of yer animals, especially horses, if'n know what I mean. You gonna get into trouble sometime up here and a horse is gonna take ya home when you ain't gonna be able to make it yerself — and remember that, if'n know what I mean."

Charlie dug out some gunny sacks and a couple of curry combs. We wiped all the horses down and gave them a good workout with the combs. By the time we were finished it was really dark but the light from the fire lit up the site while we all had a big helping of stew and some strong black tea.

"You kids better get ta bed right off," Charlie said. "We gotta big day tomorrow what with the Big Muskeg an' all, if'n know what I mean."

Chapter 4

We spread a big canvas tarpaulin under the wagon, grabbed a couple of blankets and lay down. Charlie's old man was asleep in minutes. Dad banked the fire and I could hear him talking with Charlie as the flickering light danced with shadows through the crevices of the underside of the wagon and made my eyes heavy with sleep.

"Well, I don't like it," I heard Charlie say. "If the wind doesn't change direction, we're gonna have a real pisser 'fore mornin', if'n know what I mean."

"You worried 'bout the Big Muskeg?" Dad asked quietly.

"If'n the rain holds off, we'll get us through but if'n it doesn't, gettin' this load over's gonna be a bitch, if'n know what I mean."

I must have dozed off because the next thing I remember was sitting straight up. Something like a double-barreled shotgun had gone off right over my head. Rain was pelting down in swerving sheets which changed direction with the shifting, howling gusts of wind. The thunder sounded like a million kettle drums. And lightning — I had never seen it so close or in as many forms. A blazing sheet lit up everything in sight, and in the midst of it a slender bolt slithered down and seemed to singe the trees overhead. Endless streams of chain lightning chased one another in a helter-skelter pattern across the heavens.

Nobody could sleep. Charlie and Dad stirred the fire and threw more logs on and we all sat around trying to stay warm. A real northern storm is awesome. When God's elements are unleashed it is such an overwhelming display you really know who's running things up there. Except for a couple of thunderclaps which sounded too close and one zigzag lightning bolt that hit a tree a hundred yards away it was a beautiful, magnificent storm.

Morning came and everything was drenched. There were puddles of water everywhere as we fed the horses and packed our gear. We had some tea and biscuits and helped Charlie harness the horses. The load groaned its resistance as we pulled out of Loon Lake, headed north with the wagon wheels sinking six inches into the mud.

Lloyd and I herded the cattle in behind the load and I sat on the rear wagon 'reach' as it was my turn to lead the cow. I could hear Charlie hollering at the horses as he climbed up on top the load, his hands full of reins.

The clouds hung low and moved quickly overhead, coming from the northwest. I jumped off the wagon as it was warmer walking and pulling the cow.

"Never get this sonofabitch through in one piece, Harvey," I heard Charlie tell Dad. "Gonna be tough 'nough just gettin' *to* the Big Muskeg, let alone gettin' through the fucker in this weather, if'n know what I mean."

"So? . . . whadda we do?"

"Might havta take it 'cross bit atta time. We'll see."

The horses were having trouble with the load even where the road was level. Charlie flicked their rumps every time they had to climb a hill and there was no problem holding the load going down hills as the wheels were mired deep in the muddy ruts.

Lloyd and I kept falling farther and farther behind with the cattle. The cow I was leading didn't like the ruts so I pulled her over to the side of the trail where the footing wasn't as chewed up and muddy, but she still rebelled and tugged back on her halter. My problems were nothing compared to Lloyd's. Those steers seemed determined to criss-cross half of northern Saskatchewan in every direction but straight ahead. Twice I had to tie my cow to a tree and go and help him.

I guess it was close to midday when we finally caught up with the load. They were already camped on the southern edge of the Big Muskeg and Dad had a fire going. The horses had been fed and for the first time the pigs were out of their pen in a makeshift corral Charlie had assembled from surrounding deadfall.

"Goddamn pigs'll drown in that shit, down low like that," Charlie said, pointing to their bellies. "You kids gonna havta get 'em 'cross on the timbers, if'n know what I mean."

I'd been across the Big Muskeg twice before, but what we were looking at that cold October day was a different muskeg than the one I remembered. And so was the load we had to get across. The wind had come up and was blowing cold out of the north. What had been a soft and gentle rain was now large and fluffy flakes of snow that melted as soon as they hit the ground.

Across the muskeg, about an eighth of a mile away, was a huge pile of twelve by twelve cedar timbers, each about 30 feet long. Hundreds of them had been shipped in from British Columbia as part of an election promise to build a bridge over the muskeg. Once the election had come and gone, the timbers were left stacked in big piles and nothing more was done with them. Somebody had snaked a double row of them across the muskeg to form a makeshift walkway. Some of the timbers had sunk in the quagmire and others had been spread sideways or lay fifteen or twenty feet apart.

"I want you 'n' Lloyd to get those goddamn pigs 'cross first," Charlie said, looking at me. Then looking at his father, who was sitting close to the fire, his ever-present jug at his side, he added, "Maybe ya best take the old man 'cross with ya and prop 'im up somewhere'n the other side, if'n know what I mean."

For anyone who has never seen a muskeg, let me try to describe one. Picture the biggest mud pie you've ever seen. This one is an eighth of a mile wide and anywhere from one to six feet deep. It isn't clean mud, it's filthy. It's alive with crawling creatures, including slimy but harmless water snakes. The consistency of the mud is like heavy black molasses and approximately the same colour. The mud has a tenacious holding power that sucks everything downward like quicksand. Somewhere there is a bottom, but heavy animals such as cattle or horses cannot move forward until they hit bottom and at times they have to strain and fight to keep their heads above the morass as they labour their way through. Dotted over the surface of the muskeg are tufts and mounds of grass and moss and if a person is agile and careful he may almost be able to skip from one to the next. These mounds are merely surface accumulations of vegetable life. If you jump up and down on a solid one the muskeg will ripple for 50 feet in all directions.

Lloyd and I each grabbed a pig and, with the old man in tow we hop-skipped our way from one timber to the next and got across. While I held the pigs Lloyd stacked some of the cedar timbers in a square and we put the pigs inside this enclosure. When we looked back Charlie was running over the timbers. The old man had fallen in about half-way over and only his shoulders were sticking out of the mud. One arm was high in the air holding his precious jug but the rest of him kept sinking deeper and deeper. He was helpless and screaming with fright. Charlie extricated him and we ran back to help the old guy across.

"Put 'im under a tree some'ere it ain't rainin' too bad, and see he gets a fire goin' quick's he can," Charlie said, his voice shaking with concern. " 'N' you guys hurry back cause we gotta start movin' the cattle, if'n know what I mean. Yer Dad'n me gonna havta unload some o' the heavy machinery."

Lloyd and I steered the old man over. He was soaked through to his skin and couldn't stop shivering. Lloyd and I both took our jackets off and threw them over his shoulders.

"Charlie says for you to get a fire started as soon as you warm up cause we gotta go back for the cattle," I said.

"Yeh, yeh, I heered 'im — stupid asshole! How'n hell he 'spect me ta build a fire with no axe?"

The old man gave an outburst of roaring expletives, but he was right. He couldn't build a fire until we brought an axe over, so we found a fairly dry spot for him under a big pine tree. When we left him, we saw him taking a big swig out of his jug, his hands shivering so much he could hardly find his mouth. As we jumped back on to the timbers he was digging himself a nest in the pine needles.

As we worked our way back to the southern edge the chilling rain was now snow. A whining wind rose and whipped the newly fallen snow into miniature whirlwinds that danced haphazardly over the muskeg and disappeared. The timbers were wet and slick with mud and, jumping from one to another, I missed my footing and slipped. I started sinking into the bone-chilling oozy guck. As I reached back to grab the timber I realized I was too far out and panicked.

I screamed: "Lloyd, come back! — come back! — I'm sinking!"

Lloyd was only a couple of timbers ahead, maybe 50 feet, and he was back in seconds. He lay down on the timber and stretched out for my hands.

"Take it easy," he said, as I fought frantically for his outstretched hand. "You're gonna pull me in with you!" Our fingers grasped. "Stop fighting! I've got ya. Easy now, easy."

By that time, Dad and Charlie had arrived. "Stupid little bastard," Charlie said. "Why don'cha watch where yer goin'?"

They got me back and sat me down close to the fire where I dried off as best I could but I was caked in mud and felt gritty, grimy, and cold as ice. I knew how the old man felt, for my hands and legs wouldn't stop shaking with the cold and the terrible sensation of being sucked down into that frightening mess. It could close over you so quickly and swallow everything, including the scream.

"Okay, if you kids is warmed up, I'm gonna explain how's I want these cattle handled," Charlie said. "First, ya dig out a couple o' those tuques yer Ma packed and put 'em down over yer ears."

We found the tuques and rubbers and Charlie found a jacket and mackinaw. They were about ten sizes too big and hung down around our knees but they were warm and, at least for the moment, dry.

"Ya tie the ends o' this rope 'round yer waists and let the middle of it drag behind ya. Least ya dumbbells can pull each other out if'n ya slip again, if'n know what I mean," Charlie smirked, looking at me. "Ya start with the cows. They ain't gonna act up much. Each o' ya takes yer own timber and lead 'em in. I'll whack their ass a few times till they git the idea. Keep their heads up, 'specially where it's deep — an' don't worry. I did this a hunert times. If'n they balk and pull back, whack 'em on the ass, if'n know what I mean."

We checked the halters on both cows and made certain the lead ropes were secure. I jumped on the first timber and gave the rope a yank. Lloyd was about ten feet to my left doing the same thing. As the cows stepped into the morass, Charlie gave each of them a slap on the rear with a rope and, gingerly, they stepped in.

By the time we'd reached the third timber, they were up to their bellies in mud. Charlie kept hollering and we kept pulling and got out in the middle where the mud was deeper than they were. We had to pull as hard as possible to keep their heads up and until they felt solid footing under their hooves. Then they'd vault loose from the clinging monster that was sucking them down. Slowly, we got them across and tied them to trees, then we started back for the steers.

It was getting colder and colder and except for the muskeg itself, where the snow melted as soon as it fell, all around the ground was white. The wind had died down some and at least that helped.

Dad and Charlie were sliding some of the heavier machines off the hayrack and were having a lot of trouble. They had run some log runners up on to the rack and had ropes tied to one of the big tinsmithing cutters which was made of cast iron and must have weighed five or six hundred pounds. Slowly, Charlie would feed the rope out and Dad worked to keep the machine balanced till it hit the ground. Cold as it was both were sweating profusely.

As we dug more lead ropes out and went back to pick out two steers, Charlie came over.

"D'ja check on my ol' man?" he asked.

"No," said Lloyd.

"Well wake the ol' bugger up when ya git over and tell 'im he gotta get a fire goin'. He's prob'ly sloshed with that goddamn homebrew, if'n know what I mean." Charlie took out a big pocket watch, gazed at it a moment, then put it back. He looked out over the muskeg concernedly. "Ya best hustle yer butts with them steers. It's past three, and by six it's gonna be black as sin out there."

We grabbed the lead ropes and jumped on to the first timbers. Charlie gave each of the steers a whack and in they went. I didn't have too much trouble with mine. I already knew the spots where I'd have to help pull and I made sure of my footing. Besides, the big rubbers helped. Lloyd's steer balked all the way. He spent more time whacking its rear than he did pulling but we got them over and tied them to a tree.

The old man was either drunk or half-frozen. He grunted a couple of times and told us to fuck off, so we knew he was all right.

Back we went for the next two steers. Charlie and Dad were finished with the unloading so we sat around the fire for a bit to warm up.

"Ya check on the ol' man?" Charlie asked.

"He's okay. Told us to leave 'im alone."

Charlie kept looking at his watch which was another way of telling us something without actually saying it. As soon as we stopped shivering, we got up and picked the next two steers.

"Ya get those two over 'n' when ya's get back, we'll go in with the first load. Ya can take the last two over while we load the second time, if'n know what I mean."

The steer I picked wasn't going in. Lloyd was a couple of timbers ahead of me before mine put its front feet into the mud, with a lot of help from Charlie who whacked its rump till it had no choice. I had a terrible time just trying to keep him close to the line of timbers. He was all for turning back and I could see panic in his wild eyes. Lloyd was 'way out front because the rope between us was taut. I got to the first spot where I knew the steer would be over its head. I held the rope as tight as I could and pulled the steer in close to the timber and whacked him on the rump. I figured a couple of wild jumps and I'd have his head up and out. The steer really did give it a monumental try. He went down and in and came bursting up, his eyes blazing with fear. As he went down for the second leap, the rope slipped through my frozen fingers. I was tangled up in Charlie's long mackinaw and I searched in vain for the lead rope. Without me to help the steer didn't have a chance. He sank deeper and deeper, the black ooze creeping over him. His breath agonized in a strangled scream and his eyes rolled as the muskeg sucked him down. There was no bottom without my help. Nothing to help him hold his head up. Nothing for him to push against. Nothing I could do except stand on the timber and watch the agony and the end. There was desperate turmoil as the muskeg closed over him. I could only stand there with tears in my eyes and watch. I couldn't even call Charlie.

We got Lloyd's animal over, tied it up and checked on the old man. When we nudged him he moved, so we figured he was okay. We headed back. The wind had strengthened and was hissing and raw, especially in the middle of that devastated wasteland where there was no protection from it. Our clothes were saturated and our rubbers were full of sloshy mud. Ice had formed around my collar and on the fringes of my mackinaw.

When we got back I explained tearfully what had happened. Dad put his arm around me. "Don't worry son, I'm sure ya did everythin' you could."

The horses were harnessed and hooked up. I wondered how on earth we were going to get a six-horse team and what was still a big load through that clinging, stinking mud.

Charlie came over. "Sorry 'bout the steer, kid. I was watchin'. Ya did all ya could. Nobody coulda done more." Then he started barking orders:

"I want Lloyd ridin' one of the lead team. All ya do is keep their heads outta that shit and keep whackin' 'em on the ass. I got leads from the second team and I want Harvey to run those timbers and try 'n' keep 'em in close, if'n know what I mean. There's leads from the last team and Bob can do the same as his old man. Ya all got ropes on ya so's we can get ya out if'n one of youse slips. Now let's go."

"Yehhh-hooo, ya mis'rable sonsabitches," he hollered and in we went.

A couple of hundred feet in, the horse that Lloyd was riding almost disappeared. Lloyd panicked and jumped off, fighting his way to a timber where he pulled himself up.

"Grab its bridle," Charlie screamed. "Keep its fuckin' head up. That's it, easy now." We moved slowly and when the second team went into the same depression, the lead team was on firmer footing and pulled the second team through. We reached a shallower section and Charlie stopped to give the horses a rest. We tied leads on to the front team and Dad moved up front. Lloyd moved back to the middle team and I stayed where I was.

We worked our way across the timbers, pleading, cajoling, pulling, swearing and screaming. Slowly, a foot at a time, we came through. You could feel the wagon almost stop, then jump forward accompanied by the released sound of the suction as the mud capitulated.

By the time we pulled out and unloaded it was almost six o'clock. Charlie went to check on his dad who was curled up under the pine tree. He came back, looking worried.

"We gotta getta a fire goin' and we gotta git the other stuff," he told Dad. "If'n this weather keeps up we ain't gonna git that other load over that mess of shit till freeze-up and ever'thin' up here's gonna freeze long 'fore that fuckin' mudhole."

Lloyd and I had been rubbing the horses down with some wet gunny sacks. Dad said we were to get a fire going with the cedar. He handed us an axe.

"Charlie's gotta can o' lighter fluid and yer mother packed some matches in a tin box somewhere in that stuff we just unloaded. Soon as you get a fire going, wake the old man up and make sure he's okay. Then you'd better get back over and help Charlie and me."

Charlie and Dad turned the horses around and they went back in. With the hayrack empty the going was much easier and we saw them pull out on the other side just as darkness settled.

Lloyd and I split a nest of kindling, then some bigger pieces and we had some really big pieces ready for when the fire was going well. We had to stop and stick our hands in our pockets every few minutes to try and get our fingers warm enough to hang onto the axe.

The old man hadn't moved in a long time.

I went looking through the boxes for the matches but couldn't find them. The old man smoked a pipe so I went through his clothes looking for matches. He didn't move at all. Any matches I found were soaking wet.

"What'll we do?" I asked Lloyd.

"Nothing we can do without matches. Have to wait for Charlie. His lighter'll work in a hurricane. May as well go back and help."

"Geez, the old man hasn't moved in a long time," I told Lloyd, as we picked our way carefully across the timbers in the darkness. We arrived just as the last of the load was being tied down.

"What happened with the fire?" Dad asked.

We explained that it was all ready to go but that we couldn't find the matches. As soon as we got over Charlie could start it with his lighter.

Charlie looked out over the muskeg, he looked at the load, the horses ready. He looked over at Lloyd and me shivering beside the dying fire and when he spoke there was a note of desperation in his voice: "Okay, same as last time except Lloyd and Harvey gotta hold the lanterns up high as ya can so's we know where we're goin'."

The wind had taken on a sustained overtone as it whistled and howled in a steady crescendo. It had to be below zero and my teeth were chattering as I grabbed the lead lines and followed Dad and Lloyd onto the timbers. Out in the middle, with no windbreak at all, blasts of Arctic air swept across the quagmire. I was shivering so hard I could barely pick my way along the frozen timbers. With less than fifteen timbers to go an enormous blast of air whirled around the load and everything went black as pitch. The lanterns had blown out. With no light, we had to feel our way across on hands and knees.

"Keep the teams in tight as ya can," Charlie hollered. "It's your parade, Harvey. I can't see bugger-all up front."

Just after 9 o'clock we straggled out the north side. We pulled the rig up until it was clear of the mud. We didn't even bother to tie up the horses. Charlie ran over to the tarpaulin and checked the kindling. His can of lighter fluid was sitting right where we'd left it. He squirted the gas on to the shavings and pulled out his lighter. It wouldn't light. He twirled the wheel over the flint a hundred times but there were no sparks. Either It was soaked or he had picked the worst time in his life to run out of flint.

"You gotta find those matches, Harvey, or we ain't gonna make it."

His voice trembled as he was now shivering as hard as the rest of us. Dad pulled at boxes frantically looking for the precious tin box, but to no avail. Lloyd and I pulled some wet straw under the pine tree beside the old man and snuggled close to each other in an attempt to draw warmth from each other's bodies.

Charlie ran over. "Don't you kids go to sleep — ya hear? Whatever ya do, ya gotta keep movin'!" The old man stirred slightly and his spectacle case fell out of his shirt pocket. He began mumbling and I thought maybe he wanted his glasses. He could barely move he was so cold, and he'd been lying there for hours. I opened his spectacle case to help him with his glasses and stuck under them, I felt a match! One long wooden, precious *dry* match. I snapped the case shut and held it tightly and screamed for Charlie.

He came and dragged himself down into the pine needles with us and looked at his father who was more dead than alive.

"If anythin' happens to that old bastard, "I'll never fergive myself."

"Charlie," I said, "I got the crown jewels right here. There's one dry match stuck in your dad's spectacle case."

He backed under the pine, the heavy low bows protecting him and the spectacle case.

"You kids get out there an' split a new log down the middle so's I have a dry surface to strike the match on. Give the kindling a couple more squirts of lighter fluid and when yer ready, holler."

Lloyd and I shivered our way over to the tarp and found the axe. Lloyd missed with his first, weak swing, but the second time he hit it right and the log split. I squirted the kindling which was still dry and when I looked up there was Charlie cupping his hands over the open spectacle case and the priceless wooden match. Dad had joined us and the four of us stood close together, forming a windbreak.

"Please, God," we heard Charlie say as he stroked the match down the length of the dry log. It lit and he thrust it into the kindling saturated with gasoline. The fire took hold. We hovered over it, protecting the precious flame from the wind and kept feeding it with more kindling, then bigger sticks of wood. Charlie kept squirting lighter fluid into the flames and minutes later we had the most magnificent, beautiful, gorgeous, rip-roaring, warmest fire I'd ever seen.

Charlie and Dad pulled the old man out from under the pine tree and propped him up against one of the cedar timbers where the warmth of the fire would reach him. Charlie massaged his shoulders and arms and kept slapping his face to revive him.

Lloyd and I took off our waterlogged jackets and sat as close as we could to the fire. Cedar is probably one of the best burning firewoods there is. It burns like crazy but it also spits sparks, probably in protest at its demise. We'd flick the sparks off each other like a couple of monkeys and as the fire took hold we had to keep backing off.

Charlie rescued his dad's gallon jug and was trying to pour some of its fiery contents down the old man's throat.

"Come on, ya ol' sonofabitch, open yer mouth." Some of the burning liquid trickled through the old man's clenched teeth and down his throat. He coughed a few times while Charlie kept slapping his face. The old guy finally came around and opened his glazed eyes, waiting for them to focus.

When he recognized Charlie, he launched into a non-stop tirade, half English, half German, that covered their relationship from the time Charlie was born and even included his questionable birthright. Never have I heard a son get a tongue-lashing so complete. Charlie smiled, and went off into the darkness to help Dad with the horses.

There was a wooden barrel of eggs which had been packed in oats up near the fire. The old man struggled upright, weaved his way over to the barrel and sat down on it. He took a long swig from the last of his jug and as he began to thaw out, the barrel, which wasn't all that heavy, started doing a slow pirouette on its bottom rim. He must have lost his balance because the next thing we knew he had fallen into the fire. We pulled him out and rolled him around in the mud to smother the flames and, except for his dignity, he seemed none the worse for the experience. We deposited him a safe distance from the fire and went off to help with the animals.

In the wee hours of the morning we were wakened by the creepy sonnet of howling timber wolves. They seemed to be everywhere, some far in the distance and others perilously near. We knew they'd never come close to a fire, especially one as big as ours, but we heard Charlie as he pulled on his boots and wakened Dad.

"Better check the animals, Harvey, ya can never tell with those sonsabitches — 'spec'lly with cattle tied up."

There was a chorus of howls from across the muskeg. First a staccato 'yip-yip' and then a long eerie sustained wail, falling slowly down the scale. In between we heard the frightened mooing of the two steers we had left behind. We'd left them tethered to trees and they wouldn't have a chance if a pack of timber wolves decided to attack. Charlie grabbed a .22 repeater and he and Dad took off across the timbers. Fifteen minutes or so later we heard a series of shots, a couple of yips, and half-an-hour later, we saw them stepping off the timbers, the two steers in tow.

Charlie was some kind of guy.

We arrived at the homestead the following evening, and the day after, Charlie and Dad returned the two borrowed teams. That weekend Dad left for St. Walburg in a big buggy to pick Mom and the two girls.

CHAPTER 5

EVEN THOUGH THE BARN HAD NO ROOF we busied ourselves putting in stalls and feeding troughs. We helped Charlie build a good-sized corral next to the barn and a second enclosure big enough to hold a large hay stack. Boening, our neighbour, came over with a load of hay; Lloyd and I sawed a couple of cords of wood for the kitchen stove and everything was pretty shipshape when Dad arrived with Mom, Joyce and Kay. At last our family was together again and it took a few days to get used to having females around again. The girls adjusted quickly and Mom went to work immediately, cleaning and, more important, cooking. They moved into the big tent and Charlie, Lloyd and I slept in the smaller tent, which didn't have a stove. Naturally, with my bed-wetting problem, I had to sleep alone. My mattress was made out of gunny sacks, sewn together and stuffed with straw. One end was pinned lightly so the straw could be changed periodically.

We had a bumper crop of the potatoes Gus had brought and shown us how to plant. More than 200 bushels. Charlie showed us how to dig a root cellar and we put the potatoes in and covered them with a layer of straw. Then we crossed our fingers and prayed they wouldn't freeze when the lid was closed and the cold weather set in.

Dad invited Mr. Boening over one afternoon and with his help and the aid of a block-and-tackle, we hoisted the ridge poles into place on the roofs of both the house and barn. November came, accompanied by below zero weather and more than a foot of snow. Charlie and Dad worked unceasingly, stringing poplar poles from the ridge poles down to the top row of logs which formed the walls. Once all the poplar poles were in place they were covered with a few inches of straw and over this a layer of mud, mostly clay. This would shed water within reason but, more than that, would retain heat.

While Dad and Charlie worked on the roofs, Lloyd and I spent all our daylight hours chinking the spaces between the logs with moss. The job was slow and tedious and Dad kept checking us carefully as we worked. The results were excellent and we knew that once we got a floor down and stoves going the house would be warm and comfortable.

Until then we lived in the two tents. Charlie, Lloyd and I would undress down to our long underwear in the big tent then, with only rubbers on our feet, we'd run like mad for the small tent and crawl, shivering, into bed. Somehow we had acquired a family of cats and when I lifted my mound of blankets the cats were already waiting for me. How they could breath as far down as my feet is still a mystery. It would take a few minutes to get warm but even with temperatures as low as 50 below, we managed to survive. When morning came there would be a coating of hoar frost on the walls of the tent from our breathing. Strangely, that was the only winter we spent in the north when none of us had colds.

Dad arranged a swap deal with one of the saw mills and came home with a load of lumber. We got a floor down and even though the lumber was pretty rough, it was better than no floor at all. We had two 45 gallon gas-drum stoves which Dad had converted in St. Walburg. Legs had been welded on to the drums so they would sit solidly on the floor. A hole had been cut out at one end and a hinged door with a secure clasp installed. At the top of the drum there was hole for the stove pipe.

We moved into the cabin on Christmas day, 1931. The temperature outside read 45 degrees below zero. Inside, the two drum stoves plus the big kitchen stove emitted more than enough heat to keep us warm, but burned an unbelievable amount of wood. Lloyd and I were busy from morning till night sawing wood with a 'Swede' saw.

By the middle of January we had a roof on the barn. The chinking of the spaces between the logs of the barn went faster than on the house. Along with the moss we also used fresh cow dung which, while messy, was quite adequate and made a perfect, weatherproof seal as it dried or froze.

Dad planed some leftover lumber and built kitchen cupboards which covered one end wall of the cabin. There were two flour bins, each big enough to hold a 100 pound bag, plenty of overhead cupboards and even a place for a sink and water pump, although the pump would have to wait. There were cupboards for storing pots and pans, jars for preserves and other canned food. We had brought 400 quart sealers with us and, as we got to know the ways of the north, Mom canned wild fruit and vegetables, fish and meat. While there was no need for refrigeration during the winter months the lack of it presented a big problem during the summer. There was no electricity and though we brought home a couple of loads of ice from the Beaver River it didn't last long once the weather turned warm.

When Dad was building the kitchen cupboard complex he made room in it for hiding home brew and all the elements of a complete whiskey still. Making your own whiskey was, of course, against the law. The hidden area was secreted in behind the two flour bins, which were hinged on bottom pivots. Dad never showed us how it worked but certain combinations of cupboards had to be opened and others closed before a door, which looked like part of the wall was exposed. Behind this phoney wall was enough room for the still and dozens of gallons of whiskey. Over the years we were visited many times by suspicious Mounties but they could never figure out the combination that led to the still. They did spend a great deal of time harassing homesteaders whom they suspected of having a still, and Dad was a prime suspect.

Charlie was a superb woodsman and hunter and his skills helped us to survive. We received a monthly relief cheque of $18 from the provincial government and this included the $5 for keeping Charlie. The money was spent on necessities such as shells for the two guns. We kept a .22 rifle for small game and a .303 rifle, a left-over from the first World War, for deer and moose. The shells for the big gun were very expensive but absolutely necessary or we would starve. We had to buy salt, flour, matches, coal-oil for the lamps and lanterns, sugar, used mostly for canning and if there was money left over, yard goods. These, along with the flour bags, were used by Mom to make undergarments for herself and the girls.

Charlie and I went hunting every Saturday morning in the winter months, when big game could be tracked in the snow. Dad bought a hunting license each season and to say we stretched the allowable limits would be an understatement. We ate a deer every week during the winter, having venison three times a day. When Charlie and I went hunting, he would purposely take only one shell for the .303. This forced him to be absolutely certain of his shot before he fired.

One Saturday morning we found fresh moose tracks a short distance from the house. Charlie spent a lot of time studying them.

"Gotta be a big bugger," he said. "See how those hooves spread? Gotta be a bull. Shoulda brung more shells. Quiet now, quiet as ya can."

When he sensed a prey, Charlie walked silently on the insides of his feet. He would freeze immobile in a split second and cant his head as he listened for the faintest sound. We moved forward noiselessly with me attempting to ape his peculiar, lop-sided walk. He reached down and felt the tracks with his fingers.

"Fresh," he whispered. "Can't be far ahead."

The northern wind carried dustings of newly fallen snow into the small hillocks that would build on the lee side of trees or rocks. These mounds packed hard and firm and often a light coating of ice would form as the sun shone on them. If anything stepped on them, there was a 'ping' sound. Charlie studied the tracks as we moved and listened for that 'ping.'

Over a rise we saw the marks where the moose had been lying down resting.

"Old bastard gettin' tired," Charlie whispered as we plodded along.

I always carried the .22 when hunting although I seldom used it except maybe to bag a rabbit on our way home. I carried the hunting knife in my belt and after Charlie had fired the one shot it was my job to cut the slain animal's throat. This was part of living in the north. A downed animal has to be bled immediately otherwise the blood congeals and stays in the meat.

We had one momentary glimpse of the moose, standing majestically on the brow of a hill. He was huge, with an immense span of antlers. He *was* a bull like Charlie said.

"Look at 'im," Charlie whispered. "If'n we bag that old bastard we won' havta go huntin' fer a month. Prob'bly havta track the sonofabitch all day 'fore I getta good shot, if'n know what I mean."

The .22 I was carrying couldn't even dent the hide of an animal that size and I knew Charlie was silently cursing himself for not bringing extra shells. While moose were plentiful they weren't easy to get close to, certainly not close enough to be sure you'd get one with a single shot. Twice more we saw where the moose had been lying down and twice more Charlie smiled, knowingly.

"That ol' bugger didn' get ol' by bein' stupid."

The morning wore on and the sun was off to the west. The moose was doubling back in a big circle.

"Ol' bastard ain't all that smart or he'd git his ass outta here — straight ahead."

We moved silently up a rise, with me stepping in Charlie's footprints. Charlie stopped suddenly, cocked his ear, smiled faintly, and holding his jacket over the breech of his gun to muffle the click, released the safety catch.

On the brow of the hill Charlie had his moment. The moose was downwind from us and not even looking in our direction. He was less than a hundred yards away and when he sensed the danger it was too late. Charlie steadied himself against a tree trunk, drew a bead and fired. Down went the moose.

I unsheathed the hunting knife, handed the .22 to Charlie and waited for him to say it was okay. The moose had gone down like a sack of potatoes, his leg muscles twitching their last. Charlie watched for a few seconds and motioned for me to go ahead.

I ran toward the animal. God, he was beautiful and by far the biggest moose I'd ever seen. About twenty feet away, he rose up on his front feet and, dragging his hind quarters, started pawing his way toward me. His eyes were blazing with hurt, surprise and anger, and the wild expulsion of air from his nostrils formed little clouds of steam in the crisp air. I froze. My heart stopped. A deep-rooted, guttural, angry sound came rumbling out his foaming mouth as he pawed his way toward me, leaving a bloodstained trail in the snow.

"Move ta the side, quick," Charlie screamed. He had the .22 aimed at the moose but I was in the line of fire.

I could smell the animal's breath before I jumped frantically sideways into a stand of trees. Charlie fired again and again as I cowered in behind a big birch, the moose close enough to touch. A .22 shell went right into his eye and down he went, pawing his anger to the end.

Charlie's first shot with the .303 had been too far back by a matter of inches. It had severed the spinal cord, and while the body and hind quarters were paralyzed this had little effect on the moose's front section. Charlie took the hunting knife from my trembling hand and used it. I wasn't going anywhere near it.

Charlie sent me back to get a horse.

"Put a collar on 'er and hook up a pair o' traces so's we can snake 'im out. Bring a lotta rope. An' tell yer Ma to clean out the meat box. Make sure they's no deer meat left, if'n know what I mean. All's we need is those goddamn Mounties find both deer an' moose meat in the box and yer ol' man'll do a fast six months."

A hunting license allowed us two deer *or* one moose during the hunting season. Never a deer *and* a moose.

A couple of weeks after we moved into the cabin, a team of horses pulling a light cutter came tearing up the drive and stopped in a cloud of snow as the driver pulled them around and the cutter's sleds slid in a semi-circle like a skier.

"Whoa, ya mis'rable assholes!"

It was Gus. We all ran to greet him, Charlie too, as he and Gus were old friends.

"How ya doin' ya ol' bugger?" Charlie asked as Gus jumped down and gave him a bear hug.

"Fine, just fine. Goin' up ta the lake fer some ice fishin', thought maybe some o' ya'd like ta tag 'long."

"Just in time fer a drink," said Dad. "Ran a batch a coupla nights back. Got some mash from Boening and either I got lucky or I got the best still up here. Best damn home-brew ya ever tasted, right Charlie?"

"Coupla shots," Charlie said, "and you'll be jumpin' up bitin' yer ass."

We all went into the cabin. Mom sliced some venison and Dad poured Gus and Charlie a tumbler full of home-brew.

"Tell ya what," Gus said, obviously relishing it, "Ya gimme a gallon o' this moose milk 'n' I'll bring ya's back some whitefish in a coupla days."

"Ya gotta deal," Dad said.

They sat around drinking and laughing. Dad filled the tumblers another time and halfway through the second glass, they sure weren't feeling any pain.

Before Gus left he explained to everyone that he'd promised to do something about my bed-wetting problem which, among members of my family, was not an embarrassing topic.

"Ya still doin' it?" Gus asked.

"Yeh," I replied, "most of the time."

"Well, there's two things we gonna try. Most times, as I un'erstan' it, ya only piss the bed when ya sleep on yer back. I met this young feller on a threshin' crew, years back — said his ol' man was a doctor and that's how he knew. So what ya do is tie a big wooden spool on yer back so's ya can't lie on it 'thout wakin' yerself up. See if that'll work."

"I'll try it tonight," I answered with enthusiasm.

"Meantime," Gus continued, "this young guy I tol' ya 'bout that pissed hisself till he was fifteen, sixteen, well we fin'lly sent away fer some medicine fer 'im which stopped 'im cold. Can't recall the name but my sister'll remember. I wrote her fer Christmas and tol' her if she remembers, ta write away ta Chicago fer it cause that's where it came from. Should be hearin' back any day. Meantime, try the spool."

Dad let me carry a gallon of home-brew to the cutter, which was his way of saying thank-you to Gus for all the trouble he was going to on my behalf.

The spool idea didn't work.

Spring came early that year and by April, except for a few low-lying shaded spots, the snow had disappeared. Without snow the hunting season was over. We were well into May when Mother Nature played one of her unpredictable tricks. We woke up one morning to find the ground covered in a blanket of fresh snow. As soon as Charlie saw it he grabbed the .303.

"Ya comin'?" he asked, looking at me. "We get our asses out there real quick, jus' might get lucky."

I grabbed the .22, stuck the hunting knife in my belt and ran to catch up with Charlie who was already swaggering into the trees, listing with his familiar gait.

We picked up deer tracks before we'd gone a quarter of a mile and Charlie, stalking like a bloodhound, followed the tracks briskly in the soft snow. After a few hundred yards he pulled up short and slowly raised the rifle. I couldn't see any deer.

Powww! The shot reverberated through the trees and it was only when the deer dropped that I saw it.

"Got 'er," Charlie gloated.

No more than 50 feet from the dead deer was a baby doe. Charlie had done the unforgivable; he'd shot a mother deer.

"Sonofabitch, I hate doin' that. How'n hell ya s'pposed ta know this early'n the year, if'n know what I mean."

He was pacing around, angry with himself and talking non-stop.

"Goddamn deer gotta be sexin' it up the wrong time ta have a baby this early. Go on," he said, "cut 'er bloody throat — serves 'er right."

I knew he'd have given anything to have that shot back. He handed me the .303 and caught the trembling baby, only days old, and slung it around his shoulders.

We kept it in the barn and taught it how to drink milk, sucking on our fingers. It grew and flourished and when fall came it was almost full-grown. We turned it loose but it kept coming back for weeks and we'd feed it hay and oats. As time went on its wild instincts took over and finally it didn't come back. When winter came, and with it our regular Saturday hunting forays, Charlie always looked twice before he shot. One mistake was enough.

CHAPTER 6

WHETHER WHEELER-DEALING IN EATONIA, pioneering in the bush or, later on, managing a road show, Dad was always the entrepreneur, clever with his hands and quick with his mind.

There was a strong sense of 'togetherness' in the north. It was difficult, if not impossible, for people to survive on their own. Everyone could count on help from their neighbours in a time of need. Certainly they could count on Dad. He soon became known to the surrounding homesteaders and was always on the run, helping one of the neighbours or building or repairing something. He had his blacksmith's forge and anvil and was forever sharpening plow shares by heating them in the forge until they were red hot. He used big tongs to put them on the anvil, then pounded and molded until the cutting edge was sharp again. The plow share was then reheated and dipped into a tank of water. To make sure it was properly hardened the blade had to be cooled until it was a particular colour before it was dunked completely in the tank.

Dad repaired broken farm machinery. When necessary, he would fashion a new part. There was no money to be made as no one had any. The north existed on barter. Dad was paid in many ways. If a farmer had too many pigs we might get a pig, or a calf or a dozen quarts of wild strawberries or whatever the farmer had that we could use.

Our place became a focal point, not only because people needed the things Dad could supply, but because he, being a Canadian by birth, was looked to for counsel by immigrants who were still uncomfortable with the politics and confused by the customs of the new land.

I have mentioned the refrigeration problem. If a farmer had to kill a two-year-old steer during the summer there was no way to keep the meat fresh. Some of it would have to be canned or smoked. Fresh fish and rabbits were plentiful but fresh beef was a problem. Deer or moose could not be tracked or hunted during the summer months; besides, this was out of season and rightly so, as many of the females were carrying babies.

Dad got together with three of our neighbours and came up with a plan to hold a 'butcher-bee' each weekend for a month. Each neighbour had to supply a two-year-old steer. Dad kept the records, and each farmer got a specific cut of meat each time. If he got a front quarter one weekend he might get a hind quarter the next. At the end of the four weeks each farmer had received the equivalent of a complete steer and the meat was always fresh.

As the word got around the idea caught on and before long more homesteaders were added to the butcher-bee ritual. As most of the farmers were German immigrants, pigs were added, and not only did we have fresh pork to add to our diet but a variety of delicious sausages as well.

The butcher-bees grew to include 16 farmers and became important social gatherings. They were held at a different farm each week. Farmers brought their wives and children along and it was not unusual to find fifty or sixty people together on a butcher-bee weekend.

With sixteen participants, four steers and two pigs would be butchered. Tripod hoists were built and moved from farm to farm and the slaughtered animals were strung up for skinning and dressing. Buckets of hot water were needed and huge fires built. The steers were killed with one perfectly placed blow with a heavy hammer. The pigs were put into a corral and 'stuck.' A sharp knife was used to cut the jugular vein and the pig would then be turned loose in the corral until it bled to death. This was necessary to ensure that the meat was clean and free of blood. To the uninitiated these methods may sound a bit primitive. They do to me now after all these years but it was the way it was done and probably still is in remote places.

Using a combination of pork and beef the wives made a variety of sausages and 'head-cheese.' The 'home' wife on any particular weekend took on the added responsibility of feeding everyone. Visiting wives pitched in and helped and all brought extra food with them. Mealtimes were fun. There was warm fellowship and a wonderful exchange of stories.

Women and children got to know their neighbours better while the men made barter deals, relaxed and rid themselves of the tensions which were part of living in a hostile environment.

Many of the farmers brought drinks with them, mainly home-brew which, when well distilled, was practically neat alcohol. Some of the German immigrants had the recipe for home-made beer and there was always more than enough. For those with a more exotic taste, there was a choice of dandelion or blueberry wine.

Those who had a long way to travel would begin arriving on Friday evening. By noon on Saturday everyone was there. The afternoon was taken up with the butchering and the big meal was served around seven o'clock. A dance followed with all sorts of folk tunes and singing and it would be well into the wee hours of the morning before the last visitors went off to their tents or tarps or the haystack to sleep.

The Mounties were extra busy on butcher-bee weekends. They hunted in pairs, using a light buggy and fast horses. As they were outnumbered they never raided a butcher-bee but they did stakeouts on the bush roads leading to the host farm. They'd hide in wooded areas, usually just around a bend in the road and as a wagonload of homesteaders went by, they'd come tearing out of the bush in their buggy. As soon as they were spotted the home brew would be dumped overboard. No evidence, no case. Rarely was anyone caught.

Most of the Royal Canadian Mounted Police posted into the north in those early years were young and fresh out of training school in Regina. Many had pronounced British accents and exuded a superior and paternalistic attitude — at least this is how it was perceived by many of the homesteaders.

The settlers were a rugged, unsophisticated, hard-working and earthy kind of people with little or no education. For many, English was a second language. There was a preponderance of German, Slavic and Scandinavian immigrants. Between the quasi-colonial British image portrayed by the Mounties and what seemed to be an unending harassment of the settlers the Mounties were not looked upon as your friendly neighbourhood cop.

Many homesteaders still had vivid memories of a war-torn Europe and questionable freedom in the countries they had come from. That was why they had come to Canada. Authority, indiscriminately administered, frightened them. They were easily intimidated by the Mounties, who were better educated and certainly had a better command of the English language.

With almost a total lack of communication with the outside world, the north was on its own. The RCMP were a constant reminder that somewhere, big brother was watching. They were the law — the only law. Search warrants were rarely used, except with people like Dad, who had some knowledge of law and refused to let the police into the house until they produced a warrant. This resistance did not endear him to them. They much preferred to roam around the north doing as they pleased which, in most cases, is exactly what they did.

Most homesteaders had a homebrew still and made their own whiskey. The ones that didn't had access to one through their neighbours. With Dad's expertise and tools, his still was a work of art.

All the pipes were copper and the zinc tanks copper lined. The Mounties knew we had a still but thanks to Dad's ingenuity, they could never find it.

Each fall Dad would buy hunting and trapping licenses. The trapping license covered muskrats, weasels, wild mink, fox and other furbearing animals. We were not very good trappers but we made the most of the hunting license.

When the Mounties dropped in they would head directly for the meat box. Then, after presenting their search warrant, they would go through all the buildings, looking for the still. Dad would laughingly remind them they hadn't checked the chicken coop.

We lived in the north during the time the Mounties were trying to apprehend "Trapper Johnson." Whatever his initial offence (I think it was alleged trapline encroachment) the first constable sent after him was shot by Johnson. This precipitated one of the great manhunts in the history of the north. Trapper Johnson was a superb marksman and possessed more north country moxie than any of his pursuers. A number of policemen were killed before Johnson was cornered and shot. At the time, almost everyone in the north was secretly rooting for The Mad Trapper of Rat River.

A motion picture was produced about the manhunt. I can assure you that more than a few artistic liberties were taken with the facts.

The Mounties received a salary and all the benefits of federal civil servants. The homesteaders, on the other hand, were scratching to eke out a living. The Mounties rode around the north with the fastest horses, the best buggies in the summer and the best cutters in winter. They didn't have to worry about where their next meal was coming from; the homesteaders did. To a people totally occupied with finding enough to eat the Mounties were perceived as a spectre, constantly harassing them. Sides were chosen and it became a game of the homesteaders against the police.

Many of the constables were rookies on their first posting. It was important to them and their superiors that not only did they maintain law and order but showed a record of arrests. This determined whether they would earn their stripes and maybe a better posting. They were well-trained and efficient in police work but many were too young and immature for the basic wisdom required in confrontations with the people. Law enforcement was necessary. Nobody quarrelled with that, but it would have been better served by a more judicious and mature selection of RCMP candidates. They were pompous, belligerent, discourteous and patronizing and in our little corner of the world, where human relationships were so important, and where people depended so much on one another, the Mounties I remember and, unfortunately by inference all other things British, were a pain in the ass.

Once, when a butcher-bee was held at our place, a bunch of homesteaders were sitting around a camp fire passing the jug around, all feeling kind of mellow and listening to Dad. He dominated most conversations and was certainly more articulate than most of his audience. Most immigrants were eager to learn about their adopted land and Dad, as a native-born Canadian was looked upon as an expert.

"There are really only three kinds of people in this country," he began. "There are the 'doers', the 'leaners', and the 'side-way movers'." The audience settled back, they knew more was coming. "Everybody sitting here is a doer. It's not hard to recognize a doer. They make everything but money. They're farmers, they're builders of railways, and builders of roads. They opened up the west, and they're gonna open up the north."

There was polite applause and you could see some self-satisfied smiles on the circle of faces as Dad continued. "Doers strung the cedar timbers across the Big Muskeg, and when any of us needs help, a doer is always around."

"Leaners, they're different. It was the leaners had those cedar timbers shipped in from B.C. then allowed them to lie there and rot. They're politicians, civil servants and all the bureaucratic bullshit that comes out of Ottawa. Leaners are the professional do-gooders that tell you how big or small your next relief cheque is gonna be or even if you're gonna get one. Leaners look for any kind of job that guarantees them a pay cheque. Most of 'em don't even like what they havta do but they hang on desperately cause they ain't like you and they're scared to be a doer, scared to take a chance. Compared to you people their contribution to the human race is nothin'!"

More applause, more smiles, and the jug kept moving around the circle.

"Now, the side-way movers; they make all the money, and that's gen'rally all they make. They don't build anything, and they don't grow anything. They just put things together so whoever owns it'll make more money. They sell land, they lend money, they hire people to make things and then sell 'em at a profit. They buy things, they rent things, and they sell things, but they don't make nothin' 'cept more money than anybody else. You get so's it's easy to spot a doer, and a leaner, but it's a little harder to tell a side-ways mover. They gotta be smart to make money doin' nothin'."

"You and me, and our kids after us, we're the doers! And it's gonna be people like *us* gonna open up the north!"

Chapter 7

Our family contributed much of the music to the social functions like dances after the butcher-bees and weddings. Lloyd played guitar and banjo, Kay played tenor guitar and sang. Dad usually played drums but he also played guitar and sang. He knew plenty of funny songs and many ethnic folk songs. Joyce, it seemed, could sing before she could talk; she had an uncanny, inborn sense of music. She sang all the harmony parts. When there was a piano I would play it and if there was none, I'd play violin or guitar.

Most of our repertoire was simple songs which everyone knew but we could also do popular German, Polish, Ukrainian and Scandinavian folk music.

These musical get-togethers went on into the winter months long after the butcher-bees were over. Many families would still arrive early and stay late. The men arm-wrestled and broke in young horses and steers which had never been ridden. Sometimes we had a miniature rodeo. The women brought ornate desserts and even this became something of a competition. Dancing contests were generally Ukrainian folk dances, which had difficult and physically demanding steps. By the time we went into *Home Sweet Home,* daylight could be seen breaking in the eastern sky.

We spent a great deal of time during the winter months with our music. There was little else to do once the cold weather set in. We had many different instruments and without exception, we all loved music. As Joyce grew older we marvelled at her talent. By the time she was four she could sing all the songs we knew.

When Kay sang the melody, Joyce could invariably find all the right harmony notes and sing along. I began to discover that in most songs there was a third harmony part, and by the time spring came we sang most of the songs in three-part harmony.

Every couple of months we would receive packages from my grandparents in Ontario. At least once a year we received a large wooden barrel of dried apples. There were boxes full of clothes, some used, others brand new. Styles would change and some of the new clothes were out of vogue, but these fads didn't apply in our part of the world, so there was a wild scramble to find something that fit. The items were packed between old magazines and newspapers, which were saved to be read over and over. Reading material was hard to come by when my two aunts no longer lived with us. They had supplied all the current pulp magazines and were forever sending away for new catalogues and periodicals on a 'tryout' basis.

When I no longer had access to my aunt's True Story magazines the only other reading material which sent my fantasies running rampant was the Eaton's and Simpson's mail order catalogues. They were beautiful, especially the colour pages. There were pictures of women in skimpy undergarments and night attire and I spent a good deal of time looking them over. In the north the catalogues served several purposes, so we'd go to great lengths to order as many copies as possible. Lloyd and I would use different names and have them sent care of Dad. There'd be one for Charlie, one for each of my aunts even though they no longer lived with us, and some for people whose names we'd just make up.

Dad had cut tin template patterns for all our clothes. Lloyd and I were almost the same size so we only had one set. There were sets for Dad and Charlie and Mom and the girls. A pattern for jackets and breeches for each of the men and skirts and jackets for the women. All our clothes were made from tanned deer and moose hides which we got through barter deals with the Indians. It took Dad no time at all with the tin patterns and his big sewing machines to cut and sew new outfits for all of us. The breeches went halfway down each leg and we learned how to make moccasins which covered our feet and went halfway up each leg to overlap the breeches. The outfits were practical and utilitarian but a study in monotony. Only the undergarments and hand knitted sweaters made the difference between our summer and winter attire. The flour we bought at Wagner's store came in 100 pound bags. The bright red brand name "Robin Hood Flour" had been printed so it would disappear after a couple of washings. Mom used this material for all our underwear, which was warm and comfortable.

One particular catalogue arrived with a full-colour page of boy's winter jackets. One, shown in bright red, caught my eye. It had three white bands on each sleeve and was really beautiful. But how impossible. The price was $5.25. Our whole family hadn't seen that much money at one time since we'd lived on the homestead. It was out of the question but I couldn't dismiss it from my mind.

The first cigarette I ever smoked on the homestead was a roll-your-own wrapped in non-coloured paper from one of the catalogues. But while the catalogues served many purposes, their most important function was in the outhouse. Our outhouse was rather special, with Dad being a carpenter. We had a three-holer: three seats side by side and each a different size. There was a shelf within easy reach where the catalogues and other reading material were stacked. A visit to the outhouse didn't just require the time needed to do what had to be done but added time thumbing through these wonderful pages which depicted a life-style from another world. On every visit I took a long, longing look at that wonderful red winter jacket.

One afternoon I was in town on some kind of errand. I was wandering around Wagner's store, looking at things and smelling things when Mr. Wagner hollered at me.

"Hey, squirt, come 'ere."

I walked over.

"Could you handle a load of lumber?"

"Whadda ya mean, handle a load of lumber?"

Wagner looked down at me. "There's this load of lumber I bought over at Flegel's mill in Pierceland. I wanna get it over here before it snows. It'd be two long days, eighty miles 'round trip. D'ya think yer ol' man'd letcha have a team of horses?"

"Have ta ask him but I'm sure he would."

"Okay," Wagner said, "if yer ol' man'll let ya have the team, leave early in the mornin', stop in on yer way through and I'll give ya a bag o' oats for the horses. Tell yer ma to make ya a lunch. Mrs. Flegel'll feed ya when ya get ta the mill and make ya a lunch for the trip back. They'll help ya load and make sure it's tied down. You'll need two loggin' chains — ya got 'em?"

"Yeh, we got 'em," I replied, trying to remember where Charlie had put them.

Wagner started pacing back and forth. "Now, how much money ya gonna charge?"

I looked down at the floor and half whispered. "Two days, with a team and wagon . . . should be worth . . . five dollars and 25 cents!"

The ensuing pause went on forever and I kept my eyes on the floor figuring maybe I'd asked too much. When I finally looked up Wagner was smiling and holding out his hand. That would make it a deal.

"What's the extra 25 cents for, kid?"

I didn't answer.

When I got home, after getting Dad's okay, I checked the wagon carefully and made sure all the wheels were greased. I nailed a couple of planks to the bare chassis and tied down two logging chains and the extra gear needed to secure the load. Mom made some sandwiches and packed some tea in a syrup can with a handle on it which could be strung over a camp fire. Wooden matches were packed in a water-proof tin box. That night the horses, Tony and Ben, got an extra helping of oats. Before I went to bed I took a lantern and paid a visit to the outhouse for one more look at that red jacket.

Morning dawned in all the glory of late fall. The trees were decorated in every shade of autumn: reds, yellows, rusts and brown. With the sun shining, I was on my way before anyone else was out of bed. I stopped at Wagner's store and picked up the bag of oats.

The road from Wagner's to Flegel's mill in Pierceland was an old Indian trail which followed the path of least resistance. It twisted and turned which probably added another five miles to the 40 I had to travel. It skirted Big Island Lake before turning inland to the mill. There was a Indian encampment on the shore and as I passed, I recognized Sammy, who was about my age. I turned in and passed the time of day with Sammy and his Dad, Mr. Jackson.

Across the road I could see Mrs. Jackson tending some smoke fires with five or six deerhides stretched over the frames and mounted on rough tripods. She waved at me.

Three horses, or maybe the word would be ponies, were grazing contentedly in the long grass and six assorted dogs of questionable origin were yipping and yapping their heads off.

Sammy picked up a long leather thong and snapped it. "Enough!" he said quietly, and the dogs stopped barking immediately. They crept closer, wagging their tails.

Mrs. Jackson walked across the road, smiling, and nodded a shy greeting.

"You get those hides finished," I said, "and I'm sure Dad would like to see you — maybe make a deal." Dad had made some deals with the Jacksons and had always treated them fairly.

"Come by — maybe one week — you tell your father," Mr. Jackson said. "Where you go?" he added.

"Pierceland. Pick up lumber — come back tomorrow." I found myself talking in short, clipped sentences like they did.

"Better start early in morning," he said, looking out over the lake. "Some weather comin' in."

I couldn't help but think here's one Indian who doesn't know about weather. The sun was shining in a clear blue cloudless sky. It was a perfect autumn day.

When they write about God's country, this is the part of the north they must be describing. On my right was the lake lying tranquil and totally at peace with itself. On my left, in a gentle ascent, were layers of pine and spruce, poplar and birch trees. The underbrush grew in profusion and the colours ran the spectrum of the rainbow.

I took my time drinking it all in as we ambled steadily along, the horses' hooves beating a relaxing rhythm on the twisting trail. About noon I stopped, made a fire and put some water on to boil. I unhitched the horses and fed them their oats. I ate my sandwiches and had tea. There was no need to rush. The sun was still high in the sky and the weather couldn't have been more perfect. I took off my moccasins and socks and waded along the shore with the horses as they drank the clean lake water.

Looking out over the lake, I made a mental note to talk to Gus when I got back and maybe arrange another fishing trip before freezeup. I'd never tried for deep lake trout and the lake was supposed to be full of them, but we'd need a boat or a canoe. Besides, I wanted to ask Gus what it was that made his friend stop wetting the bed and if he'd had any word from his sister.

As I hooked up the horses I couldn't help but think that here I was getting paid for something I'd gladly have done for nothing, what with the weather and scenery and all. Maybe I dallied too long because it was after seven o'clock that evening when I arrived at Flegel's mill.

Mrs. Flegel met me with her arms full of firewood. "You s'ppose' be here supper! Supper over," she said in a snarky tone of voice.

"I'm sorry, Please don't fuss about supper."

"I vorm up pork — potato — you late." Kicking the cabin door open, she disappeared inside just as Mr. Flegel approached from the barn.

"Too dark for load tonight," he said curtly. "Load in morning."

With that he turned and went into the cabin. I unhitched the horses, watered them and found empty stalls for them in the barn. I gave them some hay, wiped them down and kicked some dry straw around their stalls for bedding. When I finished, I knocked on the cabin door and went in. Mrs. Flegel was busy at the stove, muttering to herself. Boy, I thought, the Flegel's sure aren't very friendly. I sat down unobtrusively at the table and waited.

Mrs. Flegel clanked around the stove and shortly, still grumbling to herself, she put a plate down in front of me with a big slab of dried-out pork roast and what looked like worn-out potatoes. That was it. No tea, no dessert. I didn't say anything. The meat was awful but I ate what I could mostly so as not to offend her. I thanked her and went out to the barn to check again on the horses.

As Mrs. Flegel hadn't volunteered where I was to sleep, I decided I would climb up in the hayloft and not bother anybody. Besides, the smells were wonderful; not only the hay all around me but the smell of the lumber mill wafting through. Nothing smells better than freshly cut lumber.

There was a nip in the air so I pulled some hay over me. It had been a long day and I must have fallen asleep in minutes.

Next morning it was snowing. It had turned much colder and I could feel a chill in the air as I shivered myself awake. I put on my jacket, tended to the horses, and went out to help Flegel load the lumber. It was 24 feet long, one inch thick, and six inches wide. The lumber had been milled from green trees and was wet and heavy. The load would be approximately four feet high and the full width of the wagon. As we loaded, I noticed the lumber protruded a good six feet back of the rear wheels. It didn't look right, it wasn't properly balanced. We'd already loaded three or four layers when I finally spoke up.

"Maybe we should extend the wagon a couple more feet."

"Load fine," Flegel said. "You go slow — no trouble."

"It's out pretty far over the back wheels," I said, pointing. "It doesn't look right."

Flegel was annoyed as he interjected, with a note of finality: "You take time — no trouble."

There was no point in pursuing the matter. I helped him stack the boards as the snow came down heavier and the temperature kept falling. Where the sky had been blue and sunny the day before, it was now covered with low-flying clouds.

As we worked with the green lumber, the boards became frozen and slippery. When we had finished loading, I knew how important it was to tie the load down tight and secure. One logging chain was slung around the front end of the load and a long tamarack pole hooked through the links of the chain and bound down to lock it in place. As the pole was forced back and tied down you could feel the load groaning its resistance. The same happened with the second chain over the rear axle. When we were finished, the load still didn't look right to me.

"I really wouldn't mind taking the time to unload and extending the wagon. I know it's not balanced right and I don't wanta have problems goin' home," I said, trying to sound as grownup as I could.

"You smart sonamabitch kid," Flegel said, bristling with anger. "You tell Vagner next time he send man — no sonamabitch kid."

It was a losing battle. I told Flegel everything would likely be okay and thanked him, apologizing for any inconvenience I might have caused him or his wife.

By the time I had hitched up the horses it was almost ten o'clock and snowing heavier than ever. Anxious to get going, I forgot to remind Mrs. Flegel about the lunch she was supposed to give me for the return trip. I didn't remember until I was a few miles down the road and I sure wasn't going to go back. I *had* remembered the horse's bag of oats which I used as a seat as the green lumber, now frozen, was too cold to sit on.

As we pulled out, I could feel the horses straining. The load was very heavy. At the first tug of the team, I felt the front wheels lift slightly and I knew I was right about the load not being properly balanced. Flegel saw it too, but he just gave me his 'don't worry, kid' fluff-off and turned back into the cabin.

The wheels made a crunching sound in the snow, now about two inches deep and coming down heavier than ever. I should have had a sleigh.

I had only gone a few miles before I realized I was shivering. I tied the reins to the logging chain and started moving back and forth on the load in an attempt to keep warm. If Mrs. Flegel hadn't been such a crabby old bitch I would have asked her for the loan of a blanket or bear skin before I left. Lunch time passed but I wasn't hungry, I was too busy trying to stay warm.

When we hit a hilly section the horses had trouble pulling the load. Steam rose from their bodies as they struggled in the nippy air. The first time we stalled I jumped down and ran to the front and led them by their bridles. Slowly we worked our way to the top. Tony nuzzled me as we rested. He was very small compared to Ben, a big dumb clod who consistently outpulled him. I kicked around in the snow and unearthed a piece of deadfall which I threw on top the load.

Down we went as fast as I dared go, bumping and yawing, slipping and sliding with both horses high-stepping on the treacherous footing in the hope the momentum would get us up the other side. The wheels crunched and complained their way through the deepening snow and we didn't quite reach the top. I jumped down and jammed the deadfall under one of the rear wheels before the weight of the load could pull back on Tony and Ben. I untied the reins, brought them alongside the wagon and holding them in one hand like Charlie did, I snapped them onto the horse's backs. They jumped forward a few feet, and again I jammed the deadfall under the wheel. Slowly a few feet at a time, we reached the top, straining and pulling, the snow crunching with the weight of the load which compressed it into hard-pack as it squeaked and rebelled.

I unhitched the horses, took their bridles off and fed them the last of the oats. I used the empty oat bag to rub them down as they were drenched and running in sweat. I could tell by their heaving and the way they breathed that the last hill had taken a lot out of them. I rested them for almost an hour and by the time we were ready to go again the sun was beginning to set. We had covered about fifteen miles — not even halfway — and the day was almost gone. I had no more feed for the horses and I hadn't eaten all day. I began to feel uneasy, and to bolster my courage I started talking to the horses as we moved slowly forward.

"Come on, Tony — don't let that big dummy beside you outpull you — you can keep up with him — go little fella, go!"

But Tony wasn't keeping up. He was getting very tired and Ben was doing most of the work. I changed my tactics. "Atta boy, Ben," I said encouragingly, "you do it cause your buddy's runnin' outta gas, and if you can't do it, we're all gonna be in trouble. Go big fella — go!"

I started singing snatches of songs. The sound of my own voice cheered me as I was terribly alone in what was now a dangerous situation.

Down a hill we went, careening as fast as I dared with the wheels screeching and bumping through the deepening snow, praying I'd make it up the steep other side. The narrow trail turned slightly at the bottom and with all the snow being kicked up by the horses in their frantic scramble, I couldn't see very well and cut the corner too tight. The wagon tried to right itself as it slipped and skidded its way around the bend, the wheels fighting to hold the line of the narrow Indian trail but as we slithered sideways one rear wheel hit a protruding tree stump. There was a bone-jarring crunch as the load became airborne and landed like a bucking bronco. We came to a stop, the horses trembling, their withers quivering. I knew without looking that the load had slipped.

Walking around it, I took stock of the damage. I blocked all four wheels. The horses were steaming, partly from nervousness but mostly from exertion. I held their bridles and talked to them gently. They were snorting and pawing the ground and it took a long time to gentle them down. I took their bridles off, unhooked them, and tethered them in a small clearing surrounded by a stand of spruce trees where they would be protected from the biting wind. As I surveyed the damage, I knew I couldn't have picked a worse place to have hit a stump. Miles from anywhere or anyone, with the snow and cold smothering what little strength there was left in the horses. The green lumber was now frozen and slippery as glass.

The load had shifted way over to one side and if we were going to proceed I would have to unload and reload everylast piece of lumber.

I got on top the load and untied the tamarack poles binding the logging chains and slowly, one board at a time, I began unloading the lumber and stacking it, half on each side of the wagon.

Working kept me warm except for my hands. I had to stop every few minutes and put them in my pockets to get them warm again. As I reloaded each frozen, lead-like board, I moved the load forward about a foot to balance it better. If I'd had the tools I would have extended the wagon. The work was painfully slow but if I didn't do it right I was only wasting my time. It must have been two hours later when I locked the last logging chain into place and cinched it down. The sun had long since disappeared and the temperature was now well below zero. Most frightening was the eerie silence created by the thick, padded blanket of newly-fallen snow.

I fetched the horses and hooked them up. They had had a good rest and we got to the top of the first couple of hills with little difficulty. I tied the reins to the logging chain and for the next few miles, just to stay warm, ran in front of the team, leading and encouraging them as they struggled up a hill, and running around back to block the wheels when they stalled. They were very tired and even the smallest incline became a mountain.

The snow was now about eight inches deep and it clung in globs to the metal rims on the wheels.

Anyone who has lived in the north knows how ruthless winter can be. You develop a great respect for it knowing that if you make a mistake, you pay. I had made a mistake and now it became a desperate question of survival.

I broke off a long willow whip and started running alongside the wagon. Whenever the horses slowed down, I'd tap them on their rumps with the willow and holler words of encouragement. Anything to keep us moving. I'd stumble over hidden tree stumps and fall. This was foolish because a stumble in the wrong place could have thrown me under the wheels and with that load it would have been a crushing end.

Finally we reached a point where I knew we couldn't go any farther. We were only a third of the way up a steep hill and even if the road along the lake had been over the next rise, we would never make it. The horses were now totally exhausted. Tears welled into my eyes and I loved those big, dumb, wonderful animals who had tried so valiantly and now stood there, heaving, steaming and trembling with strangled nerves in the biting cold. I don't know how long I had been crying, but when I reached up to brush the tears from my eyes, some of those tears had already frozen. We still had almost twenty miles to go.

I unhitched the horses and rammed blocks behind all four wheels, then climbed on Tony's back, knowing that Ben would follow. We couldn't go very fast in the deep snow but at least we were moving, we were staying alive. I was so tired I just wanted to close my eyes and sleep but if I did, I knew it would be the end. Tony felt warm under me and it wasn't long before we were out of the bush and on to the trail that ran along the lake.

The north wind came in over the lake in frigid gusts and tore through my clothes like knives of cold steel. It had stopped snowing but the temperature was still below zero.

Thank God for the horses. They had that inborn sense that would take us home. I lay forward on Tony's back for some protection from the wind and the added warmth from his body. I was so tired I just wanted to hang on.

What happened next is a blank in my memory. Somehow, even riding bareback, I stayed on Tony, but I must have passed out. When I came to it was daylight and I was in a tent. I could hear muffled voices and someone calling in the distance. Then the voices came nearer and I realized I was in the Indian camp we had passed the day before. Images floated slowly in my mind. The last thing I remembered was climbing on Tony's back and somehow getting to the lake road. To get to the Indian camp meant we had gone about ten miles that I couldn't recall. The horses had turned into the camp only because I had stopped there briefly the day before, otherwise Tony would have tried to take me all the way home and I'd never have made it. Stopping to say hello to the Jacksons the day before had probably saved my life.

The sound of our arrival had awakened Sammy and his dad. They had brought me in and taken care of me.

I looked up and saw Sammy and his mother smiling down at me. I was warm and covered in blankets. I told them about having to abandon the load and Mr. Jackson and Sammy left immediately with their horses to pick it up. Mrs. Jackson made porridge and I reached for my moccasins which had been strung over a rack to dry. They were hard and needed a good rubbing before they were soft enough to put on. When I tried, they wouldn't fit. My feet were swollen twice their normal size. Mrs. Jackson smiled knowingly and gave me another pair.

The next day, with new moccasins and limping slightly, but with a team of well-rested horses, I delivered the load of lumber to Mr. Wagner. That same afternoon I sent in my order for the red jacket.

I was twelve years old.

CHAPTER 8

WHILE THERE WAS A STRONG SENSE of community feeling among the settlers and everyone, with few exceptions, helped everyone else, the native Indians were really not a part of it. Having been uprooted, they were sensitive and if any homesteader didn't make them feel welcome, they would avoid stopping there. The Indians I remember spoke softly with a limited and crisp vocabulary but behind their quiet facade was a fierce sense of pride.

They had a great respect for the north — not just the land but everything that grew and lived from it, and inwardly they resented anyone who abused the abundant gifts the north provided. They had learned to survive in an unpredictable, and at times, vicious environment and, using methods passed down to them from generation to generation, they had come to terms with a vast wilderness.

In 1867, the native Indians surrendered title to huge tracts of land in a series of treaties with the Crown. They were not granted voting rights and had little, if any, input into the decisions that were to dictate their destiny. They were politically naive, timid and malleable. In return for lands which were once theirs alone, they were ceded small, scattered reserves, encumbered with restrictions designed to prepare them for integration into the white man's perception of civilization. For more than a hundred years they have been and remain ghettoized on these reserves, and the white man's attempts at integrating these proud people have led to unqualified failure and frustration.

Indians pay no land or income tax as long as they remain on reserves. They are, however, obliged to pay income tax on monies earned elsewhere. The tendency therefore, in many cases, is to remain on their reserves and take advantage of the tax forgiveness, but to survive, they require government subsidies, welfare payments and other benefits.

This bureaucratic structure, by imposition, destroys individual incentives and like some rampant cancer, the frustration grows.

An unwritten code existed in the north which almost everyone obeyed. The early rules had been established by the Indians who were there first. As the settlers moved in they quickly learned these rules and most lived by them. Aside from an obligation to help anyone who was in trouble, probably the most important law was no encroachment or poaching on another man's trapline. The Indians were the best trappers, their techniques having been handed down from father to son since long before the white man came to North America.

We tried our hand at trapping with little success. The snares we set for fox would have rabbits in them when we made the rounds of our traplines. But the north teemed with wildlife and a good trapper could choose from a wide variety of fur-bearing animals.

After the ground had been surveyed and the homesteaders moved in, the Indians recognized that the land now belonged to somebody else. They moved farther north beyond the surveyed land and staked out new traplines. Our homestead was only nine miles from the end of the survey and many Indian families would stop at our house on their way back and forth.

Not all homesteaders had a welcome sign out for Indians but Dad did a lot of business with them, all barter. Indians didn't need hunting, fishing or trapping licenses. We did. For us there were rigid quotas and certain species of animals and birds could not be shot or trapped at all. Indians could hunt or trap anything, in or out of season, and rarely was this privilege abused.

Indians, however, were not allowed liquor in any form. Because there were no liquor stores in the north, most homesteaders had their own illegal stills and traded it illegally to the Indians. We bartered our homemade whiskey and the birds and animals which Dad stuffed and mounted. In exchange we got tanned deer and moose hides to make clothes with and the striped blankets made by the Indian women.

Dad was an excellent taxidermist and a mounted Arctic owl would fetch four deer or two moose hides. The Indians loved these mounted birds, especially Arctic owls. They would stop by with a frozen owl and ask Dad to mount it. Dad would explain that it was extremely difficult, as the frozen bird's feathers were too disheveled and could not be put back into place properly for mounting. The better way was to keep the bird alive for a couple of days and allow it to preen itself and get its feathers back in order.

When I arrived home after delivering the lumber to Mr. Wagner I told my parents what had happened. Dad was quick to point out that I owed my life to the Jacksons and the first time an occasion presented itself, I was to thank them properly with some kind of gift to show my gratitude and let it be known they would always be welcome at our house.

One afternoon their outfit pulled into the turn-off and stopped in our yard.

"Hi, Sammy," I said, "I'm glad to see you again." He shook hands shyly and I nodded politely to his parents. "We've been waiting for you to drop in so I could thank you again for saving my life."

The Jacksons shuffled their feet uncomfortably in the leaves as Dad watched. Mr. Jackson held up his hand as if to stop me from saying more. My words were embarrassing him.

"My Dad says I owe you."

Jackson bristled. "You owe us nothing."

"We want to give you some small token to show our appreciation for your kindness," Dad said with some finality.

Jackson nodded stoically, relieved the conversation had ended. "Maybe a stuffed owl," he said, tentatively. "That would be more than enough."

Dad explained that the owls he had mounted had been brought to him by Indians. "We don't know how to catch them without shooting them, and when we do that, the bird is too messy to work with. You people have a way of catching them alive and if you could do that, we could keep it a few days while it straightened out its feathers," he continued. "You bring me a live owl and I'll really do a nice job for you."

"It's easy to catch owls," Mr. Jackson said, and went on to explain his method. We marveled at how simple it was, if it worked.

"We go south — collect treaty money — come back maybe week, ten days."

"Okay," Dad said. "If your procedure works, we should have your owl when you come back through."

They piled onto their wagon, their extra horse tied on behind and all the dogs following, and disappeared slowly down the road.

That evening we decided to try their method of catching a live owl. We took a birch pole about 25 feet long, nailed a twelve-inch-square board across the flattened top end then attached a muskrat trap by its chain securely to the top end of the pole. We went into Boening's clearing next to our land, set the trap then carefully raised the pole right in the middle of the cleared area. We piled a few stones around the base of the pole, just enough to hold it up. If anything landed in the trap on the twelve-inch board, the pole would fall over.

Owls hunt at night and survival dictates that they be extremely careful, which they are. They don't just land anywhere. They look for lone trees in clearings so they can see all around. The pole in Boening's field was a natural. When we looked out the following morning, the pole was down and sure enough, flopping around on the ground, its foot securely caught in the muskrat trap was a live owl. It was as simple as the Jacksons had said. Dad threw a heavy gunny sack over the owl and gently removed the trap. The foot had been badly mangled but Dad knew he could repair it with his taxidermy paraphernalia.

We carried the owl back to the corral and locked a metal clasp with a chain onto its other foot. When we removed the gunny sack it immediately began shaking out its feathers and preening itself. That's exactly what Dad needed. We threw some rabbit meat into the corral and later, when we went back to check, the meat was gone.

The owl wasn't very big. Dad felt the Jacksons should have a very special bird. He threw the gunny sack over the owl again, undid the clasp and turned it loose. That night we set the trap in Boening's clearing once more to see if we couldn't catch a bigger one.

Next morning the pole was down again but this time everything was gone, even the pole. It had been dragged through the grass and we found it lodged up against two trees on the edge of the clearing. Caught securely in the muskrat trap was not an owl, but an eagle; one of the restricted species of wild life. They were quite rare, and while we had occasionally seen one flying over we had never seen one up close. This bird was awesome.

Standing, watching us ominously, it must have been over three feet tall. When we moved closer it spread its wings which must have been over seven feet from tip to tip, and hissed like an angry snake. Its claws were as big around as pie plates and its beak was a frightening and vicious-looking weapon. Dad's gunny sack wasn't going to be enough so he sent us back to the barn for two horse-blankets and a heavy rope.

Grabbing one end of the pole, Dad slowly pulled the trapped eagle until it was firmly lodged up close to one of the trees with very little room to maneuver. Circling cautiously, he threw one of the horse-blankets over its head, got the rope around both its legs and pulled them tightly together. With the eagle now literally hobbled, we got the second horse-blanket around it and carted everything back to the corral, eagle, trap and pole. Once in the corral, Dad got the metal clasp around its foot and tied the chain to the corral fence. The trap was carefully removed and the pole taken away. We all got out of the corral and zipped the blankets off.

What a magnificent, terrifying bird. And what a prize for the Jacksons when they stopped in to pick up their 'owl.'

A few scraps of meat were obviously not going to satisfy the eagle. We had a three-month-old calf that was sickly and wasn't going to make it, so Dad killed it and threw it into the corral. It was scary, watching as the eagle tore the calf apart. Its beak ripped away the hide as though it was peeling an orange. By evening, the calf had disappeared.

We kept the eagle alive for three days. Lloyd and I spent all our free time sitting safely on the far side of the corral fence watching the beauty and ferocity of this king of birds. The first day, when Dad wasn't around, we teased it with a long pole but we soon tired of this as it seemed demeaning to the eagle. It grabbed the end of the pole and snapped it like a matchstick. When the calf had been eaten we snared a couple of rabbits and threw them into the corral. They were little more than a snack and gone in minutes.

Dad never let us watch him when he killed the birds. He used some of his embalming equipment and I know a long syringe was a part of it. It must have been painless and quick because the feathers were always immaculate and we never ever heard any noise.

Dad mounted the eagle with its wings spread in a landing position. The bottom feathers on each wing jutted downwards like airplane landing flaps. The claws were open and the head was slightly tilted, looking down. It looked both real and deadly. He built a special pedestal for it and set it up in the cabin so we could all enjoy it until the Jacksons arrived.

That weekend, as luck would have it, we were visited by the Mounties. They had tethered their horses some distance from the house and sneaked in furtively through the trees hoping maybe we might be running a batch of brew, or whatever.

Dad happened to be out in the yard and saw them flitting from one tree to the next like the scenario in an old western-style movie.

"You there," he hollered, "get yer sneaky asses out here where I can see who'n hell ya are."

They walked sheepishly out of the trees and one of them produced a piece of paper from his tunic pocket.

"Look, Hahn, we have a warrant to search this . . ."

Dad was very angry as he interrupted. "When you speak to me, on my land, you say 'Mister' — understand?"

They both looked taken aback by Dad's abrasive manner. They weren't used to being talked to like this. Most homesteaders kow-towed to them and no one else ever treated them with disdain.

"Okay, ya gotta warrant," Dad said, turning his back on them. "Search to yer heart's content but if ya pick up anything, make sure ya put it back, jus' like ya found it."

They wandered around checking in the barn and chicken coop. They even kicked around the bottom row of oat sheaves in the corral. Finally, they knocked on the cabin door and Mom let them in. As soon as their eyes adjusted to the dim light in the cabin, they saw the mounted eagle.

"What's that, ma'am?" one of them asked.

"It's an eagle," Mom answered.

"An eagle? — don't you know eagles are on the protected list?"

Their eyes lit up like Christmas tree lights as they went out into the yard, looking for Dad.

"Okay, Hahn, get your things — you're coming with us and that's an order. You're under arrest!"

"On what charge?" Dad asked.

"Possession of a restricted species of wildlife, namely an eagle." The Mounties were gloating. They had been after Dad for a long time because of the still they knew he had but could never find. Now they had him cold. One of them went off through the trees to get their horses and buggy and the other carefully carried the eagle out of the cabin.

While all of this was going on, Dad was busy packing some things in a knapsack and at the same time, holding a whispered conversation with Mom. We could see her nodding her understanding.

The eagle was carefully deposited between the two buggy seats.

"Come on, Hahn, let's go!"

Dad sat on the back seat holding the eagle as they turned down the driveway, heading north to the RCMP post.

"None of you are to worry," Mom said. "As soon as the Jacksons arrive, everything is gonna be all right."

A couple of days later, they arrived. Mom explained what had happened and Mr. Jackson understood. The next day we all accompanied Mr. Jackson when he went to the RCMP post to claim *his* eagle.

"This eagle mine," he explained. "Somebody shoot — break wing — I find — bird suffer — have to kill — bring Mr. Hahn for mount — not his eagle — eagle mine."

In the face of this evidence the Mounties could only release Dad which they did, grudgingly. The Jacksons went on their way with the eagle and we all knew as we drove home that at least part of my debt had been paid.

Chapter 9

It was autumn and I was wandering along the creek bed with my dog Spot, drinking in the multitude of colors and enjoying the crisp, tangy fall air. The skies were full of wild ducks and geese on their way south to the Mississippi Delta for the winter. They were flying pretty low and the air was alive with their squawking conversations as they vied for their rightful place in the long lines forming the familiar 'V's. There was always a lot of confusion and a great deal of discussion among them as they sorted themselves out for the long flight.

These wild birds are very much creatures of habit. There were specific places they would land to rest and feed. Our homestead was not one of them and except for the odd straggler, the formations invariably overflew our place. The Beaver River Valley was a major stopping-off place and Charlie often took the .22 and rode Tony down to the river to return with three or four big fat birds.

The oats had been cut on our six-acre patch and Spot and I wandered through the trees in that direction. Suddenly, there was a whirring sound just above our heads and I held Spot quiet as a bunch of wild turkeys flew over, tree-top high, and prepared to land in the oat patch. Wild turkeys are huge, much bigger than wild ducks or geese. As they disappeared over the rise, preparing to land, I ran back to the house looking for Charlie.

"Ya gotta come quick. A whole gang of wild turkeys just landed in the oat patch."

"Wild turkeys, you say — that's strange," Charlie mused. "They don't gen'rally land 'round here, if'n know what I mean. Yer sure they's turkeys?"

"Positive," I said. "Shall I get the .22?"

"If they's turkeys, we's gonna have us some fun. Go fetch the horses.

I'll show ya how to get us a turkey, maybe two, and we don't even need a gun, if'n know what I mean."

I went and got Tony and Ben and when I got back, Charlie was putting the finishing touches on two willow clubs, each about four feet long. He gave me one, jumped on Ben, and motioned for me to follow.

We tied up the horses a couple of hundred yards from the oat patch and Charlie explained what we were going to do. We sneaked up quietly to the edge of the clearing and watched for a few minutes. The turkeys were making a lot of noise as they complimented one another on what a great feeding ground they had stumbled onto. Charlie had a quizzical look on his face.

"Them fuckers ain't turkeys!" he said. "Wild turkeys gobble and those birds is honkin' like ducks, if'n know what I mean. Never seen birds like that — they's big like turkeys but they's talkin' like ducks or somethin' — funny."

"You still gonna do it?" I asked.

"Fuckin' right," Charlie answered as he jumped on Ben. "You take Tony — ride 'round ta the south end o' the clearin' and wait. I'll take Ben an' work my way 'round ta the north end. When ya hear me holler, jump in an' make's much noise as ya can. Them birds is so big they's gonna needa a hunert feet of runnin' 'fore they can take off, if'n know what I mean. If we's quick 'bout it and come at 'em from both sides, they ain't gonna know their ass from Adam and we gonna get us a couple 'fore they get off the ground."

We mounted the horses and grabbed our clubs. I made a wide circle and approached the south end of the oat patch as quietly as I could. Spot was following close behind knowing something big was about to happen. Whatever it was, he wasn't going to miss any of it.

About 50 feet from the clearing, I stopped and waited for Charlie's cue. The birds were making a hell of a noise and were far too engrossed in what they were doing to sense that disaster was about to strike.

Charlie came charging out of the far end of the clearing, hollering at the top of his voice. I dug my heels into Tony's flanks and we charged into the oat patch with me screaming as loud as I could and Spot right along side, barking his head off.

The turkeys were totally confused. They didn't know which way to run. Charlie had been right. They were like miniature airplanes and every time they'd get going down the runway trying to get up enough speed to become airborne, either Charlie or Spot or I would be in their way. I concentrated on a big, clumsy, lumbering bird and galloped alongside. I missed with my first swing of the club and had to turn around. The field was bedlam, with turkeys and horses and dogs all over the place. I charged into the fray again and almost took a turkey's head off with my next swing. Charlie already had his. He held up his hand for me to stop and we watched the remaining birds motor awkwardly down the runway and take off.

It was only years later, when the newspapers showed pictures revealing there were only 30-odd whooping cranes left in the world that I recognized the two 'wild turkeys' Charlie and I had decapitated. As I read the account, I realized the only turkeys running around our oat patch that day were Charlie and me.

I have never understood people who don't like dogs. Dogs live on love. Not wanting it as much as giving it. Every boy should have a dog. I didn't get a dog of my own until we moved to the homestead and I didn't really *get* a dog, he sort of got me.

I was walking down by the creek one day and there was this frightened little mongrel cowering behind a log. He was nothing but skin and bones and still a puppy.

As I meandered along I could see him following cautiously, maybe fifty or sixty feet behind. When I got back to the cabin, I put some leftover rabbit stew in a dish and tried to coax him to come closer. He wouldn't. Finally, I put the bowl down a distance from the house and walked away. Slowly, he inched his way toward the bowl as I watched. His eyes were on me all the time but I was careful not to make any threatening moves. He must have been starving. Eventually he got to the bowl and the stew was gone in a couple of minutes. As soon as he finished he scrambled back into the trees but I could see him watching me from a safe distance the rest of the day.

Before I went to bed that night I put another bowl of stew out and in the morning it had been licked clean. It took a couple of days and a few more bowls of rabbit stew but that's how I got my first dog.

I called him Spot which wasn't very imaginative but the name seemed right. Spot didn't grow very big. He was assorted shades of brown with haphazard streaks of white. He looked more like a collie than any other kind of dog but he wasn't nearly as big and his nose wasn't pointed. His face was beautiful, though, and his eyes were big and brown.

Spot was mine. Really mine. When we were together, no one could take him away by calling him unless I said it was okay. If anyone else was around it was almost embarrassing to see him sitting there, looking at me with adoration shining from his eyes. His love was so obvious and he flaunted it, unashamedly. He'd lick my hand whenever he could and when he lay down, he'd do it in such a way that part of him always touched me.

Spot was very bright and learned to do tricks faster than I could think them up. He would roll over, play dead, jump through a willow hoop, shake hands with either front paw, and 'speak.' Maybe that isn't a whole lot, but I thought he had extraordinary talent and so did he. We had wonderful days together and at night he would sleep on my bed.

Spot had his bad times too. I remember the day he tangled with a skunk and that's a no-win confrontation. He couldn't understand why he wasn't allowed in the house for the next week. Another time he had a fight with a porcupine and when he came whimpering home, his nose full of quills, it hurt me more than him as I pulled each one out.

In the summer when I was sent to the store, four miles away, the fastest way was on horseback. Spot would always come along, running as fast as the horse. In winter I'd use the toboggan Dad made, which was pulled by one horse. Spot would ride inside with me, snuggling up tight not only to keep warm but so he wouldn't fall off. The toboggan had a hand brake which was used going down hills to keep it from running into the horse's heels.

Spot was my best friend, better even than my brother or sisters and certainly a better friend than Mom or Dad. He never wanted anything except to be with me and he was with me all the time, day and night. Spot transmitted his love through his big brown eyes. Except that it was more than love. It was worship. He really made me feel good.

Before a homesteader received clear title to his land, certain minimum requirements had to be met. The initial filing fee was ten dollars, for which you had the rights to 160 acres, or a quarter-section of land. Over a period of time, certain improvements had to be made to the property. You had to dig a well. You had to clear a minimum number of acres, 'break' this virgin land and put it under cultivation. We eventually had about seven acres cleared with six seeded, mostly in oats, and the other for garden vegetables. Seven acres, however, wasn't nearly enough to satisfy the requirements of clear title. Another stipulation was that a certain number of acres had to be fenced. The first area we fenced, except around our buildings, was the six-acre patch of oats. This was as much to keep wild animals such as deer and moose (although they could jump it easily) out of the oat patch as our own domestic animals.

We had plenty of fresh water. Aside from the well, which was frozen over most of the winter, we had a spring which ran summer and winter and this was the water we used most of the time, both for the house and the livestock.

In the summer we'd open the barn doors and turn the cattle loose. They'd head for the spring for a drink and then wander off to graze the rest of the day. Most of the homesteaders did the same thing. Somehow, when evening came, all the cattle were together in a herd of perhaps fifty or sixty head. At the time we had seven head of cattle — four steers and three cows.

Each day, the herd was found grazing in some new place. They could be just over the first knoll or as far as two or three miles away and seldom in the same direction as the day before. Spot always knew where the herd was. He'd lead the way when it was my turn to fetch them and I'd just follow on horseback, riding Tony. When we found them, we had to separate our seven from the others. This was a tedious and frustrating chore until I discovered how smart Spot really was. As soon as the herd was spotted, I'd find an area for Tony to graze and drop the lead on his halter. We rarely used a bridle with a bit, as both our horses were trained to 'knee-rein.' They would turn or stop according to pressure from the rider's knees. As Tony nibbled the lush grass I'd go and sit under a tree. Spot would stand 'pointing' like some high-class hunting dog, waiting for me to say it was okay.

"Get 'em, Spot," and he was off like a bullet. He'd run right into the middle of the herd, dodging horns and hooves, and start nipping at the heels of only our seven head. In minutes he'd have them strung out, headed for home. Then he'd come running to where I was sitting for a pat on the head. We'd saunter back home slowly. We couldn't go too fast because of the cows that were milking. Somehow, Spot understood this. If a steer got out of line there was hell to pay, but the cows received gentler treatment. Spot's job wasn't finished until all the cattle were either in the barn or corral.

As Lloyd and I split all the chores, we took turns finding the cattle and bringing them home. The cows then had to be milked. When I fetched the cows, Lloyd would milk them, and next day the procedure was reversed. Milking cows was not one the things I was best at. One old cow never complained and was very gentle when being milked, but I was scared stiff of the other two and they knew it. If I didn't do it just right they'd lift their legs and try to kick the pail. They were constantly flicking me with their tails and their aim was flawless. Lloyd would laugh as he watched me in my misery. Our chores had been rigidly spelled out by Dad, who didn't mind if we made our own personal deals just as long as the work got done. Lloyd agreed to milking when it was my turn in exchange for my doing some of his other chores. One of these was sawing wood for the stoves. While we had a complete wood-sawing outfit with a gasoline-fed engine, we didn't have the money to buy gas. We'd bring enough trees in during the fall to last all winter and these would then have to be sawed into two-and-a-half foot lengths to fit our stoves. One of the dumb deals I made with Lloyd was sawing his share of the wood in exchange for his milking the cows. Lloyd could milk all three in less than an hour and in cold weather, I would have to saw wood all day long just to keep up.

Another deal I made with Lloyd, in exchange for milking, was that I would cut the oats on our six-acre patch. We used a small hay mower but both horses were used for the job. The job was easy and the newly-cut oats smelled good. The horses were forever trying to sneak a mouthful whenever we got to the end of a row to turn around. With bits in their mouths it wasn't too difficult to keep their heads up but, row after row, they'd keep trying to grab a mouthful even though they couldn't chew it because of the bits. I would cut row after row with Spot running along behind. Sometimes, I would hold him on my lap as we went around the field. He loved this. If I didn't have him on my lap when we came to the end of a row to turn around, he would bark at me until I got down off the mower seat to pet him.

One day I was riding along, the cutting blades slithering along silently scissoring the oats and watching it as it fell in neat rows behind the mower. I came to the end of a row and stopped to give the horses a rest. Spot was behind me, barking to be picked up or at least petted. I acted as though I was ignoring him, which he couldn't stand. He ran around in front and stood up on his hind feet, barking and pleading, asking me to pick him up. Suddenly one of the horses put its head down to sneak a mouthful of oats and the mower blades slithered ahead a few inches. Spot was too close and it all happened too fast. Both of his hind legs were severed and he fell frontwards over the blades as my heart stopped beating with a thump. He lay there looking up at me, knowing that whatever had happened, I would fix it. Blood was pouring out in short sumping spurts. I jumped down and tore my shirt off. I tied a sleeve around each of his hind legs to stop the bleeding. He was whimpering softly, but when I lifted him up he licked my hand.

It was almost a quarter-of-a-mile back to the cabin. I ran as quickly as I could through the trees, cradling Spot in my arms. I could feel his warm blood running down my bare skin but I was afraid to look down. Surely this couldn't be happening to me — to Spot!

I hated those stupid horses. All for a measly mouthful of oats. Then I hated my brother. He was supposed to be cutting the oats; it was his turn. Then I blamed myself for playing games with Spot and ignoring him when he was still safely behind the mower blades, asking me to pick him up. Finally, I blamed Spot for meaning so much to me. He was looking up at me with complete trust in his eyes. I remembered all the wonderful times we'd had together. We'd hunted, we'd gone to the store, we'd gone fishing and we'd fetched the cattle a hundred times. But more than anything else, we had been inseparable, day and night, for more than two years.

Mom would know what to do. Surely there was some way to make Spot better again. The tears were streaming down my face as I burst into the cabin. Mom got a blanket and we put Spot on the kitchen table as she looked down at his legs. When she looked up there were tears in her eyes too as she slowly shook her head.

Oh, no! I thought. There has to be another way. I was sobbing now. Mom wrapped Spot gently in the blanket and put him back in my arms. She took the .22 off its wall pegs and handed it to me. I could feel Spot's life blood seeping through the blanket as I fumbled blindly for the door.

I walked gently down to the creek, in among the willows, and leaned the gun up against a tree. I sat down and held Spot tightly for a long time. I could feel his blood seeping through my clothes but it didn't matter. He licked the tears that were streaming down my face. I kissed him and put him down as gently as possible. He looked up and watched as I picked up the gun and backed away a few feet.

I had to keep wiping away the tears as I tried to aim along the sights. Spot just looked at me and waited. He knew all about guns; guns were for rabbits and squirrels. One last wipe of my tears and I had him in my sights.

I can still see the utter disbelief in Spot's big brown eyes as the gun went off.

Chapter 10

THE BUILDING SITES chosen by the settlers as they moved on to their virgin land were picked with great care. Generally, they were close to the main road and always on high ground. Snowfall most winters was very heavy and an allowance had to be made for the spring run-offs. If buildings were in a low-lying location they could be washed out. We were fortunate in our choice. A spring-fed creek in the northwest corner of our property was the key. This spring supplied water, summer and winter. From this spring to the building site was only a matter of a few hundred feet, up an incline to a densely wooded area. Some trees had to be cleared for the buildings but the location was perfect and only about 300 feet in from the road.

Once our main buildings, the house, barn, and chicken coop were up, the next priority was to clear land for a garden. We cleared almost an acre, close to the house, during our first summer. Then we had to clear and cultivate a section big enough to grow crops such as oats to feed the livestock. Growing cash crops like wheat was a long way off.

It was necessary to clear a six-foot-wide 'cut-line' a half-mile long connecting surveyor's stakes at the four corners of our quarter section. The trees cleared were used to build a haphazard sort of fence in the middle of the six-foot line. This also served as a fire-break.

Forest fires could mean disaster. Most homesteads had heavy timber stands and the settlers had learned from their experience on the prairies that leaving lines of trees standing between cultivated fields was insurance against drifting soil and erosion. They planned carefully which areas to clear and where trees should be left standing. A forest fire could destroy all this planning.

Once we had our garden plot cleared, Lloyd and I spent most of three summers working a six-acre patch of willows. Every morning we'd go out, each with a double-bladed axe, and hack away at them. The third summer was very dry. We were well into August and it hadn't rained in over a month. Lloyd and I were out hacking and I was feeling more than a little dejected. It was going to take forever to finish clearing that patch, and when it was done it would only begin again in some other part of the homestead. We would eventually have to have at least half of our 160 acres cultivated if we were to farm sucessfully, and we had to clear a minimum acreage to get clear title to the land. After three summers we still hadn't finished the easiest patch of all. The work was backbreaking, and when the day was over we could barely see any improvement over the day before.

At the edge of the clearing the terrain dropped gradually into a dried-out creek bed. In the spring, during the run-off, there was water in it for a few weeks but as nothing fed it, it dried up in warmer weather. The dried grass in this ravine grew very thick and a couple of feet high. Pussy willows and all sorts of other dried debris lay in profusion among the grass.

Looking down into the creek bed, the dry grass must have been piled eight or nine inches high. It no longer was green but rather a tinder-dry shade of yellow.

Suddenly, I wondered what would happen if I threw a lighted match into the creek bed. The grass would burn like crazy I knew, but it would undoubtedly stop when it got to the cut-line as we had just cleaned it out a few days before. In all likelihood, the fire would only run along the creek bed. The more I thought about it, the more fascinated I became with the idea. I decided to throw a match into the tall grass. There was a slight breeze blowing but it barely moved the dried out leaves and grass.

Though it was very hot, I was wearing a heavy pair of deer-hide pants to protect me from getting scratched by the willows. My shirt was flannel and my moccasins were not the usual knee-high length but were low cut, like a pair of slippers.

I walked down to the ravine and struck a match. I tried a couple of tufts of grass. They lit immediately and I pounded them out. Maybe it wasn't such a good idea after all. Shorter grass grew up from the creek bed into the dense timber on both sides. There were bare patches and it didn't look as though a fire could spread up from the creek bed into the taller trees. I walked part way up the side of the hill and lit a patch of grass. It burned itself out as soon as it got to a bare spot. So I was right! It wouldn't spread. The fire would run along the creek bed, just as I figured, and burn itself out when it got to the cutline.

I decided it might be more prudent, however, if I lit the fire some distance away, otherwise Lloyd would know who had started it and maybe tell Dad. I walked along the creek bed for about an eighth of a mile, crossed through the dry grass to the other side, lit a match and threw it in. It caught as though the grass had been sprinkled with gasoline. The wind, such as it was, was blowing in my direction. I backed off into the bare spots where the fire couldn't burn and watched, fascinated, as the flames moved rapidly through the grass. Smoke was rising and I decided to get back to our clearing before Lloyd found out I was gone. As I turned, I found the fire had moved up from the creek bed and was now on the hill behind me. I'd have to go around the other way until I could get ahead of it. Wrong! It was running along the creek bed and up on the hills on both sides.

The fire reached a dead birch tree standing in the midst of the willow bushes. A tongue of flame reached out, touched its paper-thin and tinder-dry bark and in an instant the tree was a blazing 50 foot torch. As it toppled earthward, it created a burning bridge across the stream, giving the fire the release it needed. The wind was no longer a gentle breeze for the fire was creating its own wind, sucking giant draughts of air and devouring the oxygen. What it didn't use spewed upward in a column of gases and dark smoke that drew a curtain across the sun.

As it moved into the tall trees and the deadfall began burning I knew there was no way to stop what I had started. Fascinated, I watched sparks fly up in the breeze to start a new fire 40 or 50 feet away. The bare spots I had counted on as a deterrent were of no use. The fire moved up both sides of the hill from the creek bed. The wind was stronger than ever and, even running at a brisk pace, the fire was gaining on me. The air was full of sparks as I ran for higher ground with the fire a couple of hundred feet away. I stopped and looked back. The smoke was much thicker but through it, as far a I could see, the fire had grabbed hold and was jumping everything in its path.

Suddenly I realized I was in strange territory. We never wandered too far from home except when hunting with Charlie. Then we had our own tracks in the snow to guide us home. I ran along the higher ground with the fire pursuing me relentlessly. I don't know how far I had gone when I saw a low lying area where the grass looked much greener. I headed down into it.

It was a creek with water in it. Now, I'd be safe. The water was about eight feet across and the grass lush and green all along its banks. Fire doesn't burn in green grass. I jumped a log and crossed to the other side. The water and green grass would surely stop the fire. The fire ran right up to the green grass and stopped, then the breeze, howling down the funnel of the creek bed, carried a few sparks across the water and a new fire picked up on my side. I ran down into the water and began wading. I could feel the heat and every few minutes I would dunk myself to cool off. The wind picked up even more.

Scrambling through the water, I came to a widening in the creek — a small pond with an old beaver dam at one end. It must have been 30 feet across and the water was much deeper. But like most transplanted prairie boys, I couldn't swim. I ran around the pond and jumped into the creek again. I knew if I stayed close to water I'd be all right.

I was bleeding from a dozen places on my arms and upper body. My shirt had disappeared except for the cuffs which were dangling from my wrists. I kept getting caught in the underbrush and with no shirt to protect me, every scratch became a spot of blood. I realized how tired I was getting as I fought my way through the willows and waded through the water. Countless dead trees had fallen across the creek and these either had to be ducked under or climbed over. At times, the creek became a veritable jungle with intertwined willows growing in from both banks. I kept running with the fire now a solid blanket on both sides of the creek and up both banks. It was not only gaining on me but was well ahead of me. I would have to stay in the water to get out of this alive. Even in the water it was no more than a few feet away on either side. The sparks were like mosquitoes and I had to keep flicking them off my shoulders. Some even landed in my hair.

Where the creek narrowed the fire was all around. The bigger trees were now burning. The sound of roaring flames got louder and louder and seemed to be coming at me from all sides. Fear nurtured confusion and I became obsessed with just staying ahead and outrunning the raging, hissing holocaust. Dunking my head under the water to get as wet as I could, I jumped out of the creek and ran as fast as I could right through the fire, wondering if I'd ever get to the other side. Finally, it cleared. I was through and the fire was behind me again. I kept running. In front of me was another pond, bigger than the first one and obviously, deeper. I tried wading around its fringe but the bottom was muddy and I could barely move.

If I could swim, I would have gone into the centre of the pond and waited for the fire to run its course. I thought of finding a dead log and pushing it out into the middle. All I'd have to do would be to hang on and kick my feet to keep the log in the middle. There were no dead logs and I was wasting valuable time. I dipped my head under the water and once more jumped up on the bank. And I ran! I ran around the far side of the pond, looking for the extension of the creek which fed it. It wasn't there! I ran right around the pond, the fire licking at my heels and suddenly I was back at the spot where I had climbed out just minutes before. The pond, obviously, was the headwater of the creek. There was no outlet on the other side. I jumped back into the water and waded out as far as I dared. Now the fire was burning in the trees right over my head. The heat was unbearable and I knew I couldn't stay there. Once again, I looked around for a dead log, anything I might hang onto, out in the middle. There was nothing and I had run out of time. The fire was everywhere.

I got out of the creek and ran right through the fire with nothing more than sheer panic pushing me as I struggled up the side of the hill, sparks spewing in all directions as I stepped on burning twigs and underbrush. My feet were searing and, looking down, I saw I had lost one moccasin. The other was torn and mangled and ready to fall off. I was exhausted but I kept running, picking my spots through the charred ground, flicking the sparks off me as they burned my bare skin. With only fright driving me, at last I broke through. The fire was behind me again.

I lost all track of time and direction. The sky was full of smoke and I couldn't see the sun except for a red haze or I might have guessed the time. I checked the moss on a few poplar trees and as best I could determine I had been running mostly south and east. This didn't prove anything as I could be turned around again in a matter of minutes. I had no idea where I was or what direction was home.

Looking back, the smoke must have been a mile high, with flames licking a hundred feet in the air. I crossed bush trails I didn't recognize. I ran through cut-lines but the six feet of 'no trees' meant absolutely nothing. The fire was out of control, burning high in the tall timber stand and nothing was going to stop it.

Running along, with the fire now a safe distance behind me, I suddenly realized I had company. I watched creatures that were natural enemies pass within inches of each other. Hundreds of rabbits abandoned the safety of the underbrush for the speed of the wide open spaces, with hardly a glance at the weasels and foxes fleeing beside them. There were four or five deer and a moose. There were skunks, ground hogs, porcupine, and there must have been a million squirrels and chipmunks. They criss-crossed in front of me as though I didn't exist. We were all in the same boat, trying to stay ahead of the fire.

I finally emerged at a place I recognized — the Beaver River, well downstream from our normal crossing point at Seeley's store. I recognized a duck blind that Charlie and I had used the preceding autumn. I had been running for almost six miles.

The fire of '34, burned for almost a week. Tens of thousands of acres of prime timber land were left scarred and lifeless. To this day, I have never told anybody how it started. But for 40-odd years my conscience has whipped me every time I read of a forest fire.

CHAPTER 11

ON THE NORTH SHORE of the Beaver River, far enough up from the valley to be safe from the spring run-offs, George Seeley and his wife built and ran a small general store. He sold staples such as flour, sugar, dry goods and beans but he dreamed of precious metals.

Seeley had staked mining claims all over the north, convinced that sheer numbers dictated that sooner or later he would strike it rich. He didn't work his claims; he just staked them and they dotted the north for 50 miles in all directions. He took ore samples from each claim and sent them away to be assayed. Some of the reports he received back were encouraging and this heightened his enthusiasm. He appeared very informed and made a great study of geology. His was an obsession. He wanted to venture farther afield and spoke about this with Dad. They worked out a deal. In exchange for a quantity of staples, Dad was to build a large freight canoe and accompany Seeley on a major exploration trip into the northernmost reaches of the province.

Dad went to work on the canoe. It was 20 feet long and though shaped like a canoe on both ends, that is where the resemblance ended. The bottom was flat and five five across. It sat in the water like a big rowboat, almost impossible to tip over.

The skeleton of the canoe was steamed and pressured into shape in vice-like molds. A thin layer of birch bark was stretched over the skeleton while the bark was soaking wet and when this dried a second layer of much heavier birch bark was molded and glued into place. Coat after coat of shellac was applied. Even the Indians who made and used birch bark canoes all the time were impressed by the size and sturdiness of Dad's boat. A lattice floor of one-by-fours was laid.

Dad and I drove the wagon down to Seeley's store one evening to let him know the canoe was ready. Seeley spread a bunch of maps out on the counter and he and Dad poured over them for a couple of hours, laying out the route they would be travelling and preparing a list of items to take with them. Then Seeley and Dad went through the store and as they picked out the items, I ticked them off the list. There was a good-sized tent, two tarpaulins, a 100 pound bag of flour, a high-powered rifle with a dozen boxes of shells, a .22 repeater, salt, baking powder, matches, a few bottles of citronella oil to keep mosquitoes and black flies away, two coal-oil lanterns, two five-gallon cans of coal-oil and an assortment of axes and hatchets. Last came a large bundle of sharpened surveyor's stakes for Seeley to mark his claims.

We loaded all this gear into the wagon and went back in the store as Mrs. Seeley was serving tea.

"We pick up the Indian guide day after tomorrow. He'll meet us at Waterhen Lake," Seeley said.

"You sure he knows his way 'round up there?" Dad asked.

"Says he's made the trip many times in a small canoe but he's sure we won't have any trouble with a bigger boat as long as we don't go beyond Ile-a-la-Crosse."

"Charlie and Lloyd went to St. Walburg on today's mail run to pick up a shipment of plow-shares," Dad said, "so Bob'll have ta take us to the lake with all the gear, and the canoe. He can drop us off and come back 'n' pick us up. How long ya figure we'll be gone?"

"Ain't gonna work that way. If we don't have no trouble and we get through, we might be as long as three weeks but if we have trouble, we might havta come back in three or four days — maybe a week."

"So how do we handle it?"

"If Bob's gonna drive us up to the lake, he'll havta stay right there and wait for us."

Dad looked at me. "Ya think ya can handle that, Bob?"

"Why not," I replied, trying to sound confident and grown-up. Inside I had this feeling that being stuck on the shores of a remote northern lake for three weeks, alone, was going to be a little different from anything I'd undertaken before.

"You'll have nothin' to do but tend the horses," Seeley said reassuringly.

"No problem," I said, with a forced tone of bravado. "You go stake yer claims and don't worry 'bout me. I'll be waitin' soon's ya get back." I could see Dad eyeing me with some misgiving.

The next morning we reloaded all of Seeley's things, our own gear and the canoe on to a hayrack. Seeley arrived about 10 o'clock and we set out for Waterhen Lake, the launching point. We drove through Goodsoil, past the Mountie post and north to where Lloyd and I had gone fishing with Gus. From there we would skirt the Waterhen River along an old Indian trail for about 30 miles east to the lake.

We were well north of the end of the survey and except for the remains of some old Indian camps you'd never know that anyone had come this way before. Ambling along, I wondered what I would do if anything happened to me like stepping into a ground hog hole and spraining an ankle, or if a bear came rummaging around. I spent most of the day trying to convince myself that this was going to be an exciting adventure but, watching the terrain, I realized that I was also trying to bolster my courage. We didn't pass any signs of life all day long.

The mosquitoes and black flies were at their worst at that time of year. I'd heard stories about people, even animals, being driven mad by black flies. As we drove along, we had the exposed parts of our hands and faces covered with citronella oil. That helped to keep the pests off us but the horses kept flicking their tails and twitching their ears as they were attacked.

When we arrived at Waterhen Lake it was getting dark. Dad and I looked after the horses and unpacked the load. Seeley built a big smudge fire slightly upwind from the campsite. We tethered the horses in the lee of the smoke and for the first time all day, they were rid of the black flies which had been driving them crazy. The odd mosquito braved the smoke and sneaked into the tent but it was apparent that the smudge fire would be effective through the night.

The campsite was in a small indentation on the shoreline. Trees and underbrush grew almost to the water's edge. Looking it over, I'd have felt more secure if it was more like the one Gus had taken us to at Big Island Lake where the treeline stopped a few hundred feet from the Lake. Something, whatever what, could sneak up as close as 20 or 30 feet and I wouldn't even see it or know what it was. The lake, just a few feet away, offered little comfort as it lapped against a shaggy rocky wall and the water was very deep.

Before we went to bed, we sat around the fire talking.

"Ya sure you'll be okay, Bob?" Dad asked.

"Yeh, I'll be fine."

Seeley poured over his maps. "I figure, as the crow flies, it's about a hundred miles to Ile-a-la-Crosse. If we do ten miles a day, up and back, works out to just about three weeks."

"We'll be fightin' the current goin' up," Dad said.

"Makes it that much easier comin' home."

From Ile-a-la-Cross to Lake Athabasca was another 300 miles north through a system of waterways even more complicated than the one they were about to travel. To make this trip was Seeley's ultimate ambition but another plan would have to be devised. The Indians told of countless portages which had to be made to circumvent the rough water. The big freight canoe was too big and cumbersome for even the shortest portage.

Seeley was fascinated by stories the Indians told of rocks on the north shore of Lake Athabasca which glowed in the night. He wanted to investigate this phenomenon. Many years later, a major ore find was made there and a town called Uranium City sprung up. Seeley never got there, but obviously his hunch was right.

Dad gave me our .22, a hundred feet of fishing line with spoon hooks and some rabbit snares. I had a waterproof box of matches and a small bag of salt.

"Ya want us ta leave ya some flour and baking powder? You could make biscuits or flap-jacks."

"Naw," I answered. "Jus' stop worryin' 'bout me. Between the fishin', huntin' and wild berries, I'll prob'bly gain some weight while yer gone." I wasn't very big for my age and I'd been striving to reach 100 pounds.

"Ya jus' remember ta keep the fire goin' — day and night. With a good fire ain't nothin' gonna bother ya. Keep movin' the horses if the wind changes 'n' try'n keep the flies off 'em. I left ya an axe an' a small hatchet. Keep lotsa wood on hand and green willows fer the smudge."

That was all. No last-minute lecture. I would be alone and in all likelihood, scared. He knew that. I would be fending for myself in an environment which could turn hostile in minutes. He knew that too. I was being given more responsibility and freedom than I'd ever had before and he knew that too.

When we awoke next morning, the Indian guide was sitting beside the fire, waiting. We launched the big freight canoe and tied it securely to a tree.

"Me load," the Indian said, as he carried the 100 pound bag of flour effortlessly onto the boat and stowed it dead centre. He was dressed in deer skins from head to toe and his jacket and moccasins were elaborately beaded. He studied all the gear carefully as it was handed to him in the canoe but he never spoke, just nodded his head or used body language to convey what he wanted. He wasn't very tall but his body was lithe and lean and it soon became obvious that Seeley had made a good choice. When he had finished, the load not only looked balanced, it was. Just before they left, Dad, in a rare display of emotion, put his arm around me as we walked down to the water's edge. I was thirteen.

As the canoe disappeared around the first bend a gnawing, empty feeling came over me and I went to tend the horses, not because they needed it but because it would be only me and them for the next 21 days.

While they were gone I didn't see a living soul but I certainly wasn't alone. Through the day, I would do some fishing, more for the fun of it than the need. The waters teemed with jackfish and pickerel. I weighted one of the spoon hooks and reached a point where I could get a loop swinging and throw the hook until all of the line was spent, all 100 feet. Pulling the hook in, I could see the fish in the clear lake water before it took the bait. I would hook a fish almost every time I reeled in and some of these fish weighed 20 pounds. I threw them all back unless I wanted fish for supper that night.

I varied my diet. One day I'd have fish and the next day, rabbit. I tried partridge and prairie-chicken but they tasted a bit willowy at that time of year. Whatever I chose, all were easy to prepare. I'd scale the fish right at the water's edge and when it was cleaned, I'd pack it in mud. I'd get a good fire going, wait until it burned down to red-hot embers, then deposit the fish in the hot coals and, an hour later, crack it open, lift out all the bones and *voilà!* — a meal fit for a king.

Rabbits were easy to snare and easy to cook. Once skinned and cleaned, I would run a long green willow through the rabbit and arrange two "Y" shaped stakes in either side of the fire. I would turn it periodically just like any present-day barbecue spit.

I picked blueberries, which grew in abundance, and wild strawberries. Between deciding what I was going to eat, looking after the horses — which didn't require much attention as their tethers were long enough to allow them to drink from the lake or graze — and keeping a supply of wood on hand for the fire, my days were busy enough to keep me from getting bored.

I relished the smells of the baked fish, the roasted rabbit, the smoke from the fire, the pine trees, and the crisp, clean northern air. My senses came alive as never before. The beauty of this unspoiled Eden was breathtaking and I realized how fortunate I was to be a part of it. Everything around me was important. It smelled better, it tasted better and I have never been anywhere since that made a more lasting impression.

The north is immense. It is friendly yet frightening. It is magnificent yet intimidating. It can shower you with its abundance in the summer and make you feel like you belong. Or it can be cruel and harsh and impersonal. All it takes is one storm cloud and a driving northern gale to make you realize how insignificant and vulnerable you really are. It can be as cruel in winter as it is generous in summer. When you live in the north, you live cautiously, as there is little room for error. One quickly learned the difference between the gentle rain that flowed like happy tears down the smiling countenance of the north and the terrifying torrent it could spew across its frowning face.

Though my days were full, my nights were scary. Being only thirteen I was quite capable of being frightened. Through the day, I wasn't conscious of the noises around me but at night, when everything went to sleep, not *everything* went to sleep.

The loons were the worst. Like the train whistle on the prairies, their cry, wavering across the lake, sounded like some lost soul in the wilderness. Somewhere a timber wolf would wail a lonesome solo, more so when the moon was full. Its cry would be picked up by another wolf from a different direction. The conversation would gain momentum until it took on the proportions of a giant fugue and I was convinced I was surrounded. Suddenly, a wolf joined the chorus no more than a couple of hundred feet away and the hair on my neck crawled. I jumped up and threw more wood on the fire, stirring the embers until sparks flew in all directions. I dipped a cat-tail in coal-oil, lit it, and flung it in the direction of the sound. I banked the fire and pulled my ground sheet as close to it as I dared.

I could hear all sorts of things moving around during the night but whatever they were I knew they wouldn't venture too close to the fire. You develop a kind automatic time-clock when you have to keep a fire going. No matter how carefully I banked it, it still had to be replenished every couple of hours. When I got up to put more wood on the fire, I could hear whatever it was go scurrying through the underbrush. The next morning, I'd check for tracks and they were there. They weren't very big but it was frightening not knowing what made them. It couldn't have been a skunk or a ground hog, as they are slow and lumbering. What I had heard ran much faster. A few nights of this and my imagination began to magnify. I lit the coal-oil lantern and kept it burning beside me until I ran out of coal-oil. The .22 rifle was always within easy reach. There were bear and timber wolves all over the north but at that time of year they had plenty to eat so there was little need for them to raid a campsite. Besides, the tracks I saw each morning were not those of bear or timber wolves.

One thing I did discover, the wilderness is not silent and lonely, it is alive, fearsome, awesome and frightening. The unexpected snap of a twig in the middle of the night is as loud as a gunshot.

As the days went by, time lost its meaning. It wasn't necessary to get up in the morning and go to bed at night. There was just me and the horses and they lived their instinctive schedules, needing little help from me. Some mornings I would be awake to watch the sunrise. The world was at its quietest then. There was an acute sense of isolation and loneliness but it was not scary. The dawn crept in slowly and the darkness turned to soft shades of grey. The mist over the lake began to burn off and the water was a giant mirror as the reflections of the trees and shoreline began to take shape. The sounds too took their time building from a first lonely chirp of a bird, followed by another until their chorus filled the air with music. As the sun made its appearance, the colors turned to pink and gold and where the trees held its rays in check a mix of purple and lavender painted a tapestry of wonder. I still remember these mornings and the awe I felt as the stars went out and the northern sun began another day.

There is something special about the northern sun. It is bigger and redder and takes much longer to disappear in the evening as though it is reluctant to leave the glorious, burnished landscape it looks down on. As slowly as the sounds begin when the sun comes up, so do they diminish as it goes down and the world around prepares itself for sleep — except, that is, for the loons and other nocturnal things.

Those moments became a time of reflection for me, a time to ponder what my life was all about. I was still only a young boy but I wondered if this was all there was. Surely, out there, beyond the sunrise, beyond the sunset, was a bigger world, and I contemplated what my role in it would be.

I remembered Eatonia; the church and the lessons learned; the moral standards instilled in those oh-so-important, formative years. It was different now. Profanity had become part of everyday language. "Thou shalt not take the name of the Lord, thy God in vain" I said to myself and vowed not to ape the people around me anymore. I would stop using profane words. I remembered the Parables and they had never had more meaning as I gazed at the magnitude and serenity around me. This astonishing setting was not an accident of nature. God was here and with me.

I kept the fire going for 26 days and nights before the expedition returned. They had run into rougher water than anticipated but they had made it to Ile-a-la-Crosse. Seeley was elated with the trip and had staked dozens of claims.

Whether it was by design on Dad's part or through circumstances doesn't matter now. Being left alone on the shores of a remote northern lake for 26 days and nights was part of Dad's legacy for which I remember him fondly and for which I have always been grateful.

It was this experience, more than any other, that awakened the first stirrings of manhood in me. I had coped with it like a grownup. With this realization came a no-longer childlike perception of the world around me, but one of budding maturity.

On our way home, Dad said, "You did well, son."

Chapter 12

Overall, our family was not very good at homesteading. Dad was not a farmer at heart. He was happier making things, building things or fixing things. He was an organizer, a super-salesman, an entrepreneur, and very creative. The physical labour needed to acquire clear title to our land was not high on his list of priorities.

We had built the buildings, we had dug the well and done most of the fencing, but clearing the required minimum acreage of trees and stumps and bringing the land under cultivation was a slow and back-breaking job. After the forest fire — *my* forest fire — the heavy timber stand would turn into deadfall the following year. This would make the task of clearing more land easier but the big problem was removing the stumps. Dad realized there were limits to what Lloyd and I could accomplish and Charlie made no secret about hating to clear land.

Charlie was some kind of guy, and because we learned so much from him during the almost three years he was with us, I want to describe him in more detail. Behind all his loud bravado, he was warm and very kind. He quickly became part of our family and was treated with great respect by Mom and Dad.

He had spent most of his life in the north and knew all about animals; he could even deliver a calf or help a sow when she was having babies. He insisted on the barn being cleaned every morning, and was always kind and considerate with the animals.

He treated Lloyd and me like younger brothers but he was never condescending. We could communicate our problems to him easier than to Dad and we spent a great deal of time listening to his earthy wisdom.

Charlie smoked "roll-your-own" cigarettes. He always had a can of fine-cut tobacco and packs of cigarette papers lying around. I guess most kids start smoking because they know they're not supposed to and because they see grownups doing it. I had been eyeing Charlie's tobacco for a long time and there was this day when nobody was around and Charlie's 'makings' were sitting there so I rolled a cigarette. It was pretty scruffy, too fat in the middle and not enough tobacco in the ends. Just when I was going to stick it in my pocket, I looked up and who's standing there — Charlie!

"Don't scratch like a dog — ask like a man," he said. "Ya wanna smoke, ya ask me. If I got it ya can have it. Same thin' with anythin' else I got, but ya don't take nothin' from nobody, even if they ain't home. Up here, nobody locks their door, if'n know what I mean."

Dad used the odd swear word, especially when he got mad, but Lloyd and I rarely used any bad words. This changed when Charlie came to live with us. His language was not only colourful, but he couldn't express himself without using certain words. When Dad wasn't around, Lloyd and I quickly fell into Charlie's patterns of expression. He had three favourite terms and depending on which one he used would determine just how serious he was: "Screw off" — "piss off" — and "fuck off." He had variations on these three themes like: "Screw 'em" — "piss on 'em" or "fuck 'em." Whatever the subject of any conversation, Charlie found some variation that worked.

Charlie's earthy knowledge had been learned by 'being there' or 'doing it.' If he had ever gone to school there was no evidence of it as I never saw him read anything or write to anybody. He had an uncanny ability to express himself so you knew precisely what he meant. If we were hot on some tracks when we were hunting, he'd say. "We gotta hurry — slowly!" Or once, when we were talking about his Dad, he said, "You'll get old too if ya live long 'nough!"

Charlie was an important part of my youth and I remember him with kindness and gratitude for the many things he taught me, and, with all his colourful crudeness, a degree of moral standards you seldom learn in church and which had a profound effect on my life.

Charlie had been with us for well over two years and was part of the family. He began acting strangely and was quiet and withdrawn. This was unusual as he had never been moody. We all left him alone, figuring that whatever was on his mind would go away. It didn't.

One evening, after we'd eaten, he dropped a bombshell.

"Bin doin' a lotta thinkin' lately," he began, and we could tell that something serious was coming. "You folks has bin fam'ly ta me fer a coupla years now. One time I figured ta jus' stay here, maybe fin' me a girl and settle down. Well, I bin lookin' the girls over an' I guess maybe they bin lookin' at me an' I don' see much happenin' with the current crop o' heifers, if'n know what I mean."

We all laughed nervously, waiting, because you could tell he wasn't finished.

"Comes a time a man gotta as' hisself some questions and I bin doin' that an' I can't find any answers ta please me, 'cept fer you folks. I gotta fin' me a good woman an' I gotta fin' me some work so when I get ol' I have somethin' and won't be beholdin' ta nobody. Gonna get ol' like yer s'pposed ta with a lil' house an' garden ta putter 'round in."

"Whadda ya sayin', Charlie, ya tellin' us yer leavin'?" Dad demanded. "Ya wanna house, we'll build ya one — ya wanna garden, ya can take yer pick o' the land, but ya can't leave us now. We jus' got it goin' right an' things is gonna be good fer all of us."

Charlie was deep in thought and I don't think he even heard Dad. "Heard up at the store, they's foun' oil down south — lil' town called Cabri in Alberta. S'pose ta be jobs aroun' an' it'd be kinda nice ta getta good payin' job and putta lil' money away. An' who knows, could be the gals in Alberta is diff'rent — maybe even fin' me a lady, if'n know what I mean."

This was undoubtedly the longest speech any of us had ever heard Charlie make. He rarely exceeded one short sentence. We could tell he had given the matter a lot of thought and that his mind was set.

"How soon?" Dad asked.

"Gonna catch me the mail run ta St. Walburg in a coupla days an' hop a freight from there."

"We're gonna miss ya, Charlie," Mom said. Kay and Joyce went over and sat, one on each of his knees.

Before we went to sleep that night, Charlie had more to say to Lloyd and me in our own little corner of the cabin.

"You guys ain't kids anymore. I showed ya all I know 'bout gettin' by up here an' jus' lookin' at ya doin' things, yer gonna do jus' fine."

There was a long pause.

"They's bin a lotta good feelins livin' with you folks. I havta tell ya I don' feel good 'bout leavin' but inside I jus' know I gotta go. If things don't work fer me like I 'spect, I could live a whole month on nothin' else 'cept rememb'rin' ya all."

He stopped again, searching for words.

"After I go, you fellas think a lil' 'bout what I'm gonna tell ya now 'cause it happened ta me with my folks and I think 'bout it now a lot. They's a lotta love here. I see it and I feel it but nobody tells it. Ya all run 'round hidin' how ya feel. Yer like them big birds stickin' yer head on a hole thinkin' cause he can't see nothin' nobody can see him. Meantime, he's got his ass up in the breeze an' the whole worl' can see it, 'cept he don' know an' he ain't foolin' nobody.

"What ya gotta do if'n ya feel good 'bout folks is tell 'em. Won' be easy 'cause that ain't how ya learned it but ya give 'er a start an' yer gonna fin' ev'rybody gonna start doin' it an' ya all gonna feel good 'bout it. I never figured that out with my own folks but I seen it here. You work a lil' at it an' it's gonna be like the measles — ev'rybody gonna catch it."

I lay in the darkness with tears in my eyes, holding back the sobs.

"Maybe it'll get ya started if'n I tell ya I ain't never lived with folks like you. I bin treated good an' yer Dad's always bin fair — I even learned yer grace. Here, I'll show ya. 'Our Heavenly Father, we thank ya fer this happy fam'ly and fer this food we're 'bout ta receive'."

We always said grace before our evening meal and we all took turns saying it. Mom would say whose turn it was. She never asked Charlie, mostly, I guess, because she assumed he didn't know the words, and she wouldn't think of embarrassing him.

"These is the things," Charlie continued, "that makes yer fam'ly come together an' ya gotta let it out 'cause they's a lotta love here but ya gotta quit hidin' it."

It was daylight before I went to sleep and I woke with Charlie shaking me "Come on, get yer ass in gear; we's goin' down ta the river an' get us a duck."

We spent the day down at the duck blind and there was no conversation at all. The sun was going down when we got home and as we were unharnessing the horses, Charlie said: "When I get back down south, I'll get some'un ta gimme a han' an' I'll write ya a letter fer Christmas."

Charlie left the next morning and I got up extra early and crossed over to the far side of the creek to watch him board the mail wagon. He stood up, looking around, and I knew he was looking for me but I couldn't face saying goodbye in front of everyone. Where I was hiding, nobody could see my tears or hear my sobbing as the wagon turned in the driveway and disappeared. When Charlie left a vacuum was created which was never filled. We never did hear from him again.

After Charlie, there was only Lloyd and me to continue with the clearing of land. Dad wasn't interested, but he insisted that we go out, day after day. We had little supervision and some days we accomplished very little. I spent more time daydreaming than working. I guess we were as comfortable as could be expected under less than ideal circumstances. As children and young teenagers, we were happy with our lives. The small things I remember make the time on the homestead an important part of my life. The hunting, the fishing, the friendly people, riding horseback, the music, Spot, the Indians, the grandeur of the north, the lakes, the rivers, Gus, our log cabin, and Charlie.

We had become resigned to our lot, but not Dad. He grew more and more restless and we often heard him talking with Mom. He was concerned about our schooling, the lack of communication with the outside world, the fact that the nearest doctor was 40 miles away and it was 80 miles to the nearest railway. He knew that none of these problems would be solved in the immediate future. Where we lived was not important politically or economically. There was no indication that the railway would be extended north. Dad's concerns grew. He went on long walks, alone, and when he returned he would be pensive and withdrawn, preoccupied with his thoughts.

My parents, not good communicators at the best of times, never discussed the birds and the bees with us. We grew up with a warped perception of sex — something nice people never talked about.

I don't remember Dad ever being sick and except for having babies, at which time we were always shipped off somewhere, Mom was never sick either. This was the background for one of the most traumatic experiences on my youth.

Our log cabin was huge. It had started as one room but as time went on, another room was added. The added space was not a separate room but rather an extension of the first. The end result was a long, but still, basically one-room cabin. Curtains were strung at various points to separate the different living areas. We all had some sort of privacy when we dressed or undressed. With my prior immersion in bible teachings, even to catch a glimpse of one of my sisters in her underwear meant a few added begs for forgiveness when I said my prayers that night.

So it was frightening when we were all awakened in the wee hours of the morning by Dad shaking Lloyd:- "Get up — quick! Ya gotta ride to Loon Lake and fetch the doctor. Take Tony and ride as fast as possible. Yer Ma's very sick."

The curtains had been pulled back and Mom lay on the bed, pale and quiet, her eyes closed. By this time, we were all in our clothes, tiptoeing quietly around the room. Dad tried to explain.

"Yer mother is hemorrhaging — bleeding, and it won't stop!"

He changed the sheets and we could see the blood on them.

"The doctor's got fast horses. Tell him he's gotta come right away or your Ma is gonna bleed ta death."

Lloyd ran out the door and we heard him galloping off on Tony with 37 miles to go.

Mothers are not supposed to get sick. This time, Mom was *very* sick. As we traipsed to her bedside to ask how she was feeling we realized she didn't know us.

All that day Dad kept changing the sheets and mumbling. "If we only had some ice, maybe that would help." Or, "maybe we should try a hot compress."

Mom kept getting weaker and weaker. None of us knew what to do to help. She didn't even open her eyes. We waited for some word of encouragement from Dad, which never came. Kay was crying softly and holding Joyce.

Dad asked me to build a good fire in the kitchen stove and be sure there was lots of wood stacked inside the house. When this was done, I had to fill the biggest pots with water and put them on the stove. In between, I had to take the stained sheets down to the creek and wash them out. The blood was scary, especially knowing it was Mom's.

The day passed and so did our normal bed time. Dad kept checking on Mom who hadn't moved for a long time. He paced back and forth, mumbling, "What'n hell could be keepin' him?"

The tension was terrible. Mom was breathing; we could see her chest moving slightly. Her face was pasty white. What scared me most was that I didn't know where the blood was coming from and I was afraid to ask. Maybe she cut herself, I thought, knowing it wasn't that.

It was almost midnight when we heard the doctor's buggy drive up. I ran to look after his horses. He grabbed his bag and went into the cabin. When I got back inside, the curtain had been drawn and we could hear him talking softly to Dad. Finally, the doctor came through the curtains. His coat was off and his shirt sleeves rolled up. He asked Lloyd and me to fetch a bigger box which, he explained, was under his buggy seat. Then he went over to the stove to check on the pots of boiling water.

We had no electricity. We used coal-oil lamps to light the cabin unless we had company, then we might light the gas lamp. The gas lamp had a flimsy mantle and an element which had to be preheated before the lamp would light. It also had to be pumped up periodically. For our chores at night, we used coal-oil lanterns.

The doctor spoke quietly. "I want you young people to extinguish the coal-oil lamps and if your gas lamp is working, light it and put it at the far end of the cabin." He fished around in the big box we had brought in from his buggy, and took out a flashlight which must have been three feet long and threw a powerful beam of light.

"You children stay on the far end of the cabin. We can't have any fumes from the coal-oil lamps as I will be using chloroform while I perform a small operation on your mother. Your Dad will hold the flashlight for me and I don't want any of you to worry. I'm sure your mother is going to be just fine."

He kept coming out for fresh pots of water and we kept filling them. Chloroform fumes filled every corner of the cabin.

The curtains were drawn back and the doctor emerged, rolling down his sleeves. He was smiling. "Your mother is just fine. I'll stop in again in a couple of days to change the packing, but in the meantime, there is nothing to worry about. She's a strong and healthy lady and you're lucky to have her."

Before he left, we looked over at Dad, who was still sitting at the side of the bed, holding Mom's hand. We had never seen Dad cry before. We had never seen him hold Mom's hand before. Our prayers were a little longer that night.

Dad changed. He looked about ten years older and his whole manner had turned firm and resolute. Mom got better but things would never be the same in our house again.

We had received a number of packages from Dad's folks back east. There was a barrel of dried apples from grandma, and another barrel from his brother, Clarence, full of burley leaf tobacco. Dad had a recipe, and from this leaf tobacco, he would make his own snuff. There was another wooden box full of secondhand clothes and storebought shoes. There were even pairs of silk socks. Not very practical in the north, but I never felt anything so soft on my feet before. The box of clothes had been packed with newspapers. Although weeks old, these were smoothed out and read carefully by all of us.

There was a double-page spread from the *Chicago Herald & Examiner*, headed Tin-Can Tourists. After Mom was better, Dad brought out the article and read it over and over. There were pictures of a homemade house trailer some man had built and the article went on to explain how he and his family used it to travel all over the country, completely self-contained. Wherever they stopped, they were home. We heard Dad talking with Mom and showing her the newspaper article and the pictures of the house trailer.

"I'm gonna build a trailer, bigger'n this one, big enough for all of us ta live in! And somehow, we're gonna get outta this goddamn country and back east. I've had enough of 'no doctors', 'no telephones', 'no railway', 'no money', 'no schools', 'no nothin'.''

He built a lean-to next to the barn and moved all his tools and machines into it. He was like a man possessed. I did not know it at the time, but we were on our way out of the north and on to Broadway.

Before Dad could begin building the trailer, he needed to build a sawmill to make the lumber. The mill required a solid foundation and Dad went through the bigger trees around our buildings looking for four which would form a base. He found three, and these were sawed down leaving the stumps about two-and-a-half feet high. Dad sawed down one more tree which didn't exactly form the fourth leg of a perfect rectangle but he was able to attach heavy timbers to it with strap-iron to position it properly. The rectangle was six feet by twenty.

We drove down to the Big Muskeg and scrounged some of the twelve x twelve cedar timbers, which we used to form the basic frame of the mill. Dad countersunk angle-iron strips into the cedar timbers to form tracks for the long carriage to run on, and then he went looking for six flywheels from Model T Fords. These were used on the log carriage which would carry and feed the logs into the saw. Parts were milled on his lathe and when he was finished, with the exception of the axles he would need for the flywheels, and a circular saw, he had gone about as far as he could.

Lloyd and I were given the job of hand picking the best looking trees to saw down and bring in. We took birch, poplar and spruce, which were stacked in neat piles to cure.

Dad still needed three axles for the log carriage to which the flywheels would be welded and a circular saw with an axle and drive pulley. Everything we had brought north with us was now superfluous. Dad had made up his mind that we were going to leave the north and nothing was going to deter him.

Everything we owned became trading bait for the things he needed to complete the saw mill and the trailer. We had a lot of things people needed. We had a practically new Hart Parr tractor. We had sets of harrows and plows, a seed drill, a stationary engine, even a brand-new binder made by Massey-Harris, still in its original packing crates.

Dad found most of the things he needed at a saw mill. The man had the axles and an old circular saw. Dad had all the tools to sharpen and reset the teeth. The saw had an axle with a good set of bearings and a pulley. The man struck a hard bargain: everything Dad needed in exchange for the new binder.

The flywheels were welded to the axles and installed on the carriage. The circular saw was sharpened and all the bearings greased.

We put a birch log into the carriage, locked it down, and while Dad controlled the speed of the fly wheel on the tractor, Lloyd and I pulled the first log through with a winch. When the first slab was cut, we moved the log over one inch and sawed our first board. It worked.

There are no hardwood trees in Saskatchewan. Dad had to work with what he had. Properly seasoned, birch, poplar and spruce are easy to work with and Dad knew his craft. When the first eight x eight was laid, Dad made every allowance for the stresses it would be subjected to. Around this main structural element, the trailer began to take shape.

Nothing, it seemed, was ever square. Everything was molded into an aerodynamic configuration. While not as streamlined as today's, our trailer was certainly ahead of its time. Dad used everything he had ever learned as a cabinetmaker. There wasn't an inch of wasted space. There were lockers with both inside and outside access, and plenty of overhead racks. The table, which seated six people, folded into two sections and disappeared up against a wall. The seats then became two single beds for the girls. It had a built-in toilet with an outside locker to empty the five gallon can which collected the refuse. A Coleman gas stove was built in, as was Mom's sewing machine.

Neighbours would drop in to watch its progress.

"Hey, Hahn, whadda ya gonna do fer wheels?"

"If ya did have wheels on the goddamn thing, how ya gonna get it through the Big Musket?"

"If ya do get it outta here, what's gonna pull it back east, horses?"

Dad just kept on working. The questions were troubling him too.

Christmas, 1935, and the trailer was finished. Ted and Lizzie Boening and our old friend Gus had been invited for Christmas dinner and Mom had prepared a feast.

We took the musical instruments out and played some Christmas carols and everybody joined in the singing. Dad served his best elixir and there was an exchange of gifts among the family.

Gus apologized for not having brought any. " 'Cept," he said, "I got one fer Bob." He handed me a box about the size of a shoe box, wrapped in brown paper. "Ya watch now when ya open 'er, it doesn't bust."

I pulled out a brown bottle and set it carefully on the table.

"Never could pronounce it," Gus said, "but if'n this magic stuff doesn't stop yer bed wettin', then ya jus' gonna havta wait 'til ya grow outta it."

The label read, MEDICAMENTUM - Harlem Oil. I screwed off the top. It had to be the worst, the most putrid-smelling liquid I had ever smelled.

"Whadda ya do, Gus, rub it on?" I asked.

"No sir, ya gotta drink it."

I tasted it, and as bad as it smelled, it tasted even worse. And that's how I finally stopped wetting the bed. I still don't know whether it was because the Harlem Oil worked or the sheer fear that if I had an accident, I'd have to take another tablespoon of the stuff, but within the next two weeks my problem went away forever.

We finished the Christmas carols around ten o'clock when the Boenings and Gus said good-night. After they'd gone, Dad wanted to play more.

Joyce would be six years old in a matter of weeks. Kay was ten, I was fifteen and Lloyd was sixteen.

Lloyd played guitar and banjo. Kay played a small tenor guitar and sang. I played piano, guitar, fiddle and sang. I was left-handed but I used to play the different stringed instruments without changing the strings around. Dad played drums and also guitar with a mouth-organ attachment. Joyce just sang.

Kay usually sang the melody to the songs because Joyce always knew where the harmony was. When the songs weren't too complicated I could generally find the third harmony and sing along. Dad knew a bunch of German folk songs and a few funny songs. He also did some narrative selections, some funny, some nostalgic and others quite emotional. Most were in some sort of poetic form. He wrote some poems about the north and even a couple of songs. Kay was best at pretty songs like *Danny Boy* or *I'll Take You Home Again, Kathleen.* Joyce sang anything and everything. She was by far the most talented.

After a few songs Dad put down his guitar and started listening to the four of us. It was as though he was hearing us for the first time. He asked for different songs and then suggested we change the voices around. He wanted some selections where I played piano and others where I played guitar. He moved the instruments about for a couple of hours, trying all the different combinations. We didn't know it then but what was running through Dad's mind as he listened quietly that Christmas Eve, was to shape the rest of our lives.

Chapter 13

NEXT DAY DAD CAME HOME with an old Hohner button accordion he had borrowed from one of the German homesteaders and asked me to try it. It felt very awkward. I not only had to push and pull on the bellows but try and find the right buttons with my right hand to play the melody. On an accordion you can't even see the buttons you play with your left hand. On top of all this, when you pressed a button with your right hand, it played one note when you pushed the bellows and a different note when you pulled. Meanwhile, the left hand button played the same note whether you pushed or pulled. It was all very confusing. Dad kept me at it for a week, after which the whole thing started to make a little sense. Just as I was getting the hang of it, the man wanted his accordion back. But Dad had heard enough. He showed me a picture of a *piano* accordion in the mail order catalogue. It was made in Italy and cost well over a hundred dollars. In the description, it was explained that when the bellows were pushed or pulled, the same note sounded, whether on the right or left hand. I told Dad that certainly would make it easier, and I was already familiar with a piano keyboard.

In February Dad jacked up the trailer and put two sets of sleighs under it, secured with bolts. He borrowed an extra team of horses from Boening and with a four-horse team we headed for St. Walburg, towing the trailer. Three days later we were there. Dad sent Lloyd and me home with the horses while he stayed and looked around. A week later he hitched a ride on the mail wagon and came back. He had found a chassis for the trailer — an axle and two wheels with hard-rubber tires.

We made up signs announcing an auction sale and nailed them on trees and fence posts for miles around. The problem was to find buyers who had cash. Everything was to go. We would take nothing with us except the clothes on our backs and the musical instruments. When the sale was over, we had just over $900. We left a maple chest behind containing Mom's wedding pictures, a big framed picture of my sister, Marie, and a gilded family Bible. The Boenings agreed to look after it until we were settled somewhere. We hitched a ride on the mail wagon to St. Walburg where Mom and Dad moved into the trailer with the girls. Lloyd and I pitched a tent which had been stored in one of the trailer's lockers.

Dad went to the post office, bought a money order and sent away to Winnipeg for my accordion. He purchased an old Reo Speed Wagon truck and began overhauling it completely. He built a new body and covered it with the same canvas material he had used on the trailer. Lloyd and I moved into the truck, which now had bunk beds.

Building the body was the easy part. It took most of the summer to rebuild the rest of the truck. By the time the chassis had been installed on the trailer and the outfit hitched up, it was August and you could feel autumn in the air.

In the meantime, my new accordion arrived. I had never seen anything quite so new in my life. It smelled of leather and ivory and came in a case covered inside with red velour. It had an instruction manual and it was much easier to play than the old button accordion. Dad was a hard taskmaster. He set aside two hours each morning and afternoon for me to practice, and no one was allowed to bother me during practice periods. He went through the instruction manual with me and day by day, I worked my way through it. The last selection in the manual was the most difficult — a rousing march called *Under the Double Eagle,* which was mostly a bass solo played with the left hand. By the middle of September, I could play all the solos in the book, and along with Lloyd on guitar, and the girls, we would play and sing maybe 50 songs.

Before we left St. Walburg, we played our first professional engagement, a dance. We didn't charge admission — we passed the hat and counting the take on the trailer table, we had earned six dollars and fifteen cents. Not a bad beginning.

In the third week of September we headed for North Battleford. The weather was perfect and the roads, which had just been graded, were smooth. When we went through small hamlets Dad would toot the horn to attract attention and people would come running. No one had seen anything like the trailer outfit before. From stem to stern it was well over 50 feet long and painted a bright green.

Our first stop was a town called Maidstone. The townsfolk flocked around, gawking at the outfit and the people who came with it. Dad checked the restaurant: nobody there. He tried the poolroom and found people playing at two tables with another six or seven sitting around watching. He spoke with the owner then came back and parked the outfit in front of the poolroom.

"Okay," he said, "get your instruments out. We're gonna play a few numbers in there and when we're finished, the girls gonna pass the hat."

This was going to be different from the show we had put on in St. Walburg, where everybody knew us. Here we didn't know anybody, and they were all staring at us as if we were a bunch of freaks. We went inside and nervously took our instruments out of their cases. By that time, there must have been 50 people crammed into the poolroom.

"I'd like you to meet four of the most talented kids a father ever had," Dad announced proudly, "an' yer gonna know exac'ly what I mean jus' as soon as they get started."

We did five songs in a row. Dad announced each one and he picked the best ones. I didn't look up. I kept staring down at my right hand on the piano keyboard as though I had to see the keys I played, which wasn't the case. I was very nervous and so was Lloyd. He kept staring at the neck of his guitar as though he, too, had to see what he was doing. The girls, however, were great. They looked right out at the people and after each song, the group applauded. When we had finished, and as the girls were passing the hat around, the crowd quickly dispersed. When we counted the money we had a dollar and 40 cents.

We didn't stop again until we got to North Battleford. Dad pulled up right beside the City Hall with the bravado of someone on an important mission and went inside to check if it would be all right for us to park there for a couple days. A man came out, looked us over and said it would be okay.

When we lived on the prairies, Dad had been an active member of the Benevolent Protective Order of Elks so he went looking for the Elks Club. He got sidetracked by the convenor of the Rotary Club and made arrangements for us to perform at their luncheon the following day.

We wore our best deerskin outfits, which were elaborately beaded and looked very presentable. There were only about 25 people in the audience but it all looked quite formal compared to playing for a dance or in a restaurant or poolroom. We were all pretty nervous as we waited.

Finally the time came during coffee and dessert and Dad was introduced. He walked out on to the stage with the confidence of a great impresario. "Gentlemen," he said, "I wanna thank ya for allowin' me the honour to present my fam'ly. We jus' came outta the north an' we're usin' our music to get us back east. This is gonna be our first important show and nat'rally, the kids are all a little nervous." He paused and looked over at us in the wings. We *were* nervous. "There's Lloyd and Bob an' Kay an' Joyce and I think you'll fin' they're a talented bunch o' kids. So please, make them feel welcome."

Dad led the applause and the four of us ran on stage and went into the first song. We knew nothing about timing when it came to waiting for applause after each number and we rushed into the next song too quickly. But we could feel something happening which none of us had experienced before. We were giving everything we had and could feel something coming back. When we finished our last song the applause was deafening. The girls didn't have to pass the hat, the Rotarians did it for us, and when the money was counted there was over $20. Whether these men felt compassion for us, because we must have been a pitiful looking bunch, or whether they were genuinely entertained, was not important. We had been made to feel wanted when we could have been destroyed. I have always remembered this experience and been grateful to this small group of men.

Dad lingered, talking with the Rotarians and we were back at the trailer, putting our instruments away when he came in.

"See, I tol' ya, didn' I? Those fellas thought you was great! It's okay ya get nervous, but it ain't okay ya don' know what'cha do up there is make people feel good! Bein' scared is part of it. I betcha there ain' nobody in show business that ain' scared or nervous. All ya gotta do is play and sing and the people gonna like it. You kids is gonna be important in show business and I wan'cha ta remember that."

That afternoon Dad went shopping and came home with all sorts of electrical wiring, wall plugs, light fixtures, even a fuse box. In a few days, he had the trailer wired. He installed an outside terminal with a weather-proof cover and a 50-foot plug-in cord.

Dad got permission to plug into the City Hall's power supply and I was told to go into the building, find a particular window and catch the cord when Dad threw it up. I went down a hallway to a door with a sign "MEN". I opened the window and Dad threw the cord up and I plugged it into a wall socket.

The job finished, I looked around. There was this big enamel thing up against one wall and beside it, a couple of wash basins with taps marked hot and cold. I turned one of them on and water came rushing out. I quickly turned it off and watched the water disappear through a small hole at the bottom. Across the room were two cubicles with doors on them. I pushed one of the doors open and there was this thing. The lid looked not unlike the shape of our three-holer but you surely couldn't do your business in anything so gleaming white and clean. Besides, there already was water in it so there couldn't have been any way for it to work. I didn't have to go but I did sit down to see how it felt and try and figure out how it worked. There was this chain with a wooden knob on the end with the word *Pull* — so I pulled. I knew immediately that I'd done something wrong because water came gushing into the bowl. It made a hell of a noise, and you could tell there was far more water flooding into the bowl than there was room for. I wasn't going to wait around until they discovered who had flooded the City Hall, so I ran. It was my first experience with modern plumbing.

When we left North Battleford after paying for all the electrical gear, we were broke again. The next major stop would be Saskatoon, but going through the village of Radisson Dad decided to stop. He parked in front of the Chinese restaurant and got permission from the owner to play. We took in almost four dollars — enough to keep us going.

Travelling was slow, as we were back on gravel roads and the washboard was playing hell with the hard rubber tires on the trailer. We'd stop every few miles while Dad checked the chassis.

About ten miles out of Radisson the trailer started towing to one side. The rubber had torn loose on the right wheel, so Dad took a hammer and chisel and removed it. We would now have to run on the bare metal rim. The other wheel was still okay but the trailer kept pulling to one side as the two wheels were now different sizes. We moved along slowly with the washboard playing havoc as we rattled along. We were still a good ten miles from Saskatoon when the sun went down.

Saskatoon was really a big city. Some of the buildings were five or six storeys tall and the Bessborough Hotel, which was built right beside the North Saskatchewan River, was supposed to have been built to look like a castle. In the distance as the sun went down, we were sure we could see the glow from the city lights on the horizon.

Again the trailer started veering off to one side and Dad had to pull over and stop. The rubber had now come off the second wheel and again we had to jack up the trailer while Dad chiseled the rubber off. Now we were running on bare steel rims on both sides and in checking further Dad found that some of the wooden spokes supporting the rims had come loose. We plodded on.

We were only about four miles short of Saskatoon, looking forward to our first big city, when the entire undercarriage of the trailer collapsed. Dad dragged it over to the side of the road and unhooked the truck.

"Ya might as well go to bed," he said. " I'll go into Saskatoon and see if I can find another set of wheels. Don' worry if I'm gone for a few days."

Dad had $14 on him. I gazed at the lights glowing in what must have been one of the biggest cities in the world. Between the excitement of being so close and the noise of the gravel thrown up against the trailer by passing cars, we hardly slept that night.

Dad returned in two days towing a beautiful new chassis all ready for installation. The wheels had balloon tires and in the back of the truck were five more tires, unopened boxes of new tubes, even a tire pump. When we asked him how he could possibly have made such a great deal, he grinned like a Cheshire cat.

"Never ya mind — I'll show ya, soon as we get into town."

We all went to work, jacking up the trailer and bolting the new chassis into place. All the tires were changed on the truck. By the time we had finished it was dark. We had to suppress our excitement for one more night as Dad told us to go to bed. Tomorrow would be our big day.

When we pulled into Saskatoon the next morning it was everything we had expected and more. There seemed to be hundreds of cars coming from all sides. Coloured traffic lights winked at us from main intersections and all the cars would stop and line up when they changed colours. We were proud of Dad as he threaded his way through the busy streets. He knew exactly where he was going and when to stop and go again just by watching the coloured lights. There were people everywhere and, just like the people in the small towns, they all stopped to watch us go by.

Dad pulled up beside a service station and told us to get our instruments. He pointed to a small building in the rear with the sign "CFQC."

"You all go in there and wait for me. I gotta short errand and when I get back we're gonna go on the radio."

We went into the building and stood around waiting for Dad who was back in fifteen minutes without the truck and trailer. He went into one of the offices and came back shortly with a man who smiled at us.

"If you'd follow me, please."

Broadcasting in 1936 predated the rigid requirements of today's formats. Now we have station-breaks, generally every fifteen minutes. Everything is timed to the second. In 1936, few of these requirements were observed and broadcasting was fairly casual. When you were ready, you went on the air and when you were finished, you went off. Newcasts were roughly timed for the breakfast and supper periods, give or take a few minutes either way. Dad went over the background of the family with the man who would be our announcer. A sheet of paper was tacked on one of the walls, giving the names of eight songs and a notation beside each title showing who would be singing or playing it. We were told to make sure our instruments were all in tune before we went on the air. Whatever happened, even if an instrument went out of tune during the broadcast or a string broke, we were not to stop — just keep playing. There was one microphone for all of us and we were shown how to stand around it, who was to be in closest and when to back off or move in.

The time came; some man behind a glass partition waved at the announcer and a red light went on. The announcer introduced us as "Hahn And His Kids" and we went into the first number. I thought we did really well. We opened with a duet with Joyce and Kay, *Button Up Your Overcoat.* Then I played *Under The Double Eagle.* Kay sang *I'll Take You Home Again Kathleen* and Dad sang a German folk song. Joyce sang *Pennies From Heaven* and we did a hoedown medley with the melody going back and forth between my accordion and Dad's mouth organ.

Joyce then sang, *The Best Things In Life Are Free* and we closed with all of us singing *Oh, Dem Golden Slippers.*

The station manager, Mr. Vern Dallin, came in when the red light went off, told us we were great and we were welcome to do another broadcast the next day. We agreed and left our instruments in the studio.

Our trailer was parked at a big tire and auto store. Two workmen with spray cans of paint were buzzing around it. On the back we read, "This Outfit Runs On Firestone Tires."

"That's the deal I made fer the new wheels an' tires," Dad explained. "Now wherever we go, people'll know we only use Firestone Tires. A good deal fer them and sure as hell, a good deal fer us, wouldn't ya say?"

He sure seemed to have a solution for everything, no matter how bad things were. This had to be one of the best deals yet.

Next day we played at the Rotary Club luncheon in the Bessborough Hotel. When we had finished, there was over $40 in the hat. We began to feel that this whole music thing was going to work.

"These kids bin workin' eight, nine hours a day fer the past three years gettin' ready fer this," Dad told the Rotarians. "They got more'n two hundred songs down pat; sing jus' bout anythin' ya ask 'em," he bragged. "Why, the two boys read music like you read the paper; and the girls, 'specially the lil' one, sing any song after hearin' it a coupla times. Hell, they could do fifteen, twen'y shows in a row and never do the same song twice." (He explained to us later that this wasn't lying, it was 'selling.')

When we arrived at CFQC for our second broadcast, Mr. Dallin handed us nine telegrams. All were congratulatory but one lady took exception to the way we had been introduced. Instead of "Hahn And His Kids," she suggested "The Harmony Kids."

"Lady's gotta good idea," Dad said. "Whadda ya think?" he asked us. We all agreed that it sounded kind of nice.

When we went on the air the announcer made the change and this name was to stick with us for the next ten years.

Before we went on the air Mr. Dallin pointed out a few mistakes we had made on our first show, such as being 'off-mike' a few times.

"Whoever is singing or playing a solo, you have to get in close to the microphone," he explained. "Not so close that no one else can be heard, but closer than the rest. When you get finished, then back up a little and let the next person have a chance. If we had another mike it would work better so you'll have to position yourselves in such a way that the sound comes out right."

"If ya put the microphone out in the middle, can't we work all around?"

"Good idea." He moved the mike into the middle of the studio. "Picks up on two sides only. Don't get too far off to the side or you're gonna be off-mike again."

The second broadcast went even better than the first. It was obvious that broadcasting would take a little getting used to as the idea of playing into a *thing,* with no contact with an audience you could see, was difficult. We were to learn, however, that that *thing* represented thousands of unseen people. In 1936 radio was in its infancy in the west but its power as a communication medium was staggering.

Mom and Dad went shopping and bought armloads of bolts of cloth. There was big roll of brown velvet, some rust-coloured silk, a smaller piece of blue taffeta, and some black, silky worsted. For days, Mom was busy at her sewing machine making costumes for all of us. She made a set of brown velvet slacks for Lloyd and me with matching skirts for the girls. We all had rust-coloured shirts. She made a long dress for Joyce out of the blue taffeta and a tuxedo for Kay out of the black worsted. Both of the girls danced — things like old-fashioned waltzes and German and Ukrainian folk dances. Dad felt this would go over when we did important stage shows.

Dad had some bearings changed on the truck and bought a new carburetor. With the cost of the cloth and the repairs we were broke again when we left Saskatoon.

From Saskatoon to Moose Jaw was about 140 miles and washboard all the way. As we were pulling into Tuxford, a small town only a few miles from Moose Jaw, the transmission in the truck gave up. We needed a new set of gears for the rear end but these were not available in Tuxford. They would have to be picked up in Moose Jaw. Tuxford did have a small garage where Dad could do the work, and the owner sent in to Moose Jaw for the parts. Three days later, we limped into Moose Jaw, minus a complete set of matched wrenches and other tools which Dad had to give up in payment for the parts and work done in Tuxford.

Scouting around for some place to put on a show, Dad found a big automobile dealer whose window signs indicated he was running a special sales promotion. Obviously the promotion wasn't too successful as there were no customers in the showroom.

"Name's Hahn," Dad said, shaking hands with the owner. "Notice yer runnin' a sale — how's it goin'?"

"You can see fer yerself how it's goin'. Haven't had ten people in here all day."

"What would ya say if I tol' ya I could fill this place up in an hour?"

"With car buyers?"

"I didn' say car buyers. That'd be yer job. What I can do is get 50-100 people in no time flat. Once we get 'em in you let me put on a show with my kids an' pass the hat aroun' when we're finished."

"That's all?"

"That's all."

"Ya just made a deal."

The local kids were already flocking around the trailer outfit. We drove slowly up and down some of the main streets, tooting the horn and picking up more and more people as we went along. It reminded me of The Pied Piper of Hamelin because when Dad finally parked, right in front of the showroom, a hundred kids must have been milling around, along with a bunch of curious grownups. As we moved into the showroom with our instrument cases, the crowd followed. I don't know if the man sold any cars but the place was jammed with people as we ran through seven or eight songs. The girls were waiting at the door with their hats as the crowd dispersed and we were $18 richer when we went to bed that night.

September was winding down and October can be a very unpredictable month month in Saskatchewan when it comes to weather. Dad felt the need to press on and the next morning we left for Regina.

Here was a new experience for us — paved roads. From Moose Jaw to Regina, 40 miles, the roads were smooth as silk. There was no dust and miracle of miracles, no washboard. I guess when you drive on washboard long enough you begin believing that's the way all roads are.

Dad parked right in front of the Legislative Building and we all went on a sightseeing tour. Regina was even bigger than Saskatoon. After wandering around and testing the public washrooms in the parliament building, we drove back into the downtown core and Dad went off on a 'fishing trip.'

"Guess what," he said when he returned, "we gotta job — tonight!"

One of the fraternal organizations was holding its annual dance at the Hotel Saskatchewan.

"I'm not sure if we're gonna be paid anythin' 'cause the entertainment has been booked for weeks. But they've agreed ta let us put on our show. Apparently all the important businessmen in Regina will be there. They've got a magician, and some cowboy group hired. Tonight, you're gonna wear the new outfits yer mother's bin workin' on."

We put on our new brown velvet costumes with the silk, rust-coloured shirts and we did look kind of nice.

The hotel ballroom was jammed with ladies and gentlemen decked out in their finery. We had never seen so many people all dressed up before. I guess we were all a little tense as we went over the list of songs with Dad.

"All ya gotta do," he said, "is act natur'l and smile. Take yer time between the songs — wait until they finish clapping. Now, jus' relax till they call ya."

A long table had been set up and the special people who were to sit there were led in by a man in a plaid skirt, if you can imagine, playing a terrible-sounding instrument, if you could call it that. Obviously, one of the notes was stuck.

When they were all in their right places, a man said grace and everybody in the room sat down. As the dinner went on we could see the other entertainers across the ballroom in another room opposite ours. They were waiting, too.

After the dinner the magician was introduced. We had never seen a real magician before and this guy was very good. He kept pulling silver dollars out of the ladies' hair. He made a rabbit appear out of a silk hat, and for his last trick he made a pretty yellow bird appear out of a big silk scarf. The audience loved it.

We were all ready to go on when the man at the head table picked up the microphone and introduced the cowboy group. They came bounding out of the wings with rhinestones glistening, their chaps flapping and their spurs jangling. I thought the girl singer was a little fat. She was wearing pretty tight pants but apparently the men in the audience didn't think she was too fat or that her pants were too tight because they whistled and applauded as she stepped up to the microphone. The cowboys stayed out there for over half an hour and did three of the songs we had picked to do.

This was disconcerting. We hadn't reached that professional stage where we could cope quickly with last-minute changes. There was a buildup of tension as we argued among ourselves choosing alternate songs. Then there were all the frantic instructions from Dad: "Make sure the girls run out first and when yer finished, back off and let the girls run off ahead of you; don't look down at the keys, Bob, look out at the people and smile." It wasn't the music that made us nervous, it was the bedlam that went with it.

We changed our routine just as the cowboy group finished and the man at the head table began introducing us.

"Ladies and gentlemen, tonight we're in for a very special treat. We have a family with us who have just come out of the far north. They've already done some broadcasts on their way through Saskatoon and, as a special favour, they've consented to do a few numbers for us tonight."

Mom was nervously brushing the ringlets in Joyce's hair and Dad was listening intently.

"The group are all members of the Hahn family, and the youngest little lady is only six years old. Let's have a warm Regina welcome for THE HARMONY KIDS."

We started the show with both girls singing *Button Up Your Overcoat*. Kay sang *My Heart Stood Still* and Joyce followed with *The Best Things In Life Are Free*. The next number was an instrumental medley with Lloyd and I playing *Umbrella Man* and *Celito Lindo*. Kay sang *Mexicali Rose* and Joyce did *It's A Great Day For The Irish* with everybody in the audience keeping time, clapping their hands.

I could see the magician and the cowboy group watching us from the wings. We were getting far more applause then they had received. The audience was really involved, and there was a good feeling in the room. We finished with *Tumbling Tumbleweeds* as the girls had the harmony down pat on that song.

As we ran offstage, pandemonium reigned. They wouldn't let us quit. The men were standing on their chairs and the applause went on in waves. Dad shoved us back out but before we could begin again, the man at the head table knocked his gavel for silence and motioned for us to wait.

"One more thing," he began. "The father of these talented youngsters spoke with me this afternoon and explained that the family was working their way back east and they're hoping their music is going to get them there. We're going to have a basket up here at the head table and if you've enjoyed their music, and I'm sure you have, it would be greatly appreciated if you came by after the show and showed your appreciation by dropping something in the basket to help them on their way."

Again the applause started and, before it ended, we began the introduction to the next song, *Till We Meet Again* which seemed quite appropriate.

When it was over, a long line began forming past the head table and we could see money being dropped into the basket. The headwaiter led us through the crowd, with the ladies patting Joyce on the head and smiling at us, into a small dining room where we were served a complete meal. Everything was great although we couldn't understand why each of us had to have two forks, two knives, and three spoons. One of each would have been plenty.

Just as we were finishing, the man from the head table came in with the basket. There was over $80 in it. He was all smiles and thanked us over and over.

Then another gentleman came in and said: "You kids were great — I mean great! If you're going to be in town for a few days, drop around to the station. I'm with CJRM — love to put you on the air. Here's my card

— drop in any time tomorrow."

Dad thanked him and put the card in his pocket.

As the man was leaving, he turned back and said, "If anybody from CKCK gets in touch with you, tell them you've already made a deal with us."

The main CJRM studio was bigger than the one at CFQC in Saskatoon and it even had a grand piano. The man with the card, Mr. Crittendon, explained that the station was owned by James Richardson & Sons which was the reason for the JR in the call letters. "We also have a sister station in Winnipeg, CJRC, and some of our more important programs go out over both stations at the same time."

Dad followed Mr. Crittendon into his office. When he came out, he announced: "We're gonna be doin' a half-hour show this Friday night and every Friday as long as we stay in Regina. Mr. Crittendon has made arrangements for us to park the outfit in behind a store within easy walking distance to the station and we can use the studio almost any time we want to rehearse.

"The money ain't all that good as they gener'lly don't pay groups for broadcasting. Most of them are happy to do the broadcasts for nothing as long as the station lets them tell the listeners what towns they'll be playin' in the comin' days an' weeks. We'll only be gettin' five dollars for the show and Mr. Crittendon himself will be our announcer."

When it came to money, we never argued with Dad. He knew how to handle our affairs. We'd come this far and we had almost a hundred dollars. Besides, getting five dollars every week for something we all loved doing was still a pretty good deal and on broadcasts we didn't have to worry about smiling or looking out at the people. We could concentrate completely on the music.

Chapter 14

MOST AFTERNOONS WERE SPENT at the radio station rehearsing new numbers for the radio show. We learned songs by listening to records in the station's music library. Hal Crittendon was very easy to work with. On the first show, we went into the wrong number and Hal turned it around to make it sound as though it had been his fault. By our third Friday show it was well into October and we had already had one light snowfall.

The station had received more than 50 letters addressed to the Harmony Kids and we could tell by the way the people at the station treated us that they were more than pleased with the reaction.

"How you people making out in the trailer, what with the cold weather setting in?" Hal asked Dad after one of the shows. "You warm enough back there?"

"Everything's just fine. Sure couldn't stay there all winter, but as soon as we get a few bucks ahead, we gotta get goin'. It's a long way back east."

Hal weighed his words carefully. "Two things. First, we've had a call from the authorities. They were very nice about it but they're concerned about you getting snowed in on the highway somewhere if you leave Regina now.

"Screw the authorities," Dad said.

"Let me finish," Hal interjected. "If you do get snowed in, you become a public charge and that's the reason for their concern."

"How'n hell they gonna stop us? One mornin' they wake up and we ain't there — whadda they gonna do?"

"They *can* stop you. And they just might — with a court order. Besides, maybe we can work something out. Your show is really starting to catch on; over 30 letters again this week and dozens of phone calls with requests. If we could come up with something — something a little more interesting, would you consider staying for the winter?"

"Whadda ya mean, a little more interesting?" Dad asked.

"Could the kids find enough songs to do a half-hour show every Friday, like they've been doing, and a full hour on Saturday mornings?"

"Look, the kids know enough songs already and they're learnin' new ones all the time. That's not the problem. We just squeak by every week on the five bucks . . ."

Hall interrupted . . . "Which brings me to the last point. Suppose we give you fifteen bucks a week. Five for the Friday show and ten for the full hour on Saturday. Think you could get by on that?"

"Okay, you gotta deal. Two shows — fifteen bucks. Only one more thing; some of the mail we bin gettin' asks 'bout pictures of the Harmony Kids — you know, do we have any and how much are they — that sort of thing. You let us sell pictures on the shows and you gotta deal."

Hal smiled, stood up and shook hands with Dad.

That afternoon Dad backed the trailer in tighter to the wall of the building and unhitched the truck. He took the truck and came back a short time later with some six-foot planks and two rolls of tar paper. We jacked up the trailer and Dad removed the wheels. He built a solid base under the chassis with the planks and lowered the trailer. The tar paper was tacked all the way around the bottom and the next day, a load of dirt was delivered. We all got busy with shovels and banked the dirt up against the base of the trailer, now protected by the tar paper.

Winter weather in Regina can be expected to dip well below zero and the small electric heaters we had in the truck and trailer wouldn't be enough. Dad found two small wood-burning stoves. One would go in the back of the truck for Lloyd and me and the other was for the trailer. Dad ran a charge account at a hardware store and came home with all the necessary stove pipes and other hardware he would need. He cut a hole in the roof of the trailer for the stove chimney and the pipes from the truck ran out one of the windows. The truck stove was bolted to the floor. The trailer had two doors, one on each side. One of these was hooked shut and covered inside with a sheet of asbestos. More asbestos sheeting was inserted right under the stove in case any sparks dropped out. We had a cord of wood delivered and we were ready for winter.

That week we started the Saturday morning show. It was going to be very difficult to keep it up every week, as we went through a tremendous amount of material. We needed eight songs for the Friday show and fifteen or sixteen on Saturday. The people at the station were more than helpful. We'd spend hours there, listening to records and learning new songs. We started cataloguing a repertoire. As we learned a new song, the lyrics were written out on a big piece of paper so we could just flip them over on a big easel board. The title was added to our master list and beside it the key. On the right side a notation was made. If Joyce was going to sing the song, "J", if Kay, "K", if it was a duet, "J&K" and so on. By using a reasonable number of repeats, which generally were justified as having been requests from listeners, we were able to keep up with the numbers we needed each week. Our days were totally consumed by music — there was no time for anything else.

Dad was a colorful conversationalist. He had a high-school education, which was more than most people in the west in those days. He had been in business on the prairies for many years and he was a good salesman, the result of being able to communicate with people on their own level. Not only was he comfortable with the local jargon, his command of the English language allowed him to add to it. He was not an aggressive or belligerent person; usually he was gentle and well mannered. When angry he became quite articulate but had difficulty expressing his feelings without a select choice of phrases, expletives and rather earthy, descriptive words.

We'd been on our new radio schedule for about a month when Dad answered a knock on the trailer door. There was a rather buxom lady and behind her a milquetoast little man with a briefcase.

"Could we come in for a minute?" the lady asked.

Dad motioned them inside. "Watch the stove," he said, "it's pretty hot."

Lloyd and Kay were at the radio station and Joyce and I were working on some lyrics at the table. Mom was at the other end of the trailer, sewing. Everything was neat and orderly and the trailer was warm and comfortable.

The little man was busy with some papers. They might be from the newspaper, I thought.

"Joyce, slide under the table and sit beside Bob," Dad said. This left the other side of the table empty. "If you'd care to slide in there," Dad said, pointing to the empty space, "I'm sure you'll be comfortable."

The lady motioned her friend in first as it was going to be a tight fit for her.

When they were finally settled, Dad asked, "Now, what can we do for you?"

"We're from the Department of Education," the lady announced. "We understand you have school-age youngsters living here who are not going to school. Is that correct?"

Dad's voice was ominously soft. "You might say that."

"Could we have the full names of the children and their ages, please?"

the little man asked, his pen poised.

"Well, there's Lloyd. He's nineteen."

The man was writing on his pad. Dad waited until he looked up before continuing.

"Then, there's Bob," he said, motioning to me, "he's eighteen."

I watched Dad. He had lied about both our ages. " . . . and Joyce. "She's only five, not quite school age."

Another lie. His last statement sounded quite final, as though that was the end of the list.

The lady looked over at the man's papers, then at Dad. "According to our information, there's one more girl. How old is she?"

Dad was caught and he knew it. His voice was a little louder as his strategy changed. "Look, we don't even come under your jurisdiction. We're merely passing through; transients would probably be the right word. If it hadn't been for a pile of bureaucratic bullshit that stopped us from leaving a few weeks back, we wouldn't even be here."

The lady's voice took on a very officious tone. "But you are here and the information we have is that you intend staying here and if that's the case, then it will be necessary for the children to register . . ."

Dad had had all he was going to take. "Look, lady — and you better have yer friend take notes 'cause I'm on'y gonna say this once." Dad was now standing. "Where were all you goddamn professional do-gooders when we lived in the north? There ain't any schools at all up there and there's all kinds o' kids of school age and all kinds o' parents'd love to send their kids to school."

The lady and the man retreated into their seats as Dad continued, menacingly.

"Fer the first time since the wheels came off this goddamn province we got somethin' goin' fer us and you waddle in here, yer fat ass in the breeze and try'n throw a monkey-wrench into it."

The man was closing his briefcase and the lady made a lame attempt at looking indignant. She moved uncomfortably.

Dad wasn't finished. "You go back'n tell yer boss my kids ain't goin' ta school. Tell 'em they can sen' a truant officer. Tell 'em ta send the cops. Tell 'em anythin' ya want. And when they get finished doin' the dance of the matin' cranes, tell 'em if they send anybody else 'round here botherin' us, I'll make a noise yer gonna hear from asshole ta breakfast."

There wasn't a sound from the other side of the table as Dad concluded, "Now, take yer muscle-bound frien' an' get ta hell outta here."

A week later, a big brown envelope arrived at the radio station addressed to Dad with a covering letter and a bunch of documents. The letter explained that it would be quite acceptable, considering our 'transient' status, for the girls to take government correspondence school courses. The lessons would have to be returned on a regular basis and further lessons would be sent as long as we stayed in the province. Once Dad went over the material with the girls, his attitude changed. Part of each day was spent with the girls to ensure that all lessons were completed and returned on time. The program was continued long after we left Saskatchewan, and those lessons were the only formal education my sisters received.

There weren't enough hours in the day to do all the things that needed doing. I bought a more advanced instruction book for my accordion and although the compositions in it weren't all that interesting, I did discover that with only 48 bass buttons I was severely restricted on how much farther I could develop, musically. We traded the 48 bass model in for one with 120 bass. It took some time to get comfortable with the new accordion but I could now use seventh and diminished chords and a whole new musical vista opened up.

Lloyd, too, had to work harder. We bought a more advanced guitar book and spent hours learning the new chords I was now able to use. Dad had long since stopped playing with us as he couldn't begin to cope with the chord sequences we were now using. We moved on to more sophisticated songs like *Begin the Beguine* and rarely did a song come out that we couldn't learn in a couple of hours. Even Kay got caught up in the challenge and was able to perform most of our repertoire on her small four-string guitar.

Dad enrolled the girls in a tap-dancing academy and each Saturday, after the broadcast, they'd spend two hours there. They mastered the basic 'waltz-clog' and a couple more flashy steps. What was more important, they learned a few ballroom dances like the tango and a really beautiful version of a Strauss waltz.

Mom made more long gowns for Joyce and a super tuxedo for Kay. Dad found a silk top-hat in a pawn shop that fitted Kay perfectly.

Our fan mail was averaging over a hundred letters a week, and while most were specific requests for songs, many would ask that we dedicate some special song to this person or that person on their birthday, anniversary or whatever. We'd let Hal pick out the ones he wanted to use and found that we could cut our Friday show down to seven numbers by judiciously sorting out the dedications and requests. This gave Hall more time to talk and we got away with one less song. We were learning.

Then we discovered that if we learned the right song when it first came out we could play it once as it was building in popularity, once when it reached its peak, and once again as it started to fade.

There were weeks when we didn't have time to learn new material. We would then do a complete program of 'repeats' by inventing some excuse such as: "Tonight's program will consist of the most requested songs during the last six months."

At least half the letters asked about pictures. People wanted to see what the Harmony Kids looked like, especially Joyce and Kay. Dad hired a professional photographer to take pictures. We already had a good shot of all of us with the trailer outfit in the background. We picked five more: Joyce in her long gown, Kay in her tuxedo, the two of them in skirts and blouses with Kay holding a banjo and Joyce holding a guitar, Lloyd and I with our instruments, and all of us, including Dad, in the studio. When Dad tried to arrange a deal with the photographer, he found that the mark-up, after paying for the prints, wouldn't allow us enough profit margin to make the selling of pictures worthwhile. So he bought the negatives and a do-it-yourself book on photography. He found an unused storage room at the radio station and set up his own developing lab. In a week, he was cranking out pictures of The Harmony Kids by the hundreds.

Hal started plugging the pictures on the Saturday show. The price was ten cents apiece or three for a quarter. If you wanted the complete set of six, it cost 40 cents.

The power of radio was unbelievable. It seemed as though everyone in Saskatchewan, plus hundreds more in the bordering states of Montana and North Dakota, had been waiting to see what the Harmony Kids looked like. The post office began delivering our mail to the station in our own mail bag. It took hours to process and the barrage was ceaseless. Within a month, not counting the $15 a week we were being paid by the station, we were making well over $150 a week just selling pictures. Only those who lived through the Depression, especially in the west, can appreciate how much money that was.

When nobody was looking, Lloyd and I would stick a couple of quarters into our pockets from the picture envelopes, and on nights when there was nothing else to do we'd play pool. We started on the small "Boston" tables until we got the hang of it and then moved up to the more difficult snooker tables. After a few months of this, playing three or four nights a week, Lloyd was pretty good, but I became a real pool shark. I started taking on the best players who came around and soon nobody could beat me. I insisted on playing 'call shot' which meant that no 'flukes' were allowed. If it was 'red ball in the side pocket' that's precisely where it would have to be made. If an opponent was really tough, I'd not only insist on playing 'call shot' but we'd have to call the next ball we were going to play also, and the pocket we would play it in. I could make three-quarters of all one-cushion bank shots and at least 50 percent of three-cushion bank shots. I loved the game and I played it exceptionally well. We got into three-cushion and 'Russian' billiards but I refused to gamble except for the odd game of 'pea-pool' which we played for nickels and dimes on the small tables.

In our mail bags, along with the requests for songs, dedications, and the unending orders for pictures, we'd receive inquiries from civic groups, asking how much the Harmony Kids would charge to appear in person at their annual fair, curling bonspiel, local stampede, church supper, etc. Dad kept these inquiries in a file. We hadn't put together a formal show presentation although we had discussed it and everything we were doing was leading us in that direction. If we *were* going to put on shows and charge admission, we would have to have a two-hour program ready.

All music for two hours wasn't the answer. The girls now had a series of dance routines, three of which were pretty good. Mom was still making new costumes. Our problem was not one of content but of presentation. We didn't know how to get on and off stage without bumping into each other, and nobody in the foursome could talk in a spontaneous manner or even introduce the songs.

Simple things like, "Thank you ladies and gentlemen, and now Joyce will sing one of our most requested numbers, etc., etc . . .," were too much for us. And knowing when to quit is something you learn only after a great deal of experience. How to take bows gracefully with all four of us was a mystery. We needed a professional choreographer but there was none available. We didn't know the importance of waiting for applause, let alone how to generate it. Curtain calls generate and perpetuate applause. While we felt quite professional in our music, to expose ourselves to situations where we felt and looked awkward and clumsy seemed ludicrous and unnecessary. When we talked this over with Dad, he agreed. Professional 'in-person' shows would have to wait until we were ready.

Little did we know how ingenious Dad's solution was going to be. Somewhere, he had picked up a book on magic and illusions. It didn't explain in detail how the illusions really worked but it did detail what transpired as the audience watched. This was all Dad needed to get his creative juices flowing. He started with rough drawings on a writing pad and the next thing we knew, he had rented a heated storage shed with a 25 foot ceiling. He bought a quantity of one by two lumber, some one by fours, and a large bolt of black velvet, and went to work. All his free time, when he wasn't developing pictures or processing picture orders, he spent in the storage shed. He was surrounded by large wooden frames, some hinged in sections and all covered in black velvet. Soon he had a complete stage set-up which could be folded up and stored.

He built a V-shaped frame about three feet high with sides three feet long, and a square box the same height and three feet square. There were trapdoors in different areas of the stage scenery and in both the 'V' and the box. Everything was covered in black velvet.

One evening we all went to the storage shed for a rehearsal. Dad had Kay disappear into the 'V'. Joyce got into the box and Dad closed the lids. Then he showed both of them how to slither out of the trapdoors and through the matching trapdoors in the scenery. They had to close the traps quickly behind them and Dad made well-hidden devices for this. Lloyd and I watched from out front. It wasn't going to work. When the trapdoors in the scenery were opened, you could see the light from backstage. Dad went back to the drawing board and built something on the same principle used in a diving-bell. Once the girls went through the trapdoors in the scenery, they were in another small enclosure. They could then snap the trapdoor shut and no light would show. They'd slither out through a curtain. When Dad opened the box, Kay, not Joyce would jump out and Joyce would pop out of the 'V.' The trick was going to work. Dad wrote out a script and memorized it. Later, when he became more comfortable with the trick, he discarded his rehearsed script and ad-libbed his patter.

The girls reached a stage where they could change places in a few seconds. Not only could they change places, but sometimes they would disappear or appear in the same box. In today's world of magic illusions I don't think it's the kind of trick that professional magicians go to bed worrying about, but in 1937 it was spectacular.

People would sneak around backstage after the show to see how it worked and if there were any trapdoors. Dad immediately solved this by building identical models of the 'V' and the box which didn't have any trapdoors. These would be left sitting in the wings for anyone's inspection and believe me, they were gone over with a fine-tooth comb. The ones used in the show were safely stowed away in tin boxes and locked up.

Lloyd and I worked out some 'tension' music which we played softly off-stage to heighten the suspense as Dad worked the audience, setting up the trick. When he began floating around the stage, brandishing a big red silk cape, Lloyd and I would walk on stage and our music became louder. The distraction of the swirling cape, our appearance and the music was all that was needed. By the time the audience looked back at the boxes, the girls had already changed places. Dad would open the lids, the girls would pop out, and the trick would end with a musical finale as we were then all on stage.

When Dad worked the trick well, and if he played his audience right, it could be stretched comfortably to about 15 minutes. More than anything else, Dad got very good with his presentation and he felt better, being a part of the act again. Fifteen minutes of magic, however, was not nearly enough.

We kept working in the storage shed. We set a complete routine using our best musical numbers, three different dance routines with the girls and the magic illusion. Counting the time needed for Dad's introductions and waiting what we felt was a reasonable time for applause, the most we could come up with was an hour and 15 minutes. We were still 45 minutes short.

One evening, in the trailer, Dad went over another idea with us. He produced a small writing pad and a box of well-sharpened pencils. He wrote his name on the first page with one of the pencils, tore the page off and put it in his pocket. We were all watching as he spoke to Mom.

"Now, when the people start comin' in, you'll be takin' the tickets at the door. Ask 'em if they have any questions they would like answered. If they say yes, ask 'em ta write the question on this pad but make sure they use one of these pencils. The paper in the pad is very soft and the pencils are very hard."

Mom looked a little puzzled.

"When they've written down the question, tell 'em to put the paper in their pocket. That way, they will have the only copy. Now, somehow, Mary, you gotta tear off the next page from the pad and drop it in a box under your table. Before the show starts, one of us'll come out an' collect these blank pages. As soon as we get backstage, here's what we do."

Dad then proceeded to shake a light dusting of charcoal over the blank page. He blew it off and you could clearly read, "Harvey H. Hahn."

"Tell 'em to keep the questions short and not even sign their names."

The first time we tried this trick was in a small town with about a hundred people in the audience. About 20 had written out questions which they had pocketed. We had the copies backstage, all dusted and clearly legible. Dad realized that more than a little discretion would be required, as one of the questions read, "My uncle disappeared eight years ago. I think he was murdered. Where is his body?" This type of question had to be discarded. Dad would work on five or six questions which were hidden under a large 'crystal ball' mounted on a special velvet covered table. He would, supposedly, look into the crystal ball and say, "There's someone in the audience who has lost her wedding ring and wants to know where it is."

You could see a small segment of the audience react as they listened. You would invariably see the lady who had asked the question showing it discreetly to those around her. How could Dad know, on stage? After all, she had the written question in her hand!

"Your wedding ring slipped off your finger when you were doing the laundry. Look where you throw out the laundry water and you will find your ring."

These questions weren't risky, for the answer, right or wrong, couldn't get Dad into trouble. He'd only pick this type of question, always giving an innocuous answer, like your friendly neighbourhood teacup-reader. "You're going to get a letter" or "You're going to get some money" or "I see a death in the family." Everbody sooner or later is going to get a letter or receive some money or have a death in the family. Even when it happened two years later, people would say, "See, the teacup-reader was right."

Every once in a while Dad got lucky. A lady actually did find her wedding ring where she threw out the laundry water and these kind of 'happenings' spread like wildfire through the small prairie towns. When this segment went well, Dad could easily add another 15 minutes to the show. Now we were up to an hour-and-a-half. Another half-hour and we'd be ready.

Chapter 15

One Sunday afternoon Lloyd and I were busy stuffing envelopes with pictures while the girls licked envelopes and stamps. Mom was sewing and Dad was lying down, gazing into space.

"I got it!" he said, jumping to his feet. "I just figured out the last half-hour for the show. It'll be the greatest bit of magic ever seen — mental telepathy — and I just figured out how to do it!"

When he explained it we had to agree. Dad did indeed have a great idea. If he could work it right with Joyce, it would be the high point of the show.

"We'll start in small towns not too far from Regina so we can get back every night. That way, we'll only need the truck. Once we get it all ironed out, we can start booking ourselves on longer trips, Monday through Thursday, and we'll use the truck and trailer. As long as we get back for the Friday broadcast, we can blanket the province."

Breaking in the full two-hour show was terribly important to Dad. With few exceptions, our bookings consisted of playing for dances. Most smalltown prairie dances started around eight o'clock. They would stop around midnight for about an hour and everyone would go to the local Chinese restaurant, which would stay open on these occasions. This was called the 'supper hour' and was part of all dances. After that the dancing would resume for a couple more hours, and we seldom ended before two or three in the morning. Counting the supper hour, a dance would last as long as seven hours and it was tiring work, especially for the girls. That was why getting the show set was so important. There would be no dancing afterwards and you could charge more money for a show than a dance.

Working through a local civic group, Dad booked us into Moose Jaw. The show would be held in a theatre. Arrangements were made for us to do a half-hour show on CHAB, the local radio station, the night before. We drove to Moose Jaw, did the show, and drove back to Regina. The next night we did another broadcast at 6 p.m. and we plugged the show on both broadcasts. When the curtains opened at eight o'clock on "Music and Magic" the theatre was sold out.

The first hour went like clockwork. We did our musical numbers; the girls did their dance routines; I played an accordion solo; then we did the magic illusion bit. We had footlights for the first time and there was a man following us with a spotlight.

After a ten-minute intermission, we opened with a 'flag-waver' musical number, then Dad went into his act with the crystal ball, answering questions. He answered four and used up 15 minutes. This was the weakest part of the show. The questions were insipid and Dad wasn't all that comfortable with the ad-libbing required to keep the momentum going. This was followed by all of us back on stage in another change of costumes, doing *Mama Don't Like No Music Played 'Round Here* which gave us all a chance to switch instruments around and show off a little. While we were doing this number, Dad changed costumes.

It was time for the mental telepathy routine. For it to work, there had to be a minimum of two aisles running through the audience. One middle aisle with people on both sides wasn't nearly as effective. All this had been checked by Dad when the booking was made. The audience was in three segments, separated by two aisles.

Dad walked to centre stage in a light-blue velvet suit, trimmed in sequins. He looked very elegant. There was no doubt this was the way it was done in *real* show biz. He raised his arms for silence.

"Ladies and gentlemen, tonight we are going to try something for the first time." Standing in the wings, I noted that Dad was being very careful with his diction. He had said 'for' instead of his usual 'fer.' He even put the 't' on 'first'. He continued: "I have found that under the right circumstances, I can communicate with Joyce through the medium of mental telepathy."

Some of the audience began shuffling their feet. Others showed their skepticism in other ways. Dad waited for the rumbling to stop before he went on: "In order for this to work, I must have complete silence."

More rumbling. There were, fortunately, more believers than skeptics and the audience disciplined themselves as the believers shooshed the skeptics. Dad waited until the theatre quieted down.

Because little Joyce was the main reason people came to the show, the audience was at least one-third children. Some mothers had even brought babies along.

"If any of the babies start crying, I would ask that you take them out into the lobby until Joyce and I are finished," Dad said. "There can be no noise whatsoever."

One mother with a restless child got up and went out to the lobby.

"I will be coming down that aisle," Dad explained, pointing to the left side of the audience, "and asking some of you to name your favourite song."

He jumped off stage and quietly asked a lady to name her favourite. *"Home On The Range,"* she whispered.

Dad was holding a piece of heavy paper folded over to about half the size of a normal business letterhead. He wrote down the number '1' and beside it, *Home On The Range*. He showed it to a few people sitting close to the lady, then walked down a few rows, squeezed his way into the centre and asked a second person to name a song. When he had worked his way to the back of the theatre he had written down ten titles.

All this time a spotlight had been following Dad and the stage was bare. From the very back of the theatre Dad again asked for silence and waved the paper around so everyone could see it.

"You have all seen me go down that aisle and write down song titles requested by ten different people. I am now going to ask Joyce to come on stage."

Joyce walked to centre stage and waited, a spotlight now on her too. She had no idea what was going to happen.

"Now, I am going to work my way down the opposite aisle and ask some of you to pick out, at random, any of the song titles written down on this piece of paper."

In the meantime, when attention had been focused on Joyce's entry, Dad had discreetly folded over his piece of paper. This substituted the requests he had written down in the audience to ten song titles of our own which were identical to a list we had backstage. Working two sides of the theatre, there was no way the audience on the right side could know which songs had been requested by the people on the left.

Joyce, in the meantime, was trying to become transfixed. She'd close her eyes, then open them again. Dad kept holding up his hands for silence. The smallest distraction and Joyce would open her eyes and shuffle around, looking annoyed.

"Please — if there is any noise at all, there can be no communication. Try and be as quiet as possible," Dad said. No one moved.

Dad had now worked his way in to the third or fourth seat in the second-last row. He discreetly showed the list to the woman sitting there and asked that she pick any one of the titles on the list. She pointed to the number '7' and Dad made certain that a few people nearby saw her pick the number.

By this time Joyce was totally absorbed with her role, absolutely rigid with her eyes tightly closed.

Lloyd, Kay and I were backstage listening. The first time Dad used the word "concentrate" would be our cue. Dad had memorized all ten cues. Lloyd and I just read them from our sheet. Joyce was the only person who had no idea what was going on. Our cue sheet read as follows:

1. Concentrate: *Home On The Range*
2. Please concentrate: *Button Up Your Overcoat*
3. Kindly concentrate: *Lady Be Good*
4. If you will concentrate: *I Wanna Be Happy*
5. Try and concentrate: *Danny Boy*
6. Now concentrate: *Beautiful Dreamer*
7. It's time to concentrate: *Oh, Dem Golden Slippers*
8. I ask you to concentrate: *Tea For Two*
9. Will you concentrate: *Silver Haired Daddy of Mine*
10. Close your eyes and concentrate: *Listen To The Mocking Bird*

Dad held his arms out to the stage and closed his eyes. "It's time to concentrate, Joyce — please, shut out everything around you and . . ."

Lloyd and I checked our list. *It's time to* concentrate was number '7' and the song was *Oh, Dem Golden Slippers.*

Suddenly and dramatically, Joyce made her body jerk, as though emerging from a trance and beckoned to the wings for us to come out. She supposedly whispered to Lloyd and Me the title of the song and we immediately went into the introduction of number '7.' Only then, when Joyce heard the intro did she know which song she had to sing.

It worked! There was applause from the audience and the confirmation of nodding heads from the people around Dad when he showed them the list and the song the lady had picked. Dad worked his way down the aisle and had two more people pick songs from the list. By this time, the believers would have thrown the skeptics out of the theatre had they made any noise. Joyce acted out her role like a seasoned pro, and to say our mental telepathy act worked would be an understatement. We killed 'em.

Word about this strange power between Joyce and Dad quickly spread around the province. Wherever we went, people always made a big fuss over Joyce. Now, along with the "Isn't she cute" or "What a dear little thing," there was a note of awe. She wasn't just a cute little seven-year-old singer anymore, she was someone special.

Dad got busy writing letters and in a month we were booked all over southern Saskatchewan. We'd play dates on Monday, Tuesday, Wednesday and Thursday. The Thursday date was never too far from Regina so we could get back in time for the Friday broadcast. We plugged our upcoming dates on both the Friday and Saturday programs, and wherever we played the theatres and halls were filled.

All of our bookings were arranged through some local civic group. They received fifteen percent of all ticket sales but they had to pay for the hall. So the local group got out and hustled the presale of tickets. Even when the weather turned out bad and people didn't show up, the money was still there. While Dad might have been termed a show business neophyte he was fast becoming a very adept impresario.

We received two letters from the United States. Wolf Point, Montana, asked if we would appear at their annual stampede. They were prepared to pay $300 for a 30 minute grandstand show. The letter went on to explain that our radio signal came into Wolf Point loud and clear and we could be assured of a full house as people would attend on the strength of our drawing power. We had been getting a lot of mail from that area but to be told that we had 'drawing power' was new. The letter suggested we telephone — collect! It all sounded very big-time and Dad placed the call. The man in Wolf Point was delighted. He would send one-third of the fee immediately and we would receive the balance after the performance.

The second letter was from Minot, North Dakota. Their date was two days after the Wolf Point stampede. It was 230 miles between the two towns but looking at the map, good highways all the way. We would be performing as part of the entertainment at the dedication of a flag to a new Scout group. A half-hour show would be plenty and they were prepared to pay us $250. Dad agreed.

We crossed the American border at Regway, feeling like real celebrities. The customs and immigration men knew us. "We listen to your programs every week," they said as they waved us through.

The truck and trailer attracted a lot of attention as we moved through the small towns and it became apparent that everyone had heard of us. They would holler at us as we went by: "Welcome to Montana — where's Joyce?" Joyce would wave at them through a window and if we stopped, they would flock around the outfit asking for autographs.

We had been well received wherever we played, but now we were being made to feel important. Closer to Wolf Point we saw big posters with our pictures all along the highway, nailed to telephone poles. As we pulled into Wolf Point the whole town seemed to be gathered as a welcoming committee.

"Welcome to Wolf Point — welcome to Montana — and welcome to the United States of America," a stampede official said.

We weren't ready for what happened as we drove into the stampede corral with a police escort. Hundreds of people were standing and cheering as we moved around the circuit of the corral, the police sirens blasting. As we moved onstage with our instruments, the applause was overwhelming.

We couldn't suppress our smiles as we looked out at the sea of faces smiling back. An official stepped up to the microphone and it must have taken him five minutes to get the crowd quieted down so he could be heard. Lloyd and I went into a 'vamp till ready' introduction and all the man was able to scream above the din was "LADIES AND GENTLEMEN — THE HARMONY KIDS."

The applause, the screaming and the feet thumping on the wooden grandstand was ear-shattering, but as soon as the girls stepped up to the microphone, the noise stopped. This was repeated through all eight numbers. The hushed silence while we performed and the bedlam which followed each song were emotional highs none of us has ever forgotten. How kind these people were and what an impression they left with us. They wouldn't let us quit. We did three encores before an official led us off. Dad drove two circuits of the corral before exiting through the gates — the crowd still screaming as the gates closed behind us.

As we were led back downtown by our police escort, we looked at each other in disbelief. No one spoke except Dad and he sounded as though he was talking to himself: "If I ever had any doubts, I don't have 'em anymore — not after what I jus' seen."

That night we did a show in a saloon for the first time. None of us had ever been in a saloon before. We were ushered in through a back door and onto a small stage behind what had to be the longest bar in Montana. It must have been a hundred feet from one end to the other. It was so crowded no one could move. The minute we made our appearance the applause began. People were clapping their hands over their heads they were so crammed together. Bartenders were running back and forth along the bar serving drinks, which had to be relayed to the back rows by the people in between. Payment was sent back the same way and the bells on the cash registers never stopped ringing. There was a great air of fun and fellowship.

While we were performing the bartenders stopped serving drinks and held up their hands for silence. The room was hushed and you only had to look out to see how much they seemed to be enjoying us. When the song had ended they showed their appreciation in wave after wave of applause.

At the stampede show the people were far back in the grandstand seats. Now you could reach out and touch them. Most were farmers and ranchers with tanned faces from countless hours under the sun. Their smiles lit up the room as we went into our third song. When it ended, a big rugged man could be heard hollering over the din:

"Hold out your dress, honey!"

Joyce picked up the hem on her gown and the man threw a silver dollar in it. They started coming from all directions. People too far back passed their silver dollars to the bartenders and these were deposited by the handful into Joyce's dress. When we finished about an hour later, there were more than 500 silver dollars in a pile on the stage.

That night we sat around the table in the trailer gazing at all this money. Under the pile of silver dollars were two $100 bills, the balance payable from the stampede booking. We were looking at $735 and it was ours. We had earned it with our music and because a bunch of generous people had enjoyed it. My thoughts went back over the many hours of frustration and practising, the squabbles and the bickering, the struggle to keep up with the broadcasts. Now we were here. We had just ended the best day in our young lives.

We left Wolf Point, Montana leaving behind a million dollars in good will and taking with us memories which have endured over many years.

Minot, North Dakota, was different. Fewer than a hundred people were at the function in a church hall. The mayor welcomed the guests which included "our renowned guests from Canada — the Harmony Kids." He waited for the polite applause that followed our introduction, then he went on to extol the virtues of the Boy Scout movement. Lesser dignitaries were introduced who were cited for their contributions to the Scout movement and the community. Then some state dignitary took the podium and covered all the bases right up to the president of the United States.

Fifteen Boy Scouts in uniform moved to the front of the hall. A colour-guard of three men in military uniform marched in the flags. A lot of saluting and 'coming to attention' followed as the flags were deposited beside the podium.

We were then introduced and did our eight numbers. Our reception was less raucous than in Wolf Point; nevertheless the audience enjoyed our show. When we were finished, we were shown to four chairs lined up next to the flags. The Scout leader thanked us and proceeded to introduce the Reverend Garside. He mounted the podium and intoned the glory and the honour of the Scouts which ended with the actual dedication:

"Brethren in the Lord, because men at all times have made for themselves signs and emblems of their allegiance to their rulers and of their duty to uphold laws and institutions which God has called us to obey, we, following this custom meet here this evening before this assembly to ask God for his blessing on this flag . . . (he paused as one of the Scouts took the flag from its receptacle and turned to face the audience) which is to represent to us our duty to Him, to our country and . . . (he spread his arms towards the Scouts) this Troop."

The flag was re-deposited and the colour-guard marched up to the podium and everyone in the room stood up. As the colour-guard and the Scouts stood in salute, everyone in the room spoke in unison:

"I pledge allegiance to the flag of the United States of America, and to the Republic for which it stands, one Nation under God indivisible, with liberty and justice for all."

With everyone still standing the Scout leader looked at us and said, "And now, ladies and gentlemen, our National Anthem!"

Everyone in the room turned to look at us and the silence was deafening as they waited for us to start playing. Lloyd and the girls were shuffling uncomfortably and I stood immobile, looking out at the audience, not knowing quite what to do. The only anthem I knew was "God Save The King" and I knew it wasn't that. We didn't know the American national anthem.

There was a restless stirring in the room as the Scout leader looked at me impatiently and said, "If you please!"

Instinctively, I sounded a note on my accordion and waited. With the note as their starting guide, everyone began singing "The Star Spangled Banner." I had sounded a 'C' and I couldn't have picked a worse note. It was too high for the ladies and too low for the men. The American anthem is a demanding piece of music that has extreme vocal range and if one starts it off in the wrong key it can be a disaster — and it was!

What came back was a combination of the Chipmunks and the Red Army Chorus. It was awful. We stood there wondering when it would end.

Minot, North Dakota, did not end in a blaze of glory but it did prompt us to learn one more number to add to our repertoire.

As the weeks went by the stage shows ran smoother and smoother; the magic segments became flawless, our music library grew and grew. We kept up with all the new songs as they came out and we knew most of the old standards. We could perform dozens of ethnic folk songs. The halls were filled wherever we played, the broadcasts drew hundreds of fan letters and the orders for pictures poured in. We had five complete costume changes, a brand new truck; Lloyd had a gold-plated banjo and both girls had new guitars. We had our own public address system and we gained experience every day. Everything was great and life for the Hahn family had never been better.

As soon as we pulled into a town, Lloyd and I would set up the stage for that evening's performance then I would head for the local pool hall. My game kept improving to the point where I could take on all the local champions and when I was playing well, rarely did anyone beat me.

One week after the Friday evening broadcast, Hal said he had some good news. "Guess what, we've sold the show."

Dad looked a little puzzled. "Whadda ya mean — sold the show?"

"You now have a sponsor. O.G.D. — Out Goes Dirt, The Wonder Cleanser, will be paying all the bills from now on. You'll be going out over this station and our sister station in Winnipeg."

Dad looked more puzzled than ever. "What will this mean in the way of money?"

"O.G.D. will double your fee because of the two-station feed, then double it again because of their commercial involvement. Instead of $5 you'll be getting $20. There'll be three commercials on each show advertising Out Goes Dirt so we will have to put a limit on how many of your own public appearance announcements are used, otherwise there'll be no time for music. Somehow, we'll try and make up your own plugs on the Saturday show.

The success of O.G.D.'s sponsorship was felt immediately. Stores couldn't keep enough stock on hand to satisfy the demand. Within two weeks they had picked up an option on the Saturday show (that we didn't even know about) and our normal ten dollars a week went to $40. Now we were making $60 a week on our broadcasts alone.

However, all was not well. After one of the Saturday broadcasts, Hal looked uncomfortable as he told us: "The sponsor has asked that the announcements plugging your up-coming personal appearance dates be taken off the Friday night show completely. He feels it cheapens the overall sound of the program and there are too many interruptions, counting his commercials."

Dad tried not to sound angry when he replied: "Look, Hal, we've built this show over a long period of time. We appreciate what you're saying and we know a commercial program is very important to the station but we make much more money from our personal appearance dates and selling pictures than we get for broadcasting. If you take the plugs off the Friday show, our earnings are going to suffer."

Hal looked down as he continued. "The sponsor also wants to limit your Saturday plugs to four 30-second spots."

Dad was angry. He knew Hal was only relaying a message but it was obvious that Hal was the only channel of communication back to the sponsor. "We can't possibly cram everything we have to say into four 30-second spots. You tell him that."

The following Friday we were asked to be at the station early for a meeting. Hal explained that while he had tried to reason with the sponsor, the sponsor remained adamant. "No plugs on Friday, starting tonight and only four on tomorrow's show. You can appreciate this is important to the station, especially with the two-station feed, and we hope we can find a way to work this out."

"Why can't we all meet with the sponsor?" Dad asked. "These demands are not reasonable, and if the kids get unhappy 'bout this situation it's gonna be reflected in their music."

Each week new instructions were relayed to us from the sponsor. We were asked to change our opening and closing themes, and the commercial announcements which were supposed to plug O.G.D. sounded as though the sponsor owned The Harmony Kids. We all became conscious of a tension which had never been there before and doing the shows was becoming a chore. The fun was gone.

Then came a request, relayed through the station manager. "The sponsor caught one of your stage shows and asked me to tell you he was very impressed."

"Hallelujah!" Dad said, "The sponsor's impressed. He stops in to see one of our shows and doesn't even let us know he was there. In the meantime, he's screwin' the whole thing up."

"He's asked, what with his sponsorship and all, if we could arrange to have two big O.G.D. signs placed on either side of the stage during your stage shows."

"Absolutely not!" Dad replied. "This whole sponsor thing has gone far enough."

"Give it some thought. It was only a suggestion because he was so impressed with your show."

Dad gave it some thought and the next week he asked Hal to relay a message back to the sponsor. "Tell 'im we'll use his signs but he pays for the hall. That seems more'n fair." The offer was refused.

Although Hall still presented the program, a new commercial announcer was added for the O.G.D. commercials. The *pièce de résistance* came when we heard him telling the listeners: "If you would like a picture of The Harmony Kids — suitable for framing — buy the Jumbo Size box of O.G.D., 'Out Goes Dirt' — The Wonder Cleanser — the picture is right on the box."

We were still clearing over a hundred dollars a week on our picture sales and now all you had to do to get one of our pictures was buy a box of O.G.D. Within a month, the sale of pictures dropped to a trickle and the sales of O.G.D. soared.

This was too much for Dad. He gave the station two weeks notice.

"We wan'cha ta know how much we appreciate everything you did for us," Dad told Hal. "We came here sixteen months ago, fresh outta the north and not knowin' a whole lot about anythin'. We learned a lot here at the station and we thank ya for the chance you gave us. It's time ta move on. We wanna thank everyone, espcially you, Hal, for your kindness and help."

We piled into our brand-new truck, headed for Winnipeg and points east. It was spring, 1938, and a new horizon loomed.

1. Mum and Dad, 1919

2. Main Street, Eatonia, 1920

3. In the north, 1931   4. Building the trailer, 1935

5. *On our way, 1936*

6. *Homework in the trailer*

7. *Winter, Regina, 1936*

8. Joyce and Kay
   One of the pictures we sold

ADMIT
ONE CHILD

HARMONY KIDS
Entertainment and Dance

Don't fail to see the
SHIRLEY TEMPLE
of Western Canada

9. On "We the People" with Pat O'Brien
   New York, 1940

10. New York, 1941

"The Harmony Kids with Major Bowes"

11. The family, 1942

12. *The war's over, back with Joyce, 1946*

CHAPTER 16

LLOYD WAS NOW NINETEEN, I was eighteen, Kay twelve and Joyce eight. We started lying about Joyce's age as soon as we left Saskatchewan. With her pixie-like appearance, we kept her at six years old until she was ten. When we started working in bars in the U.S., and later in Montreal, it was necessary that we grow her up as quickly as possible and she went from ten to sixteen overnight.

We took our time going east. We had quite a bit of money saved and Dad just sort of piddled along. We spent a couple of days in Winnipeg, looking around. Dad dropped into the radio station but the reception wasn't all that warm. Apparently they were still upset about our quitting the show.

Then we headed east for Lake Of The Woods. The scenery was breathtaking and the shoreline adorned with coves and inlets. Trees and shrubbery ran down to the water's edge and the lake was dotted with islands. In those years it was completely unspoiled.

Just off the shore from where we had parked, a huge yacht lay at anchor. Long and sleek, it epitomized the luxury and ostentatious nature of those who owned it or those went on board. Small power-boats ran back and forth, transporting beautiful people in elegant attire. At night an orchestra played on deck and you could see men in white evening clothes and ladies in long flowing gowns, dancing. The music wafted over the still water as I listened and watched and wondered if I would ever be part of such a fairyland setting.

I realized that some of the fantasies I'd read in Aunt Carrie's True Story magazines were true after all. Dad tried to get us onto the yacht to do a show but was not successful. He did find out that the yacht was owned by a man named Dodge, whose family had something to do with making cars.

We stayed at Lake Of The Woods for a couple of weeks just lolling around. One night, we tuned into "We The People" with Gabriel Heatter. The broadcast came from New York and was sponsored by Sanka coffee. The program was made up of 'human interest' vignettes featuring people with unusual stories to tell. As we listened, a musical family not unlike ours came on and professed to be "the most trailer-travelled family in the world." They went on to say how far they had gone and their segment ended with them doing a musical number.

Dad blew his top. He worked furiously with a pencil and paper and calculated that we had travelled farther in our trailer outfit than they had. "Can't figure out how they let people like that on the air without checkin' 'em out first," he ranted. "We've travelled twice as far as they have and there they are, tellin' the world - on 'We The People' — sonsabitches didn't even check with us. An' d'ja hear their musical number? Christ, we could blow 'em right off the stage."

The program always ended with the announcer saying something like, "If you have a story to tell, write to us, "We The People" — 285 Madison Avenue, New York." Well, you can bet Dad wrote them a letter. By the time he was finished, it was smoking with lines like, "Why the hell don't you check up on these things before you let them on your program" — "We've gone farther" — "Musically we're better," etc., etc. Luckily, before he mailed the letter he included a return address — General Delivery to some town we knew we would eventually be going through, and Dad added 'Hold For Arrival.'

As soon as we left Lake Of The Woods we forgot the episode. We received mail as we went along but it was generally two or three months old, as we seldom got to where we were going as planned. We weren't in any hurry to get anywhere and we took our time as we went along, sightseeing and staying longer in places we enjoyed.

We would have to cross into the States to get to Sault Ste. Marie, where we would again cross back into Canada. Dad wrote to his folks in Ontario telling them we were on our way and they told us a big family reunion was planned as soon as we arrived. It would be held in the park in Waterloo. Sadly, a subsequent letter from Ontario brought the news that Dad's mother had passed away. Grandma had been very kind to us during the bad years in the north and we were all sorry we would never get to meet this dear lady.

We crossed the United States border at Fort Frances/International Falls, Minnesota, then drove south and east into Michigan. We hadn't played professionally for months and we hadn't been in the U.S. since the flag dedication in Minot, North Dakota.

Across the border everything felt different. The cars were bigger and newer. The roads were better and you could buy Camel and Lucky Strike cigarettes. The only thing that didn't measure up to Canada was the pool halls. It was as though all American pool players were beginners. Everyone played on the small "Boston" tables and we were lucky if a pool hall had one snooker table. On the small tables I could run three or four racks of balls before I missed. It was great fun having everyone watch me as I "ran the table," but not very challenging.

We skirted the northern shore of Lake Michigan stopping over in a town called Escanaba where Dad arranged for us to play in a bar-and-grill setup. We were back to passing the hat again, something we hadn't done in a long time, but this was quite acceptable in the U.S. As we knew we would never be back that way again it wasn't embarrassing. We came out of Escanaba with a few extra dollars, which Dad said would come in handy as we were running kind of low with all the travelling and not working.

The news on the radio was full of what Hitler was doing in Europe. We listened with great interest. But even more startling was the news that Mom was pregnant. We were about to have a new brother or sister who would be 20 years younger than Lloyd and me.

Dad wrote home to say that we expected to arrive sometime in August and they could go ahead and set up the reunion. We would have been right on schedule but when we got to Sault Ste. Marie, we couldn't get our outfit across the river — it was too big. We would have to retrace our steps and go via Milwaukee, Chicago and Detroit. We would also have to work our way along, as we were fast running out of money. Dad wrote home and suggested they postpone the reunion for at least a month.

We marked our route carefully on the map and picked out towns to stop in that looked big enough to have a place where we could put on a show. Dad would stop in front of the liveliest bar-and-grill and usually arranged for us to perform. The girls would pass the hat and we did well enough to keep going, generally with a little to spare.

We stopped in Milwaukee, where Tony Martin, a motion picture star, and his orchestra were playing. Lloyd and I got some money from Dad and went to see the show. This was the first big band we had ever seen and it was thrilling. The lighting, the sound, the sheer slickness of the presentation made us realize how far we had to go before we would be ready for this kind of booking. When we explained this to Dad, he just laughed.

"What you kids don't know is you're ready for anything!"

While his confidence was reassuring, he hadn't seen the Tony Martin show and I knew he was wrong. We still had a long way to go.

Travelling through the States was no different from Canada. The trailer outfit was just as spectacular and everywhere we went, traffic and people would stop. But we weren't ready for what happened when we drove down State Street in Chicago.

Two motorcycle cops with sirens screaming appeared from nowhere and pulled us over. "You can't drive that thing in the city of Chicago," one of them hollered. "It's against the law. We'll either escort you through the city or, if you're planning to stay over, we'll direct you to a parking lot."

Dad said he'd like to stay over for a few days, and with sirens at full blast they led the way to a parking lot, right in the downtown core. "When you're ready to leave, call this number," a cop said, handing Dad a slip of paper. "We'll give you an escort out of town."

Chicago was immense. I couldn't believe any city could be so big. It was a mecca for the big bands. Looking in the paper, you could take your pick of any number of clubs and venues where big-name bands were playing. But there was no money from Dad.

"Much as I know you'd like ta see some o' these bands, we're runnin' low on cash and we still have a long way to go."

Wandering around that evening, I found myself outside the Chez Paree, where Duke Ellington and his famous orchestra were appearing. Well-dressed people were flooding in so I sort of mingled with a large group and entered with them. I could hear the band playing but I couldn't quite see over a partition into the main room. A cover charge was required to get all the way in and I didn't have it. I just wanted to go back and tell everyone I had seen the Duke.

I grabbed hold of the partition, pulled myself up and there he was, Duke Ellington, smiling graciously. Then someone grabbed me by the back of my pants and I was unceremoniously ushered out. But I had seen the Duke.

Dad bulldozed his way into CBS, taking our scrapbook with him. They were suitably impressed and suggested that Dad bring us all in for an audition a week later. After checking our money, we agreed it would be better to leave Chicago and work our way back through the smaller towns.

"Ya know," Dad said, "ya can't work anywhere in Chicago, 'thout joining the union. Clubs won't let ya in and ya can't do any broadcasting. The union checks all the clubs and if they find anybody don' belong, the club owner can lose his license. Sometimes, they even blow the joint up — this guy was tellin' me."

Dad called the number the policeman had given him, and with sirens wailing, we left Chicago with all flags flying, on our way to Gary, Indiana, and Detroit.

Working our way across southern Michigan, we found some place to perform every night but passing the hat was becoming an uncomfortable way to make money. While this was going on, Dad would sit at the bar bragging about "his kids" to the patrons. He seemed oblivious and completely insensitive. Disquieting inner feelings began to emerge. They were not only concerns that I was experiencing but everyone in the family, except Dad. We were beginning to develop subtle and unexplainable hang-ups.

They started with me, while walking around Chicago. I was conscious of my clothes. Ever since I could remember all our clothes had been handmade, mostly by Mom. Because she was an excellent seamstress we were, more often than not, better dressed than the other kids. Our stage attire had to be attention-getting. Mom spent hours creating configurations of baubles, bangles, and beads for our costumes and it worked. Unfortunately, these sartorial efforts were carried over to our everyday street clothes. We had never felt uncomfortable in Saskatchewan, where we were well known. We were expected to be different.

We had long since graduated to "store bought"shoes, but the rest of our clothes were out of step with the world around us. The people we mingled with in downtown Chicago wore suits and ties, and while our family still attracted a lot of attention it was now for the wrong reasons. My intuition told me it was not because we were being recognized as the famous Harmony Kids from Saskatchewan but rather being perceived as the waifs and strays we were.

Talking with Lloyd, he echoed these new and disquieting feelings. The girls, being younger, were less sensitive. Their street clothes were not unlike their stage clothes except for Kay's tuxedo and Joyce's long gowns. Mom dressed them both in 'cutie-pie' frocks adorned with ribbons and bows, and their hair was always curled. Mom and Dad seemed insensible to the turmoil Lloyd and I were beginning to experience.

Other feelings began to manifest themselves. Lloyd had to work harder at his music than I did. Things which came easily to me required more hours of practice for him. He started to complain. I would hear a new song and work out an arrangement for it. Lloyd resented the extra time it took him to learn all the chords. A gap was growing, not only in our music but between us as brothers.

"Geez," he'd say. "We got enough songs. We could play for the next six months and never havta do a repeat."

"Yeh, but we havta keep up with all the new songs as soon as they come out. What if we get a request?"

"Tell 'em we don't know it. I'm gettin' tired of havin' ta learn new songs ev'ry time you hear somethin' on the radio."

As long as we were performing on stage in a set, rehearsed and disciplined order we felt secure and self-assured. Working our way along, we hadn't done our stage show for months. In bars and night clubs, Dad's contribution was limited to arranging for us to perform. A sequence would be determined, depending on the makeup of the audience, and we all had our moments in the spotlight. We'd generally start with a song which featured both girls, then a short interlude featuring Lloyd and me. When *we* were performing, the girls would clap their hands or stand to each side just smiling. The second song would feature Kay and was usually slow and pretty. The next song was an instrumental with Lloyd and me and, as our musical proficiency grew, we chose more difficult and demanding selections. Then came Joyce's spot and without even trying she stole the show.

Lloyd and I began developing musical complexes. We had no problems when the girls were out front but it became increasingly difficult to hold an audience's attention during our instrumental spots — they were really waiting for the girls. More than that, they were waiting for Joyce.

Lloyd and I had worked out a complex arrangement of the *Poet and Peasant Overture*. It had taken hours of practice and was by far the most ambitious instrumental we had ever attempted. During our first public performance of this piece somebody at the back of the room hollered, "Bring back the girls! Bring back the girls!" We were destroyed. More and more, Lloyd and I began hiding behind the girls.

Then Kay started to feel insecure. When she sang a solo the audience was generally attentive but you could detect a certain restlessness. They were waiting for Joyce. Slowly, Kay began to recede, and before it was over we were all hiding behind Joyce.

Kay began to rebel. "I don't like that song," she'd say when we began rehearsing. "Give it to Joyce; it's more her style."

"It's exactly right for you," I'd say. "You always liked the slower, prettier songs."

"Well, I don't want to sing it as a solo. If you want to do it as a duet, okay, but I don't want sing it by myself."

Joyce was too young to understand what was going on. She was not only the youngest, she had an enchanting personality and enormous natural talent. She had spent her formative years in a fairyland world of "Isn't she cute," and of the four of us she was the most unaware. She only had to walk on stage and she had the audience in the palm of her hand.

As all this confusion began meandering through my mind, there came a realization, a glimmer of understanding of what was going on and what was motivating the people around me. In my struggle to evaluate our obvious hang-ups without mature insight I went back over the facts as I knew them, searching for answers. The relationship which existed between my brother and sisters and the resultant complexes we were developing began to sort themselves out in my mind. Mom, through no fault of her own, had little education in a formal sense. While she could read and write, she had gone from a girl-child to a child bride, and in the first four years of her marriage three children had been born. She just wasn't equipped to deal with the emotional labyrinth we were attempting to negotiate. Mom epitomized everything altruistic. She was the most unselfish and self-abnegated person I have ever known. To give and do for her family while ignoring her own needs was to her what life was all about. She expected nothing in return and her giving pleased and satisfied her.

Dad was totally preoccupied with our becoming successful in the world of entertainment. He was single-minded in this purpose and would not tolerate the smallest deviation which might affect the goals he was determined to achieve. He refused to recognize any of our shortcomings, such as the fact that we bordered on musical illiteracy and the prime reason for our acceptance might be because we were just kids. He equated our talent and ability with those of the biggest names in show business, convinced we were every bit as good as anyone out there and that time would prove him right.

He was stubborn and obstinate and no amount of logic could sway his obsession. His feelings seldom, if ever, were discussed with the family, and as this lack of communication grew it followed that we rarely discussed our feelings with him. He was the boss and he ruled with an iron hand. Only in the choice and style of music we performed did he leave us alone. He was completely inadequate in this one area as we left him farther and farther behind.

He was an unabashed braggart and the cause of many embarrassing moments as he extolled the virtues and talents of "his kids." I have never known a person more certain of the pot of gold waiting for him at the end of the rainbow. His life had been an unending cycle of ups and downs. The fact that we had done well before leaving the west but now had little to show for it was merely another curve in the cycle. He blamed God and the elements for any setbacks in life. In his view, he had not been a failure in any of his endeavors; rather, he had been a victim. While a degree of cynicism would assert itself from time to time he was a generous, outgoing extrovert in his dealings with people *other than the family.* For Dad everything was just fine. We had our own stage show, we could play anywhere, and wherever we stopped was home. The rest of us, however, became more and more conscious of the abnormality of our life-style.

Joyce couldn't remember having any childhood at all. Moving constantly from one place to another, she had never had time to make friends. Hers was a grown-up world with hundreds of fans, but what she wanted, what she needed, was a school buddy or to belong to the Girl Guides.

Sibling rivalry between Joyce and Kay went far deeper than the normal sister relationship. Kay was competing on a professionl level as well, and it was a losing battle. Joyce was naive. She spent her childhood oblivious to what was going on around her and the resultant havoc. It would take years to repair the emotional erosion and how sad for us all because it all became so transparent later.

We crossed back into Canada at the Detroit-Windsor border and headed for Tavistock to meet the Hahns. It was the middle of September but Ontario was still green and alive. The Niagara peninsula, bordered by parts of the Great Lakes, is the richest, most diverse farming and industrial area in Canada. Almost anything can be grown, including tobacco and such fruit as peaches, grapes and plums. We had never seen fruit trees and the only peaches or plums we had ever eaten were out of cans. We passed market gardens scattered all along the route. There were dairy farms and cheese processing plants and canneries with their smokestacks belching.

Small towns supported a myriad of industries such as furniture plants, chocolate factories, plants which manufactured rubber tires, automobiles, and farm machinery. Some farms were dotted with tobacco kilns. It was easy to see that during the worst of the Depression years things could never have been as bad in this part of Canada as they had been in the west, where the only cash crop was wheat.

Though we were now back in Canada it felt alien and strange. Where everything in the west was new and crude, clapboard and tarpaper or logs and sod, southern Ontario was different. Houses were made of bricks and stone. Its people looked comfortable and established. Everything looked 'used' and old. Tombstones in southern Ontario went back into the 1700s and many of them, we were to find, were marked Hahn.

When we arrived in Tavistock all Dad's family were waiting. They were quite impressed with the trailer outfit but their welcome felt forced and illusory. At a welcoming dinner the conversation was dominated by Dad explaining how well we were doing. I sensed a defensive tone when he spoke of our many successes. The meal finally over, we adjourned to the "drawing room" where the real inquisition began.

"Well, Harvey, now that you're finally here, what plans have you made for getting on with the children's education?"

"Whadda ya mean?"

"You can't go on neglecting the children's schooling," one of my aunts persisted, "you're going to have to settle down somewhere and have them all enrolled."

"And live on what?" Dad asked.

My aunt sputtered the beginning of a response as Dad continued. "We've been making a good living with our music and we're very good at it. It wasn't easy getting started but we've reached a point where if we continue working hard, we could become important in show business."

My aunt was making clucking noises.

"The boys did very well with their schooling. They started in Eatonia when Lloyd was five and Bob was only four. They both jumped grade two and they did grades seven and eight in one year. When Bob was only ten, he was in grade nine. Then after we moved up north there weren't any schools."

"And what about the girls?"

"They've been taking 'mail-in' courses through the Saskatchewan government and doing very well. Both of 'em can read and write if that's what ya mean."

"That's not all there is to it, Harvey, and you know it. There's more to education than reading and writing." She clucked to a stop.

Dad restrained himself with difficulty as he explained the problems we had been through and how fortunate we had been even to survive. "I recognize the importance of education," he continued, "but it hasn't been very high on our list of priorities during the last few years. Besides, the kids are learning things being on the road they don't teach in schools."

"I'll bet they have," my aunt smirked.

"We intend to continue a career in show business," Dad said with finality. "If an opportunity presents itself where the kids can go to school, fine, but if it doesn't, the first order of business is to carry on with our music."

The vaunted Hahn reunion was set for the end of September in Waterloo Park, Grandpa would see that everyone was notified in plenty of time.

The next day we arrived in Hamilton and Dad learned quickly that working in Ontario was not going to be easy. No clubs or bars existed where we could just drop in and put on a show. Ontario had the most antiquated liquor laws in North America, and while you could buy liquor in government-owned stores, you could only consume it in the privacy of your own home. With no clubs available, we would have to arrange bookings in a traditional manner in theatres and dance halls.

Our first job in Ontario was as the opening act for a wrestling match in a sports arena in Hamilton. The ring was strung out over a swimming pool and we had to walk a narrow ramp into the ring to do our show. There was a P.A. system but the sound rolled around in the tiled surroundings and kept repeating itself. Even with the bad acoustics, the promoter asked us to do a few more numbers during an intermission. He put us in touch with a promoter in Kitchener where we were booked as part of a wrestling match again and the timing was perfect. On our way, we did a couple of broadcasts in Wingham and picked up a couple of dates through Dad's association with the Elks. What little money we had was fast disappearing. The night of the wrestling match, our opening half-hour was picked up by the radio station as a live remote. Grandpa was sitting in the front row. He had never seen us perform and we could see how pleased and proud he was as the applause echoed through the auditorium. Out of all the relatives who knew we would be appearing locally that night, Grandpa was the only one to show up.

On the day of the reunion we parked beside the bandstand in Waterloo Park. By three o'clock, over 400 Hahns and other relatives were congregated. As they arrived, they took the time to gawk at the trailer outfit and have a few words of welcome with Dad. Speeches were made by some of the elders, one of whom was a minister. The loudspeaker system was barely adequate and we knew we would not be able to perform our magic illusions as the bandstand was circular. The one thing we knew *would* work, aside from our music, was the mental telepathy routine.

The audience was very attentive and we were all quite aware we had a lot to prove to the assembled Hahns. No one could quarrel with our presentation — it was just too slick. Few of them had ever seen an act that was more professional. We covered a broad spectrum of music including some old German folk songs, with many of the older people singing along. But the capper was the mental telepathy bit. By this time we had memorized all the cues and codes. We could not be caught. Dad worked among the picnic tables which surrounded the bandstand and the people were astounded by his amazing communication with Joyce. For years after, we were looked upon with wonder by many of our relatives and by others as some sort of spooks.

Overall, Dad was very disheartened by our reception. He had been away from home for almost 30 years. He was proud of the family he had brought back, *and* their accomplishments. However, many of our new-found relatives frowned on the way we were conducting our lives and made little allowance for what we had been through to get where we were. There was no understanding when Dad attempted to reason with them. He spent little time defending himself, realizing it would be simpler to leave them in their little two-by-four worlds, surrounded by their own small-town definition of 'the right way to live,' and move on.

We headed for Toronto and the Big Time.

Chapter 17

THE BIG TIME FOR US, was not to be Toronto. Our only important date was at the Top Hat in Sunnyside.

Mom's baby arrived in January, 1939, after a very difficult delivery. For the second time, we came very close to losing her. It was weeks before she was allowed to come home with Donnie, the only baby in our family who was born in a hospital — the Toronto Western. The rest of us had all been born at home.

With all the furor in Europe and the imminence of a confrontation with Hitler, things were beginning to boom in Canada. Industrial plants were working around the clock and the Depression, for all intents and purposes, was over. Even with this upturn in the economy we were still having problems trying to find places to work. We had covered all the service clubs. Passing the hat wasn't done in Ontario and while we could find lots of places to perform there were few places where we could make any money.

When Donnie and Mom were well enough to travel we hooked up the trailer and headed north to the mining districts and northern Ontario.

In September, 1939, Canada was at war with Germany.

We were in Sudbury at the time working mining towns as far away as Timmins. We felt more comfortable. We were back with an earthy type of people. We realized that our problem wasn't the attitude of our relatives who frowned on our way of life or the people in Toronto who didn't seem to care. It was us. *We* were the misfits.

Dad was still the law, and he rode roughshod over anyone or anything that stood in the way of our making it to the big time. While we were good at what we were doing we knew that something was missing, and we wouldn't find out what it was until years later.

"I don' wanna hear any more bitchin' an' crabbin' from any of you, anymore," Dad would say, pounding his fist on the table. "There ain't a fam'ly in this whole goddamn country got more goin' fer it than ours. We sure ain't selling' bullshit, we're sellin' talent. You can see it wherever we play. I know, cause I'm sittin' out there an' watchin' the people with their eyes glued on what yer doin' and ya jus' havta listen to the applause to know how much they enjoyed it. If that Nazi bastard and this bloody war don' screw things up, and if we all stick together, there ain't nothin' in the world gonna stop us!" He not only convinced us with these kind of pep talks, he was totally psyched himself.

We went on, night after night, week after week, and we were making a living. By November the weather in the north had turned very cold and we decided to head back to Toronto. On our way back south we stopped in North Bay and did a couple of broadcasts. After the first one, the station received a telephone call from the postmaster in Orillia advising us there was a big bag of mail being held there for the Harmony Kids. It was only then that Dad remembered giving Orillia as a forwarding address. That was before we found we couldn't get our outfit across the border at Sault Ste. Marie. So we stopped in Orillia to pick up or mail. There were hundreds of letters from as far back as Regina and the bag had been held for months. Dad threw it into one of the lockers and we proceeded to Toronto. Christmas was coming and unless something unforseen happened this was going to be a lean Christmas. We were able to get a couple of weeks at the Top Hat again but aside from that, nothing.

One evening we got the bag of mail out of the locker and went through it on the trailer table. Most were requests for songs and dedications forwarded by the radio station in Regina. Some were requests for pictures, some to wish us well but amongst the deluge was a letter from Young & Rubicam, the advertising agency which produced "We The People" in New York. It was in reply to the snarky letter Dad had written from Lake Of The Woods, months before. First, they apologized for letting the other family make the claim of being the most trailer-travelled family in North America. The letter closed by asking if we were available to come to New York to appear on the show.

Dad wrote immediately and they replied with a telegram. Could we be in New York the following Tuesday? We were to wire our availability immediately and advise how we would be travelling.

Dad replied that we would be driving.

"I'm gonna drive this rig up Broadway an' park it in Times Square — right in the middle of the Great White Way," Dad said as we pulled out of Toronto headed for Buffalo.

When we woke up the next morning Buffalo was covered in eight inches of new snow and western New York state had ground to a halt.

Dad wired New York and they wired back, instructing us to go to the railway station — prepaid tickets were waiting and a man from the agency would meet the train when it arrived.

We had entered the United States on a week's visitors permit. We left the trailer outfit in a parking lot after paying a week's parking in advance. We took the bare essentials — our scrap book and instruments — and headed for the railway station. We needed two taxis to get us there. When we boarded the train, we had less than $3 among us. As soon as we arrived in New York we knew everything would be taken care of and, somehow, $3 would get us through. The money was spent for milk for the baby on the train. The rest of us went fourteen hours with nothing to eat.

With the huge snowfall, the train to New York was delayed. When we pulled into Grand Central Station it was three in the morning. A very kind man from the program staff was there to meet us. Dad explained that we hadn't eaten all day and when we arrived at the Lincoln Hotel on the corner of 45th Street and 8th Avenue, he insisted the dining room be opened and we could order anything we wanted. Before leaving he said that someone would be around at noon the next day to take us to rehearsals and that we could order anything we wanted in the hotel, just pick up the phone and ask for room service. The program would pay for everything. He gave Dad $100 spending money and said goodnight.

Before we went to bed Lloyd and I walked the one block to Times Square. The impression endured for years. New York was overwhelming. Even in the middle of the night you could sense an excitement that exists nowhere else in the world. The huge animated and glittering signs around Times Square made an unforgettable imprint. The theatre marquees showed names that just couldn't be real. These were not movies, the people were actually here. Here indeed was the fantasy land of Aunt Carrie's True Story magazines and I could reach out and touch it.

On the button at noon, the phone rang to tell us the man from the program was in the lobby. We grabbed our instruments and followed him to a waiting limousine. It seemed kind of silly having to take a limousine the short distance to the studio. We could easily have walked.

There was no orchestra, just a piano player and a black man singing *Serenade* by Enrico Toselli. His powerful tenor filled the almost-empty theatre but it was the sensitive playing of the piano accompanist that caught my attention as he flawlessly chased the soaring voice through to the end of the piece. The black man would be opening the program and his story was that he worked as a window washer, but had stopped 5,000 commuters by singing Toselli's *Serenade* in the concourse of the Pennsylvania Station.

Two music arrangers were sitting in the front row writing furiously on large pads of music-scoring paper. A girl kept track of timings on a stopwatch. I found out later that between the time the arrangers started writing down the notes the black man was singing and the dress rehearsal, they would score complete arrangements for all the music to be performed that night for the full orchestra. To me this was incredible, with the broadcast only hours away.

We were called next. There was a sea of microphones around the stage. The girl with the clipboard said: "The two boys on this mike, both on this side. Work out to the audience. The girls will use this one," she continued, walking to a second microphone. "What's your name, honey?"

"Joyce."

"We'll need an eight inch rise for the little one," she hollered into the wings. "We'll get a little box for you to stand on or they won't even see you over the footlights." She patted Joyce on the head and disappeared into the wings.

We were about to be a part of one of the biggest programs on network radio and I had the feeling that this was where *the* standards were set. I wondered how we were going to measure up.

We had chosen *Oh Johnny* which was very popular at the time. While it was basically a solo for Joyce, I had arranged it in such a way that we all had some 'ooohs' and 'aaahs' stuck in here and there and Kay played her small guitar.

"Okay, Hahn family — let's hear a run-through for timing," the scriptgirl shouted.

We went into the number and didn't make one mistake. There was scattered applause from the 20 or so people in the theatre. Even the blasé piano player applauded. The two arrangers were looking up at us, smiling, and the script girl was dancing around. "Dynamite! — Dynamite! — Don't change a thing," she said as she gave both Joyce and Kay a hug. "Two minutes and eighteen seconds — perfect!"

One of the arrangers motioned for me to come and sit beside him. I took off my accordion and found my way down the steps. "I don't think we should use any orchestra at all," he said. "Maybe add bass and drums — give it a good feeling."

"You're right," the second arranger said. "We'll need eight bars with a repeat sign as a run-off over applause 'cause these kids're gonna kill 'em tonight."

"You've done this before, eh kid?" the first one grinned.

"Not *Oh Johnny* — this is our first time with this song, but yeh, we've done quite a bit of broadcasting."

"I didn't even know they had stations up there in Canada."

When we arrived back at the theatre for the dress rehearsal, we were greeted by a 35-piece orchestra and the sound was unbelievable. The black man's rendition of Toselli's *Serenade* soared above the strings and woodwinds and was a far cry from what we had listened to at the piano rehearsal.

We were handed copies of the script and a girl went over the questions with each of us to make sure we had the answers down pat. She was friendly and super-efficient.

"Try and sound as natural as you can when Mr. Heatter talks to you," she said. "Make it sound conversational and relaxed." Most of the interviewing would be between Gabriel Heatter and Dad. The rest of us only had one or two lines each.

"Okay Hahn family," someone hollered, and we took our places at the microphones and waited for the signal to begin. I kept my eyes riveted on a man wearing earphones with his hand raised. He flung his arm in our direction and we went into the introduction. The bass and drums joined in. We were only a few bars into the vocal, with Joyce singing her tail off, when there was a loud, static-like sound as someone on a talkback from the control-room interrupted us.

"Segue into the next segment and have the Hahn family go into Rehearsal 'A' backstage," the voice said.

We stopped playing and I wondered what had gone wrong. I was positive none of us had played any wrong notes and I knew we had checked the tuning carefully.

Two men, obviously very upset, were waiting for us backstage. "There's been a strike call by ASCAP," one said, "and you'll have to find another song for the show." None of us knew what he was talking about.

"We don't have very much time to explain," the second man said, "but basically, the story is this: Almost all songs are written by members of ASCAP and they've called a strike on the networks, which means we're not allowed to perform any ASCAP songs. That includes *Oh Johnny*."

"So, we'll do a different song," Dad said.

"It's not that easy. Almost any song you can think of was written by a member of ASCAP. Do the kids know any Stephen Foster songs?"

Dad looked over at me. "We know all of Stephen Foster's songs," I replied, "but surely there must be something else we can do on a program as important as this." I named several songs.

"You can't do any of them — they're all ASCAP."

The rehearsal pianist rushed in with a handful of music manuscript. "Here's a bunch of new songs that aren't ASCAP, but can you learn one in time for the broadcast?"

"If you work with us until we get the notes down, we'll have it ready on time," I said.

He went over to a small upright piano and started running through the song, singing along in a gravelly voice so we could hear the lyrics. We stopped him when we heard *There'll Be Some Changes Made*. A half-hour later, we did it onstage so they could get a timing. Then we went back into the rehearsal room and kept working on it until we were called for the show. One of the arrangers sat quietly as we rehearsed and wrote out parts for the bass and drums.

We discovered later that ASCAP, the performing rights society that controlled almost all of the songs in the U.S. was having a big fight with the American broadcasters. Because of its popularity, "We The People" was one of the shows picked where no ASCAP songs could be performed. This resulted in the beginnings of Broadcast Music Incorporated, which was structured by the broadcasting industry in an attempt to offset what they felt were unreasonable demands by ASCAP. I was to learn more about these matters in later years but at the time, the whole fiasco was nothing but confusion.

By showtime, we were ready for the song. We watched from the wings as Harry Von Zell, the announcer, did the audience 'warm-up.' The orchestra had not run through the themes during the dress rehearsal as the producer knew the timings from previous shows.

The theatre was packed and when the red lights went on all over the house, signalling we were on the air, and the orchestra went into the opening fanfare we were all nervous for the first time in many months.

VON ZELL . . .
SANKA COFFEE presents WE THE PEOPLE
(THEME)
HEATTER . . .
Good evening everyone. This is Burgess Meredith speaking for Gabriel Heatter welcoming you to WE THE PEOPLE for SANKA COFFEE. Tonight you'll meet a family of musicians who've travelled fifty thousand miles in a trailer. And a taxi cab driver is going to bring you some never-before-told stoies about J.P. Morgan. You'll meet a colored man who sang before an audience of 5,000 commuters in Pennsylvania Station. You'll meet Colonel "Wild Bill" Donovan, war-time Commander of the famous regiment the Fighting 69th! And with him is one of Hollywood's best-loved stars — Pat O'Brien! These and many more — real people come to tell experiences you hear only when WE THE PEOPLE SPEAK.

This is a transcript of Page One of the script. For some reason, Gabriel Heatter did not do the show. His place was taken by a much younger man named Burgess Meredith, After Parker Watkins, the window-washer, performed his *Serenade,* Siegfried Blum, who was J. P. Morgan's chauffeur, was interviewed. Then came Zebulon Tilton, the 74-year-old skipper of a two-masted schooner who had an interesting story to tell about a lady who waited 50 years to marry him. Next came a lady named Rose McMullin who was presented with the American Legion Gold Medal for Bravery, 1940, by Colonel Theodore Roosevelt Jr., one of the founders of the American Legion. Then it was our turn.

Burgess Meredith was warm and friendly. The over-written and melodramatic script sounded genuine the way he read it and his timing was superb. We did the musical number with no mistakes and enjoyed the help of both the bass player and drummer. The full orchestra played a short 'run-off' of the same song over the applause when we finished. Watching the rest of the show, we knew we had done our work well.

The closing segment featured Colonel "Wild Bill" Donovan of the Fighting 69th. The motion picture of the same name was opening on Broadway that week and Pat O'Brien, who played the role of Father Duffy was on the show.

When the show ended we had our picture taken with Pat O'Brien. I've often wondered if big stars realize how important it can be for some unknown to be shown with them. Our picture took a few seconds out of his life and opened countless doors for us over many years.

As the theatre emptied, a flashily-dressed little man introduced himself to Dad. "I'm a booking agent. If you people're gonna be in the New York area, gimme a call. There's gotta be a lotta work out dere fer a small group like yers." He gave Dad his card.

The limousine driver was waiting to take us back to the hotel. A man came over to Dad to tell him he would stop by the hotel the next morning to settle all the bills and that the program would be paying our hotel rooms until the end of the week. He also gave Dad an envelope with $200 spending money.

The day after the show was a tremendous psychological let-down. All sorts of people had been looking after us, making sure we had everything we needed. We had been picked up in big cars and deposited safely back at our hotel; we had been doted over and showered with accolades; we had been applauded and patted with affection; we had been complimented and adored; and suddenly it was over.

Without consulting any of us, Dad went across the street and arranged to rent rooms at 261 West 45th Street. Next, he went to Grand Central Station and cashed in our return tickets to Buffalo. He took the ferry to

Ellis Island, which was still the major port of entry for immigrants to the United States. The next day we all had to go to Ellis Island with Dad to appear before an immigration officer. Luckily, he had heard us on "We The People" and he extended our permit for a month. For the initial period we had to report at Ellis Island each month, then we were told only to report if we changed our address.

To me, it was all very exciting. We hadn't bumbled our way to New York. We had arrived, all expenses paid, because someone felt we had an important story to tell. "We The People" was an important calling card. With the tremendous professional aura exuded by the broadcasting fraternity in New York, I was more and more conscious of our musical shortcomings. We were a bunch of country bumpkins in a very sophisticated city. But Dad didn't know this or if he did, it only fired his ambition more. He knew we were now where he could make it all happen and he grabbed for the brass ring as though we were the only people riding on the merry-go-round.

We moved into the rooms across from the hotel on the Sunday following the broadcast. Although a sign No Cooking Allowed was prominently displayed in the hallway, the first thing Dad bought was an electric hot plate. Next was a crib for the baby.

Two beds folded into the walls and a bedraggled old chesterfield opened into a double bed. The place was alive with cockroaches — something we had never seen before. The landlady gave Mom some white powder to spread around but it did little to allay the invasion. She put mosquito netting over the crib to keep the cockroaches away from the baby.

We ate a lot of Chinese food as there was an inexpensive restaurant downstairs. The hot plate was only used to keep food warm or re-heat it. We had an old icebox which we used for milk.

All in all, when we looked around, things weren't all that bad. The rooms were pretty rundown but we had a lot more room than we had had in the trailer. The beds were bigger and although a little lumpy, quite comfortable. We had our own "toilet" so we couldn't complain about that, and we lived right in the core of the most exciting city in the world. Even the cockroaches were tolerable — better cockroaches than blackflies any day as far as I was concerned. The street was noisy with the constant traffic and the honking of annoyed drivers, but after a while we even got used to that.

Dad sent me over to CBS to see if any mail had arrived as a result of the broadcast. Among some fan letters was one from the parking lot owner in Buffalo advising that the immigration people had had our trailer outfit towed back to Canada because we had exceeded the time limit set when we entered the States. A bill was included to cover the towing charges. Another letter came from the owner of a parking lot in Fort Erie, Ontario, advising us the outfit was now parked in his lot and would we kindly remit the first month's fees. We didn't have the money so Dad ignored the notices. It was never his intention to ignore these bills indefinitely but somehow we never seemed to have the money to pay them. The bills from Fort Erie got bigger and bigger and more impossible to pay. We never saw the trailer again. We heard some transients broke into it, and that it was ransacked and destroyed by fire.

The young lady at the CBS reception desk was very friendly. She asked if I would like to go to any other CBS shows and over the next few months, I was able, through the CBS and other network ticket offices to see most of the big network shows. Harry Von Zell was everywhere. He was the announcer on three or four shows a week.

I went to the Burns and Allen Show a number of times but my favourite was the Fred Allen Show. He was a truly funny man and the characters on Allen's Alley have never been duplicated. We went time and again to see ''We The People'' and although all the big programs had orchestras I never ceased to be amazed by the musical excellence of that one. All the broadcasts were free, and as I went from one to another I realized all the more how far we still had to go before we would be in the same league. Not so with Dad, who was convinced we were ready for anything. He came home one afternoon all excited to tell us we had an audition for NBC. We would be trying for a feature spot on a major new show being considered by the network.

The next day we were ushered into a small audition studio at NBC. At one end of the studio was what looked like a black window but you couldn't see through it. We were sitting there, waiting, when a voice came booming over a 'talk-back.'

''Okay, let's get on with it!''

We couldn't see anybody but we assumed that somewhere behind the black glass, people were watching us.

''What about mikes?'' Dad asked.

''Don't worry about mikes,'' the unseen voice boomed.

We were about eight bars into our first song when the voice on the talk-back interrupted us. ''Can you do anything slower?''

We went into *Mood Indigo*. After a few bars, the voice interrupted us again.

''Can you do any original songs — something you've written yourselves?''

Dad stood up awkwardly looking for a microphone. He looked as though he was talking to the ceiling as he explained: ''We have a few original songs about the north but most of them have a kinda country feelin — here's one called *The Loon Lake Trail.*"

We heard someone laughing as the voice came back on. "Okay, let's hear a few bars of *The Loon Lake Trail,* the voice said, with measured exaggeration on each word.

We had hardly finished the introduction when the voice began to interrupt again. It was very intimidating because it was very loud and it's impossible to communicate with someone you can't see, especially when the person is as ill-mannered as this person was. Dad was seething as he motioned for us to pack up our instruments.

Looking into the black window, he exploded. "How would ya like to stick the whole NBC network up yer ass and some day when I got a few minutes I'm gonna write a book on NBC called "Who Needs It." I'll try an' remember ta send ya a copy."

From that day on, we never did another audition.

Dad called the flashily-dressed little man who had introduced himself the night of the broadcast and said he was a booking agent. "Sammy" was very pleased to hear from us and assured Dad that he could get us all kinds of jobs in the New York area. "Gimme a coupla days. Lemme see what I can come up with. In the meantime, why don'cha bring the kids 'round to the office — meet my partner, Rose."

We trooped over to a third-floor walkup on 9th Avenue to discuss our future with Sammy and Rose. Sammy was Jewish. He must have weighed all of a hundred pounds and he couldn't have been a inch over five feet. Rose was Italian. She had been a strip-tease dancer when she married Sammy and though now well into her forties, she still did the odd stag.

Their office was adorned with autographed pictures; mostly of burlesque queens and comedians. We were a little embarrassed by the pictures of semi-nude girls smiling down at us. Burlesque had been closed down in New York and Sammy admitted things were not all that good in the booking business. He and Rose booked an array of schlock acts into third and fourth-rate clubs. "I'll have to do some scoutin' 'round for you people — what with the kids and all," he said. "Mos' o'tha clubs where we got connections wouldn' be right fer ya. Lemme think 'bout it — I'll come up with somethin'."

They were warm, kind people and when we needed it most they always came up with a gig. The money was never that good but in the beginning they had us working three or four nights a week. But the William Morris Agency they weren't.

I guess we'd been clubbing around for a month or so when Sammy dropped in, all excited. "I think I jus' struck oil," he said. "Got'cha a booking — three nights a week over on Madison, near 74th Street. Nice guy runs the joint and he caters to a perty jazzy clientele. Ya can't pass the hat though as he won' stand fer any buskin' in the joint. Wants ta see how yas work out and if he likes ya, we'll work outta deal fer a sal'ry."

We opened the next Thursday and Sammy was right. The clientele was above average and the boss liked us. While the salary wasn't all that much, at least it was all going to the same place and we could get along very well. Besides, the tips we received for playing request numbers sometimes amounted to more than our salary. Sammy and Rose would drop in at least one night of the three we worked, and not just to collect their commission. They would sit around giving us hints on how to improve our presentation.

"You kids is fantastic," Sammy would say. "I gotta lotta irons in the fire and all I need is ta get the right cat in here ta see ya an' you'll be on yer way. Did I tell ya, I think I got ya booked on Major Bowes? Should hear back any day now."

Things were too good to last. One night, after we'd finished our first set, a man and a woman came over to our table and introduced themselves. "We're from the Garry Society," the lady said. "Ever heard of it?"

Dad wasn't in the club that night and it was up to us to cope with problems. "Never heard of it," I answered.

The man took over. "The job of the Garry Society is to make sure that no under-age children are exploited in the New York area when it comes to show business. Children can work, but only if very rigid requirements are met."

I sensed I was in over my head and suggested he would have to talk with Dad or our agent as we only played and sang. "We don't bother with the business end of what we do. Our agent does all that."

"Who's your agent?" the lady asked.

Lloyd gave them Sammy's name and they left.

The next night, Sammy came in before we went on.

"You can't go on tonight. If the Garry Society comes in again, and you're still here, they'll start proceedings where the club could lose their license and they can put me out of business in this town forever."

Sammy told us he could handle some out-of-town bookings for us but he wouldn't be able to book us anywhere in New York now that the society knew of his connection with us. The job folded and our association with Sammy ended, except for a one-nighter in Poughkeepsie and the booking on Major Bowes Amateur Hour.

We were offered one of the Major Bowes tours. The pay would be $140 a week ($35 for each of us) but we would have to pay our own travel expenses. When we sat down to work this out with Sammy, we all agreed the deal was ridiculous. While we turned down the tour part of it, we did do the broadcast and had our picture taken with Major Bowes. This became another important calling card in our portfolio.

With the Garry Society on our tail, we started going farther afield. We'd leave our rooms around seven o'clock each night, all dressed in our costumes. In New York, this didn't attract any attention. We'd get on the subway and ride it to the end of the line, somewhere like Far Rockaway. Then we'd wander around, carrying our instruments until we found a bar that looked promising and Dad would go in and see if they allowed busking, which was just another term for passing the hat. Busking was quite acceptable with most club owners and we started doing very well. Many of the clubs we wandered into became regular stops as the weeks went by. We'd get home around two in the morning, dragging our tails. These were physically taxing nights. My accordion was by far the heaviest instrument, and because I played it I was expected to carry it.

As time went on, we found that trying to find places to play early in the week wasn't worth it. We got it down to Friday, Saturday and sometimes Sunday, and it wasn't unusual for us to work as many as three or four clubs in the same night. Working in the remote areas from subway stops like Pelham Bay, Van Cortland Park, Coney Island and the Far Rockaways, we never ran into anyone from the Garry Society but we *were* aware that we were being watched as we left our rooms some nights. This led to a game of cops and robbers and we devised numerous tricks to avoid detection. We'd sneak through Shubert's Alley, lose ourselves in the milling theatre crowds, and catch the subway on the next street.

CHAPTER 18

I WAS NOW TWENTY YEARS OLD. When we left the north, I wasn't quite sixteen. Behind us lay thousands of miles and hundreds of one-nighters in club after club and town after town. It was a more puritan time, and while we had our share of groupies who would hang around after a show, I just wasn't aggressive enough to develop any kind of relationship with a girl in the few hours we'd be in a town. I was quite inexperienced and terribly naive.

New York was inundated with pretty girls who had gravitated there hoping to make it in show business or the fashion world. Many were assertive and ambitious, and to tide themselves over, waiting for that big break, many worked at menial jobs. Some of the prettiest girls in New York worked clearing tables at the Automats or behind the counter at Nedick's Orange Juice stands.

I'd never had a girl friend and I would back off if a girl so much as smiled at me. I was shy and withdrawn. Even with all the excitement going on around us, New York was a lonesome town for me.

Standing outside the Circus Bar of the Piccadilly Hotel one evening, listening to The Three Suns playing *Twilight Time*, I was conscious of another young guy looking in the window too. We got to chatting and I detected a strange accent. He took all the 'R's off where they should be and put them on where they didn't belong.

"You from New York?" I asked.

"Boston — name's Bruce — you?"

"Name's Bob," I said. "Canada."

"Canader, I was there with my folks. Drove up to Montreal. Had to be the craziest drivahs in the world up thah — we just pahked the cah and took taxis. Wanta coffee?"

We had three or four coffees. He had come to New York to make it in commercial art. Though I was to know him for well over a year, I never did get to know his last name. He told me he had been in New York for almost two years and was still waiting for his first assignment.

When I asked him how he managed to get by, he explained there were a million ways to make a living in New York.

We left the restaurant and walked down 45th Street towards Times Square.

"Like ta go to one of the shows?" Bruce asked.

"You gotta be jokin'." To go to a Broadway show was out of the question. I'd stood and watched the taxis and limousines pull up night after night, disgorging their beautiful people. The admission prices were ridiculous.

Most Broadway shows are split into two halves and as we walked by it was intermission time when a lot of the patrons go out in the alley for a breath of air or a cigarette, or grab a fast drink in one of the bars. A warning bell sounds to let everyone know the second half is about to start.

When the bell ran Bruce grabbed me and elbowed his way into the milling crowd. We got caught up in the flow and ended up inside the theatre. No one was taking tickets.

"Find yahself a seat and I'll see ya aftah the final curtain," he whispered, slipping away quickly.

I waited until everyone was seated and found a single empty seat. Quite a few single seats were interspersed throughout the theatre and I was to find this held true even in the biggest hit shows. People went to the theatre in twos, threes, fours, or larger groups. Rarely did anyone go alone. Single seats were always available and impossible to sell. Tuesdays, Wednesdays and Thursdays I started going to Broadway shows. Only once did I get bounced for not having a ticket. I have yet to meet anyone who has seen the last half of more Broadway shows than me.

The Paramount Theatre played first-run movies and had a live stage show featuring all the name bands. I saw them all. If you went in before ten in the morning, it only cost 25 cents and you could stay as long as you wanted. I saw *Gone With The Wind* the day it opened on Broadway, staying up all night to get a good place in the line and sleeping through the first couple of shows.

I saw Tommy Dorsey, live, with Frank Sinatra and the Pied Pipers, Glenn Miller, Harry James, Duke Ellington, Kay Kaiser, Benny Goodman, Bob Crosby, Claude Thornhill, Count Basie — just to name a few.

Sometimes I went alone but more often with Bruce. When I wasn't working we were constantly together. He sure knew his way around. He knew all the hucksters on the different corners along Broadway and on 42nd Street. He knew all the ticket-takers at the peep-shows and girlie-shows and we never had to pay to get into these places. Bruce also knew most of the girls who plied their trade in the Times Square area.

"If ya see anything ya like," he'd say, jokingly, "let me know. Maybe I can get it wholesale."

Although I knew he was being facetious, I did tell him about one girl who worked on the corner of 47th Street and who I thought was the prettiest girl I'd ever seen.

"Her name's Elisa," Bruce said quickly. "She's biding her time waiting for a part in a chorus. Says she's a dancah — who knows. She's from Gary, Indianer, or some place just outside o' Chicago."

We ambled along with Bruce chattering away.

"Everybody in this town is from somewah. Nobody is from New Yahk. No mattah where ya from or what ya aspah to, if ya really wanna make it big, ya have to come to New Yahk.

We got to the corner of 47th Street and Bruce stopped. Elisa wasn't there and I was kind of relieved as the thought of meeting her made me nervous.

"Let's go in and have a coffee — she won't be long."

He was right. Elisa came breezing around the corner and Bruce tapped on the window to get her attention. She came in and sat down.

"Hi, Bruce! What's up?" she asked, with a smile that lit up the room.

"I wancha to meet a friend of mine who thinks you're very pretty. Bob, say hello to Elisa."

"Hi," I said, sticking my hand out. I must have been blushing.

Bruce started a non-stop conversation to put me more at ease. God, she was gorgeous! As Bruce and she kidded around, laughing and chatting about nothing in particular, I just sat gazing at her. She smiled constantly and unless she was putting me on, I had the feeling she liked me.

We became a regular threesome the night I wasn't working. I found myself resenting Bruce's being there. I was becoming possessive. Elisa was only eighteen years but with all the necessary accoutrements that attract men. It really bothered me when we'd finish our coffee and she's say things like, "Gotta get back to work — see you tomorrow."

I'd watch her from a distance and in a matter of minutes, she'd disappear up 47th Street with some guy. One night when Bruce wasn't there, I brought the subject up. Her response was so matter-of-fact it even made sense to me.

"It's another way to make a living. Nothing more. You see 'em once — you do your thing — you get your money — he's happy, and that's all there is to it. You don't even remember what they look like."

I began to hate all the unknown men who, for a few dollars, had access to this beautiful girl who was beginning to mean so much to me. I wanted her more than any of them and I told her so. She just smiled.

"You're the best friend I've got in this big dumb city. I don't look forward to anything as much as having coffee with you the nights you come around. So let's not screw it up by making suggestions you'll only regret. You're not one of the out-of-town rubes looking for a good time. You're very special so let's not spoil it."

Elisa was my first real girl-friend, the first love in my life, and first loves are always remembered. Our relationship never got beyond the coffees we shared except for one memorable Sunday afternoon in Central Park. Even then we did nothing more than hold hands as we wandered through the leaves. I wish the story had a happy ending, but it doesn't. It has no ending at all. I'd known Elisa for over a year and one day, she was gone. Bruce helped me check but we were never able to find where she had gone. I do know a part of me went with her but a part of her stayed with me for a long, long time.

One evening, Bruce and I wandered over to 42nd Street.

"Let's go up and see if anybody's around to hustle," he said, as we went up a flight of stairs to pool hall. I'd never told him about my pool playing.

"Evah played?"

"A little, but not since I've been in New York."

"Come on — my treat," and we busied ourselves picking out cues.

The pool room must have had 50 tables but there was only one snooker table tucked away in a far corner. Nobody played snooker in New York, or so it seemed. All the other tables were the Boston types. The game played most was "break-ball." A good player could run balls down the edges of the table, which was almost impossible on a snooker table. The pockets on the Boston tables were much bigger and you really had to hit a bad shot for the ball not to go in.

While the balls were numbered from one to fifteen, they were not played in numerical order. A player could shoot any ball he chose. You played until fourteen balls had been pocketed and the one remaining ball was used as a 'break ball' for the next shot. The objective was to shoot the last remaining ball, make it, and hopefully break the neatly tracked fourteen balls. Then you just kept going. Good players could run more than one rack if they played the right position on the last ball — the "break ball."

I watched Bruce chalking his cue. He broke, didn't make anything, and I "ran the table."

"Jesus Christ, kid! Where in hell did ya learn to play like that?" He eyed me questioningly with more than a little admiration.

We played for a couple of hours and by the time we were ready to quit, there were a couple of dozen people standing around watching. One of them was the boss, Pucci.

As we were racking our cues, Pucci looked me over carefully, and said, "No charge — it's on the house. Any time you wanna play, jus' come in an' hang aroun'. It won't cost ya nothin' — win or lose. I'll fix ya up wid a game anytime if ya can't find nobody to play witcha."

On off-nights, I started hanging around the pool room near the first two tables where the big money games were played. The lights over those tables were brighter, the cushions more alive and the playing surface immaculate. When things were slow, Pucci and I would play. I'd try all kinds of two and three-cushion bank shots and combinations. Pucci was impressed. My game came back quickly as I began to get the feel again and it was a real pleasure playing on the two front tables. I found a cue I especially liked which Pucci put aside for me. With it, I could get tremendous action on the cue ball, and I'd show off by pointing to Pucci where the cue ball was going to end up after every shot.

One night a guy came in looking for a game and Pucci motioned me over.

"This gentleman is lookin' for a game — wouldja like ta accommodate 'im?" He gave me a discreet wink as I went over to get my cue.

We flipped a coin, and I had to break. I didn't make anything. The stranger took off his jacket and I caught a glimpse of a big belt buckle. He had a midwestern accent. Pucci had warned me about professional hustlers who knew all the tricks including looking like country hicks.

The guy played pretty well. We made eight balls in a row. I could see Pucci watching intently and as I walked past, he whispered, "Let 'im win."

I promptly missed the next shot and the man, who said his name was Jack, ran the rest of the table.

He felt pretty good and wanted to know if I cared to make the next game a little more interesting. When I told him I didn't have any money for betting, Pucci jumped in.

"One hundred points — I'll take twenty-five bucks on the kid."

"Yer on," Jack said confidently as we flipped for break. Jack won the toss and asked me to break. I didn't make anything and he promptly ran three racks. He was much better than I had him figured. Pucci again whispered to me to let him win. Jack had little trouble reaching his hundred points and beat me handily. Pucci asked for a chance to get his money back.

"Anythin' ya want — name yer poison," Jack drawled as he busied himself chalking his cue.

"Double 'r nuttin'."

"Ya gotta bet, sir."

This meant we would be playing for 50 bucks. Pucci sidled over and whispered discreetly, "Let 'im win, but make it close."

I pulled off a couple of bank shots to keep a string going but they looked more like flukes than planned plays. "Lucky again," I said, as I proceeded to run two racks before missing what looked like an easy shot. I had 87 on the board when Jack went over the hundred mark.

"Ya gotta lil' lucky there, kid. Damn near beat me," Jack said as he chalked his cue, waiting for Pucci's next move.

"I've only got time for one more game," I interjected. "I gotta go ta work."

"If the kid has the time, let's make the game three hunnert points," Pucci suggested.

"How much ya wanna bet, sir?" Jack queried, his face beaming.

"I'll leave it up ta you."

"Last game, how'd ya like ta make it 500?"

Pucci looked over at me with barely a flicker, but it was enough.

"All right with me," I said, "it's your money."

Jack only had five shots during the game, and on three of them I had him frozen to the rail and he missed. He had less than a hundred points when I went over the three hundred mark. Jack was ready for more but I insisted I had to go. I waited across the street until I saw him leave then went back upstairs. Pucci gave me 50 dollars.

"Ya did good, kid."

I was in. Now I had a private source of income I could more or less count on when nothing else was happening. The nights we weren't working I'd hang around the pool hall and Bruce would usually sit there and watch. On my way to the pool hall I'd go out of my way to walk the two extra blocks over to 47th Street, just in case. There was a new girl on the corner.

I looked very young for my 20 years and more like a country boy than a pool hustler. Pucci had little trouble setting up games for me and only once, out of the dozens of players we hustled, did we ever get taken. I knew I was into something with that guy though and I tipped Pucci off to be careful with his bets. Pucci lost a hundred bucks.

It must have been seven o'clock one morning and I'd been playing since nine o'clock the night before. When the game was over, Bruce suggested we go and have breakfast.

"Besides," he said, "I wanna show ya something."

While we were eating, Bruce said, "You've often asked me what I do fah a living — well this mahning I'm gonna show ya."

He led the way down 42nd Street to 7th Avenue and along to 34th Street. "You stay on this side of the street and watch me."

He crossed over to the other side. People were opening their stores and as they fumbled with the multiple locks, Bruce went into his act. He must have been very good because only one person out of the dozen or so he approached turned him down. He was bumming. Within a half-hour, he had 30 dollars.

"Ya get ya spiel down pat — don't look like a panhandlah — project an air of embarrassment, like it's sort of degrading to be doing what yah doing — nevah too pushy — always say sir and try to sound sincere." He projected a $30 smile.

Bruce was very good at his profession. That's all he ever did all the time I knew him.

When summer came, we took the boat excursion down the Jersey shore. One of these outings stopped over in a resort area called Red Bank. While the rest of us sat on the beach, Dad took our scrap-book and went looking for a club. Ever since the Garry Society chased us into the New York boondocks, we hadn't worked in any nice clubs. That day Dad booked us into two clubs and we played up and down the Jersey shore the rest of that summer. When fall came and the resorts closed down, we found there were dozens of clubs just across the Hudson River from New York, in places like Jersey City, Hoboken, West New York, Union City, even Secaucus, with the smell of the pig farms.

Dad, as he was scouting around, got us a booking at the Hudson Theatre in Union City. We didn't know it was a burlesque house until we got there. But there we were, sandwiched in between the comedians, the strippers and the candy salesmen. When New York closed down burlesque the industry moved to New Jersey. The Hudson Theatre was one of the more important venues on the burlesque circuit and all the bigtime strippers and many name comedians played there.

In Union City we found our home. Across the street from the Hudson Theatre was a club called The Red Robin and the night we closed at the Hudson Dad arranged for us to busk the Red Robin. Everybody from the theatre came over to make sure we would have a friendly audience. The cast had adopted the two girls. They doted over Joyce and treated Kay like a younger sister.

The patrons of the Red Robin were pretty rowdy and the place was jammed. Maybe because Joyce was so tiny the room quietened down when we started our set.

The owners, Dave and Gus, watched, fascinated.

"We really like what we jus' saw," Dave said afterwards, "and we'd like to have ya work for us, steady."

"I don' know," Dad said. "We do pretty well movin' 'round from place ta place and we never havta worry 'bout gettin' fired. The money'd havta be pretty good 'fore we could consider somethin' steady."

"Look," said Gus, "how much can ya make buskin'? Thirty, forty, even fifty bucks a night an' ya gotta break your tails runnin' all over the place ta do it."

"We'll pay ya two hundred a week — clear." Dave said.

"An' I'll lay ya odds, ya do better'n that with tips." Gus added.

"Ya can start next Monday — whadda ya say?"

Dad looked around at us and he must have read the enthusiasm written all over our faces.

No more subways, buses, ferries, and lugging our instruments all over the place, I thought.

Dad was still noncommittal. "I don' know — tonight the people were great. What happens if a bunch o' sailors come in from the docks an' start tearin' the joint apart. Sure no place fer kids."

"Between me an' Gus and Al, the bartender, we don' have no problems at the Red Robin. We can have the place flooded with cops in five minutes. That jus' ain't one of our problems."

"Why don't we try it," Joyce chimed in. "The people are really nice."

The next day we moved out of the rooms in New York and into a nice apartment at 412 - 37th Street just down the street from the Red Robin. Dave had big pictures of us made up and a huge flyer announcing our opening.

The world, except for the United States, was at war. But that didn't mean the States wasn't involved. Convoys were running the U-boat blockades in the North Atlantic and many of these ships were loaded in Hoboken. The seamen who ran these blockades were being paid a lot of money and when they docked one of the first places many of them headed for was the Hudson Burlesque Theatre. We got most of them in the Red Robin, either before or after the show. And Dave and Gus had been right about the tips.

The head bartender was Al Bernardi. He was a big, jovial, outgoing man with a permanent smile etched on his face. Some of the seamen who had been cooped up for days on a floating bomb on the North Atlantic run vented their tensions by over-indulging. Al had a knack of pacifying the most belligerent type by reasoning with them in his quiet and unruffled manner. He looked after us as though we were his own children, especially the girls. Kay was no longer a child. She was almost sixteen and growing into a beautiful young lady. Al watched over her like a hawk the minute he detected any interest that went beyond appreciation for her singing. And Dave and Gus were never far away.

We had a neat, carpeted stand built for us in the centre of the circular bar. It turned slowly, and while we were far enough back to feel protected, we were, nevertheless, very close to the people. The sound system was excellent and we could be heard all over the room no matter how softly we played.

The Red Robin was the best job we ever had. It was our first steady job and nowhere had we ever been treated better. The people from the burlesque world were our most ardent fans.

One night, a Canadian crew from one of the freighters which had just run the North Atlantic U-boat blockade, came in. They had no way of knowing *we* were Canadian. They kept asking for requests like, *There'll Be Bluebirds Over The White Cliffs Of Dover* and *When The Lights Go On Again All Over The World*. We played everything they asked for and the tips kept rolling in.

A big, burly fellow with tattooed arms said loudly, "I'll give ya 500 dollars if you can play *my* favourite song."

I told him we would be very pleased to play it and I just hoped we knew it.

"You can't possibly know it, kid," he smiled.

"Try us."

He put five $100 bills on the bar and said with a bravado-like flourish, "Okay, play me *The Maple Leaf Forever*."

He almost fell off the bar stool as I hit a chord and the two girls sang his song.

Dad had advised the authorities at Ellis Island of our change of address. Because Canada was at war, we were told to register with the Canadian Consulate in New York. We all trooped into New York one afternoon and did just that. The weeks went by and we heard nothing further. In the meantime, because we were now salaried employees, Dave and Gus arranged for us to apply for Social Security cards and a portion of our pay each month was paid into this fund. We began feeling quite American. Everything around us made us feel as though this was where we belonged.

About this time we started having problems with Dad. He was no longer active in getting us bookings. The only outside work we did as a group was arranged by Dave or Gus and was mainly local police or firemen's functions.

Nevertheless, Dad came to the club every night. He had this favourite spot at the bar and he'd sit there and drink and brag about "his kids."

We were very conscious of this, especially when the room was quiet and all you could hear was Dad relating some incident from our travels. The more he had to drink, the more animated and ebullient he became. He was rapidly becoming a source of embarrassment as we listened to the same stories over and over. The more comfortable he got in the telling, the more embellishments were added. While he might have been an interesting conversationalist to a new or unsuspecting customer, he became a source of annoyance to the regular patrons. Finally, Dave spoke to Lloyd and me.

"I think you're gonna havta ask yer ol' man to stop tellin' his stories 'round the club. Some o' the customers are complainin'."

Even though Lloyd was now 22 and I would soon be 21, we found this a very awkward situation to cope with. Dad had an overpowering personality and none of us had ever dared question his authority. We watched as Dave and Gus became increasingly irritated and the second time they spoke to us about it, we knew something would have to be done.

Lloyd somehow found the courage to bring the subject up with Dad as we were all walking home from work one night.

"Dave has asked us to talk with you 'bout sittin' in the club and drinking — he says you're botherin' the customers."

Dad, who was weaving a bit from too much to drink, stopped cold in his tracks.

"Now, ain't that somepin'. Here I deliver those assholes the best goddamn group they're ever gonna have in their joint an' all of a sudden I'm not good enough to be sittin' with their customers."

"He said it was more 'cause ya drink too much," Lloyd persisted.

"Screw 'em. If there's one thing I can do it's handle my liquor. I can drink anybody I ever met under the table. You ever see me when I had too much ta drink? Well, have ya?"

None of us said anything.

"Well I don' drink too much," Dad said answering his own question. "An' if they don' like me hangin' 'round their two-bit club, I'll find us another one an' ya can tell the bastards exactly that."

Now we faced an impossible dilemma. The next night Dad was back in the club, louder than ever although he only had a couple of drinks. We could see the subtle interplay between him and Dave as the night wore on. He was daring Dave to initiate a confrontation.

The four of us often went across the street to the restaurant between sets and as we piled into one of the back booths, Dave came in, very angry.

"If you guys can't keep yer ol' man outta the club, I'm gonna havta tell 'im in no uncertain terms. Did ya's talk to 'im?"

"We talked to 'im last night and he's all ready to hand in our notice an' find another job," Lloyd said.

"But that's not what any of us want," I added. "You're gonna havta give us some time to try an' figure a way to straighten this out. We don't want to leave the Red Robin."

Gus came in and joined us. "The ol' bugger musta said somethin' to the people he was sittin' with cause they jus' up and left. I don' know why we can't just tell him to get ta hell outta the club and stay out. You kids sure don' need him hangin' 'round screwin' up yer job."

What Dave and Gus didn't know was that Dad was not trying to put our job in jeopardy. He was drowning — struggling to stay afloat with us. We were leaving him behind and Dad was clinging on desperately trying to justify his usefulness. The whole scenario was really quite obvious and although we could rationalize Dad's behaviour — even defend it, to Dave and Gus the problem was black and white.

"Well you kids're gonna havta do somethin' an' the sooner the better," Dave said. "Tell 'im if he doesn't stay outta the place, we're gonna let ya go. Maybe we can scare 'im."

What they didn't know was that nothing scared Dad. If we couldn't handle this crisis we stood to lose our job and everything that went with it. We were more than satisfied with the money we were making. All the things we'd ever wanted were now possible. Mom loved the apartment and the new furniture. She had never had this before. We each had our own new beds and our clothes were fashionable and smart. Though we had little need for it, a new car was parked in the driveway. We were a short bus ride to the middle of Manhattan and the throbbing, pulsing heartbeat of the most exciting city in the world. For the first time ever we had the good life.

Lloyd and I talked about how we were going to handle the problem but it was almost like the children's story *Belling The Cat*. All the little mice agreed that if they were to put a bell on the marauding cat they would be warned of its coming and their problem solved but who among them was going to put the bell on the cat. So it was with us. We agreed that under no circumstances could we allow Dad to terminate our engagement at the Red Robin but who was going to tell him and make it stick?

We were determined not to let Dad do anything to endanger our job. He had to understand that *he* was the problem.

As we were all walking home Lloyd looked directly at Dad and said, "Both Dave and Gus told us tonight that if you come in the club anymore, we're gonna be fired."

We were in front of our building. Dad quietly opened the front door and sent the girls up to the apartment. Lloyd and I waited on the sidewalk. Dad came back and sat on the front stoop. He seemed very composed but we knew that he was ready to explode.

"D'ya know how many of yer so-called customers only go to the Red Robin because of me?" he asked quietly. We didn't answer. "Well a lot of 'em go 'cause they enjoy *my* company! D'ya ever think o' that?"

"The only thing that's important," Lloyd said calmly, "is what Dave and Gus think. And they told us to tell you we're gonna be fired if you come into the club again."

"We're not little kids anymore," I said. "You're gonna havta accept that. Just let go of us — let us be. You can't help us anymore. But don't persist in creating a situation where everything we've all worked for, ever since we left the north, is gonna go down the drain."

"Look, you two guys wanna quit, go 'head! You think you're what make the Harmony Kids tick? I'll take the two girls, with a New York piano player and have a job in ten minutes. How long d'ya think the two o' you would last on yer own?"

"We've already talked with Mom and the girls about this and we're all gonna stay together and keep doin' just what we've been doin'," Lloyd answered. "The girls don' wanna work without us and we don' wanna work without the girls."

"We're gonna start a family bank account," I said, "and all the money we make is goin' into it. Mom is gonna be the only one who can sign cheques. So, from now on, you're gonna havta talk with her when it comes to money."

None of us had even raised our voices. Dad sat looking at us, dumbfounded.

"From now on, everything we own is *ours*. Nothing is Lloyd's or mine, or Mom's or yours, and that includes the car," I said. "Tomorrow Lloyd and I are gettin' our driver's licenses and Mom will decide whose turn it is to have it. An' if you've been drinkin', you can't have the car."

Dad was silent for what seemed an eternity, then got up slowly, nodded, and without another word went inside and up the stairs. We looked at each other, surprised how simple it had been.

Dad never came to the Red Robin again. He would only talk to us if we talked with him first. Something was empty in him, destroyed. There was no feeling of gloating as though we had won some long-fought victory but a pain that we had to hurt him so much. Mom understood, knowing we were growing up and what had happened had to be.

In the meantime the job at the Red Robin went better than ever. Every night was like Saturday. The line-ups waiting to get into the club went halfway down the block. We got a substantial raise in salary and apart from our concern about Dad's reclusive attitude, life for the Harmony Kids just kept getting better.

Then came December 7th, 1941 and Pearl Harbor. It was Sunday and Lloyd and I were in the car with the radio on when we heard the news. We were as stunned as the whole American nation. Two days later, Dad got a call from the immigration people advising us our status was now changed — the United States was at war.

Lloyd and I were eligible for the draft, so we were given the option of returning to Canada immediately or registering for U.S. military service. Canada had declared war on Japan a matter of hours before the U.S. and despite the warm feelings we all felt for the Americans, down deep inside we were still Canadians.

We held a family council, Dad included, and decided to return to Canada. In going over our maps, Montreal looked like the closest part of Canada to head for. For the first time in weeks Dad emerged from his shell.

We gave two weeks' notice to the club and Dave and Gus made arrangements for a "Farewell to the Harmony Kids" to be held every night during our final week. A huge banner was strung in the window of the club and a flyer posted in the lobby of the theatre. It seemed as though everyone who had ever seen us found time to come in and say good-bye. Al was in his element as master-of-ceremonies, declaring, "One day, all being well, our dear Canadian friends will return again to the Red Robin."

The only flaw was Dad's stubborn refusal to go near the club, even though Dave came to the apartment to invite him.

We realized the happiest and best days of our lives were coming to an end. We sold our furniture and bought a two-wheeled trailer to hook on to the car. With only our instruments and clothes and a pronounced feeling of *déjà vu,* we piled into the car and took off for the Canadian border, and another unknown beginning.

Dad was driving . . .

EPILOGUE

WE DROVE TO MONTREAL and that was the end of the Harmony Kids. Lloyd and I enlisted in the Royal Canadian Air Force. He signed on as an airgunner, became an officer in six months and was posted overseas, attached to the Royal Air Force.

I became an airframe mechanic and was posted to No. 9 Repair Depot in St. Jean, Quebec, attached to "salvage operations" which, in essence, meant our crews picked up crashed aircraft in the whole of No. 4 training command. I served all my service tenure in Canada.

Dad spent the war years working in an aircraft plant.

The girls tried singing on their own but it didn't work too well. Joyce got a job in a department store and Kay became a shoe model.

When the war ended there was a feverish and desperate striving to return to normal, but for the Hahn family and the Harmony Kids things could never be the same.

When I got my discharge I joined an orchestra in Hamilton, Ontario and spent the next three years going through the Hamilton Conservatory of Music.

Just before Lloyd was eligible for home leave his plane was shot down over the North Sea. His squadron had been sent in to bomb a German battleship anchored in the harbour in Gydnia, Poland. The 'Pathfinder' squadron which was to light up the target arrived late. Twelve bombers went down that night. Lloyd and his crew were picked out of the North Sea the next morning by a German E-boat as they were rowing for Sweden in their rubber dinghy. One of Lloyd's arms had to be amputated and he was taken prisoner-of-war. Just before V.E. Day, he was freed by General Patton's Third Army. He returned home, got married, adopted five children, and spent his career in the civil service. He is now retired.

Kay married an airforce buddy of Lloyd's, a commercial artist. They had two beautiful daughters and lived in one of the Montréal suburbs. In 1961, when she was only 35, Kay died of leukemia.

When television came to Canada in 1952 Joyce was a natural for the new medium. She became one of Canada's first major television stars. She is now married with a grown daughter, Beverlee, and a son, Graham, who is autistic. When her television days ended, she dedicated her life to Graham and the cause of autism. She lives in Los Angeles with Graham and her husband, Peter.

Donnie, the 'baby' in the story, went on to become one of the world's top recording engineers. He spent thirteen years in New York at a major recording studio and now lives in Los Angeles where he is director of studio operations for A&M Records. His name can be found on scores of albums in almost any record store. His den is adorned with Gold and Platinum albums. He is married, with three children.

Mom lives in a senior citizen's home in the same town as Lloyd. She is 85, but if Dad were to knock on her door tomorrow and announce he had just filed on a homestead in the Australian 'outback', she'd be packed to go in an hour.

When I returned to Montréal after my three years in Hamilton, I went into the commercial "jingle" business and wrote and produced over 1,500 sessions. I went into record production and music publishing and am involved peripherally in the motion pictures business. My wife and I have three children — all grown-up.

And that leaves Dad. After the war he worked at a large lumber firm. In 1957 he had an accident at work. As it was explained to us, a load of lumber slipped and Dad was caught under the pile. One of his arms was injured and there were unknown internal injuries. He went on workmen's compensation and was not able to do very much. He was very unhappy but we were all too busy with our lives to take the time to find out how serious his injuries really were. One afternoon he complained of feeling tired and went into the bedroom to lie down. When Mom came to call him for dinner, he was dead.

He had touched a great many people on his rocky way through life and it is unfortunate that more people didn't get to know this exasperating, effervescent, courageous, at times brilliant, obstinate and proud man.

It has taken a long time to recognize the gigantic efforts he made to keep us all together as a family, the hurculean job he did in overcoming obstacles seldom encountered by most men. His loneliness, his brilliance, his ingenuity in devising ways to get us out of the north — not only to survive, but to grow. Most of all, I remember his immense pride in us all.

He made a lot of mistakes but he also made a contribution to the beginnings of this country which few can match. His only legacy is the family he left behind, and some footprints made by a pair of shoes impossible to fill.

The Land That God Forgot

From the dried out, dust blown prairies
In an old and battered truck
Along with countless others
We headed north to try out luck.

The year was nineteen-thirty
And God had stopped the rain.
A barren, arid desert
Replaced the fields of grain.

It makes a person wonder
What he's done when things go wrong.
When his world is torn asunder
Can he cope — Will he be strong?

All unanswered questions
You just do what must be done
With four complaining pistons
Groaning t'wards the northern sun.

The telephone poles are far behind
The railway disappears.
We're not too sure what we will find
One thing, for sure, is clear.

We own a virgin homestead
Somewhere north of Beaver Bluffs.
When the northern lights are south of you
You've gone 'bout far enough.

No telephones, no doctors,
Some happiness, some tears.
No one can say we didn't try
We hung on for six long years.

Somewhere is a distant past
In a long forgotten spot
And one abandoned homestead
In THE LAND THAT GOD FORGOT.

Harvey H. Hahn (Dad)
1890 - 1957